ARAMAIC LIGHT
ON THE
GOSPEL OF JOHN

Aramaic New Testament Series – Volume 3

Books in print by Rocco A. Errico

Setting A Trap for God: The Aramaic Prayer of Jesus
Let There Be Light: The Seven Keys
And There Was Light
The Mysteries of Creation: The Genesis Story
The Message of Matthew: An Annotated Parallel Aramaic-English Gospel of Matthew
Classical Aramaic – Book 1

Spanish publication
La Antigua Oración Aramea de Jesus: El Padrenuestro

German publications
Acht Einstimmungen auf Gott: Vaterunser
Es Werde Licht

Books in print by Rocco A. Errico and George M. Lamsa
Aramaic New Testament Series: Volumes 1 – 3
Aramaic Light on the Gospel of Matthew
Aramaic Light on the Gospels of Mark and Luke
Aramaic Light on the Gospel of John

Books in print by George M. Lamsa
The Holy Bible from the Ancient Eastern Text
New Testament Origin
The Shepherd of All – The 23rd Psalm
The Kingdom on Earth
Idioms in the Bible Explained & A Key to the Original Gospels

ARAMAIC LIGHT
ON THE
GOSPEL OF JOHN

A COMMENTARY ON THE TEACHINGS OF JESUS FROM THE ARAMAIC AND UNCHANGED NEAR EASTERN CUSTOMS

Aramaic New Testament Series – Volume 3

Rocco A. Errico / George M. Lamsa

Noohra Foundation, *Publisher*
4480H South Cobb Drive SE #343
Smyrna, Georgia 30080

First Printing September 2002

ISBN: 0-9631292-8-7

This volume is dedicated
in loving memory of
Nina Shabaz

CONTENTS

THE COMMENTARY

FOREWORD
by Rocco A. Errico

Aramaic Light on the Gospel of John, like its predecessors, *Aramaic Light on the Gospel of Matthew* and *Aramaic Light on the Gospels of Mark and Luke,* acts as a Near Eastern guide, revealing to the Western mind a more intimate view of the socio-religious and psychological environment of Semitic peoples.[1] It reveals to us the human Jesus, his teaching, apostles, disciples, followers and opponents in the light of his own language, people and times.

FORMATION OF THIS COMMENTARY

Aramaic New Testament Series Volume 3 is not founded on contemporary academic analysis of Scripture. It does not use critical source/historical and literary methods of interpretation. However, on certain passages there are references to some of the these findings in the footnotes.

This work is not a verse by verse commentary. Nor does it repeat the verses and comments that have already been explained in the synoptic gospels of Matthew, Mark and Luke, Aramaic Series Volumes 1 and 2. The reader must keep in mind that this commentary works with the received text—that is, with the gospel as we now have it in its present form—and does not attempt to provide the reader with source/critical study. As much as possible, each comment is written in story form, using layman's language and not theological, specialized terminology. This style is maintained throughout the volume.

All scriptural excerpts at the beginning of each section are from the King James Version of the New Testament. I also quote scriptural passages from *The Holy Bible from Ancient Eastern Manuscripts* by

---

[1]See Errico and Lamsa, *Aramaic Light on the Gospel of Matthew*, "Foreword by Rocco A. Errico," pp. xi-xvi.

Dr. George M. Lamsa. Each quotation is identified as the "Aramaic Peshitta text, Lamsa translation." There are other citations of Scripture in the body of the comments that I have translated directly from the Aramaic Peshitta text. These passages are identified as "Aramaic Peshitta text, Errico."

I have attempted as much as possible to avoid a collision with denominational belief systems and interpretations as well as various schools of theological studies. Nevertheless, in certain scriptural passages cited in this volume, it became unavoidable. Apparently some biblical interpreters have unwittingly created and established monumental dogmas and confusing notions on verses that were only Semitic idiomatic phrases, metaphoric expressions or biblical customs. The expressions in John's gospel are Semitic; it is, therefore, helpful if we understand them from their Near Eastern, cultural perspective. (Throughout the commentary, references to Semites are to Near Eastern Semites and not Westernized Semitic peoples.)

ACKNOWLEDGMENTS AND FINAL WORD

My deep appreciation and sincere gratitude to Mrs. Nina Shabaz, niece of Dr. George M. Lamsa and proprietor of the Lamsa estate, for her kind and most gracious permission to edit, expand, annotate and prepare Dr. Lamsa's previous commentaries, *Gospel Light* and *More Light on the Gospel*, in a new format. I have also added material that he and I had only drafted before he passed from this earthly life on September 22, 1975. There is also additional information derived from my continual research into Aramaic word meanings and Near Eastern studies.

My very genuine and heartfelt thanks and gratefulness to Ms. Sue Edwards, Ms. Ann Milbourn, Ms. Linetta Izenman and Mr. Hanny Freiwat for their constructive suggestions and assistance in preparing this manuscript for publication.

These comments that help clarify the Gospel of John are the only works based solely on Aramaic and Near Eastern Semitic culture. They were written not to leave the impression that we have not understood Jesus' gospel of the kingdom but to present a clearer picture and setting in which that gospel comes to us. May this commentary be a light and guide to those who seek to understand more fully the blessed truths which were once spoken by the Semitic, Galilean prophet and wisdom teacher—Jesus of Nazareth.

To all the readers of this commentary, I say to you: *taybootha washlama dalaha nehwoon amhon hasha walmeen.* "The grace (loving kindness) and peace of God is with you now and always!"

Rocco A. Errico
September 2002

INTRODUCTION

THE KING JAMES VERSION OF THE BIBLE

When the King James Version of Holy Scripture was produced, Europe was just emerging out of dark clouds. The political and religious situation was still chaotic. Nation after nation was eagerly striving for freedom. The ecclesiastical structure and its hierarchy were weakening under the impact of scientific and religious research. The time was ripe for a spiritual resurgence in all lands. There also was a fervent demand for Scripture and this was quickly met by devout scholars who offered various translations of the Bible.

Industrial and commercial activities greatly stimulated these changes, giving hope for a better understanding of the Near East and the world at large. Since the rise of Islam and the growth of the Turkish Empire and power, the Near East became isolated from Europe. It was this isolation that prompted Columbus to make his notable voyage in search of a way to the Orient, which resulted in the discovery of the Americas. At that time there were only a few adventurers who had crossed unknown seas and lands in search of fame and fortune. In those days travel was hazardous and expensive. Transportation was beset with severe difficulties. The world was uncharted and a few good roads were found only in some regions.

Near Eastern races were hostile to the people of Europe, undeniably from the devastations caused by the Crusades in the name of Christ. Whenever an individual undertook a long journey, he was hardly expected to return alive. It took Marco Polo, the Italian adventurer, twenty years to visit the great Khan in the Far East and return home. The delay was, no doubt, created by wars, revolutions, a lack of caravans and harsh winters in the countries through which he passed. While he was learning Asiatic languages, he forgot his own mother tongue.

It was only after the conquest of India by Great Britain and the rise of the British Empire that any worthwhile contributions came from the Near East. In this particular period European nations were more interested in the search for gold and the acquisition of new lands than investigating the wisdom of the Near East.

NEAR EASTERN CUSTOMS AND MANNERS

Under these circumstances, it is apparent how Near Eastern manners, customs and religious beliefs continued to be as mysterious to Western people, as those of the latter were to Near Easterners. This misunderstanding still prevails in our modern world. (Ironically, the movement we call Christianity originally was a Near Eastern religion begun by Semites, and the New Testament is a Semitic Eastern book.)

Because Western peoples did not fully understand the Near East, we can see why early and medieval artists portrayed Jesus and his disciples at the last supper sitting on chairs at a luxurious table in European style. The Eastern style would portray Jesus and the twelve apostles sitting on the floor forming a circle around a large cloth, with their legs folded under them, their hats on their heads and their shoes removed. There would be a large tray containing two dishes, a few spoons and a cup placed on the cloth with a jar of wine in front of them. These artists and authors of books were not aware that many things which were in good taste in the Western world were in bad form and even repulsive in the Near East.

COMPARATIVE DIFFERENCES

Here are some examples of the cultural and social differences between the Western world and the Near East. In the West men help and honor their wives. But until the middle of the 1900s, wives in the Near East were virtually the servants of their husbands and never sat at a common meal with them. In some Eastern regions today, they still continue this practice. A Semite retains his hat and removes his shoes when entering a house. This courtesy is reversed among Westerners. In the Near East, where old customs are still prevalent, it would be scandalous to play music during Church or Mosque services. The absence of music is almost inconceivable in Western religious services. If a Westerner observes a Near Easterner praying five times a day, he might think that the person is lazy or crazy. On the other hand, an Easterner is puzzled when a Westerner has to be urged to pray.

In some Near Eastern areas, women are still purchased or acquired through matchmakers. Men often marry girls who are under age, but with an oral and solemn pledge that the men will not perform the conjugal rights until the girls reach the age of physical maturity. Often, wives are driven from their homes by their husbands with or without cause. All this is totally different in Western lands, where women usually have more respect and input in the affairs of their families and households.

Surely customs constituted a great barrier between the East and the West, and to this was added the barriers of distance and psychological perspectives. These are some of the reasons so much misunderstanding exists between the Near East and the West and also constitutes a barrier to understanding biblical episodes.

For instance, many narratives and locations in the Bible are exaggerated. To Easterners the small lake in Galilee appeared to them as if it were an enormous body of water, and the tiny boats seemed to appear as large ships. Small states of only a few square miles were regarded as kingdoms. Joshua conquered thirty-one kingdoms east of the Jordan that had territories of not more than a few hundred square miles, whose inhabitants were mostly shepherds and farmers.[1] Travelers are sometimes disappointed when they see biblical lands because they appear so different to what they had imagined.

These and similar differences illustrate the difficulties of Westerners in understanding the languages and customs of Near Eastern Semites. All the greater is our indebtedness to those

---

[1]See Joshua 12:24.

translators of Scripture who, in the face of insurmountable difficulties, have given us versions that stand as monuments to their scholarship, zeal and devotion, and who challenge us to follow in their steps.

TRANSLATING AND CLARIFYING THE BIBLE

Prior to and since the Reformation many attempts have been made to translate Holy Scripture and to explain its message. The Bible in its original language was simple and lucid. In spite of numerous translations and commentaries attempting to clarify scriptural passages, the Bible still continues to perplex people. This explains why new translations of Scripture continue to appear every so often.

During centuries of scholarly endeavor and controversy, the Near East has practically remained silent. Hardly anything has been said for or against what the West has done with the Bible. This silence has been maintained from the days of Assyrian writers such as Tatian, Ephraim Syrus, and Narsis, who were noteworthy commentators. The reason for this was not lack of interest in what constitutes the basic principles of religious thought; it came about because of certain unavoidable circumstances.

EASTERN CHRISTIAN MOVEMENT

Near Eastern Semitic Christianity was accomplishing its work with vigorous enthusiasm. Its leaders had the assured confidence that their spiritual movement would soon become a universal religion in the East and the West. In those early days the Persian Empire alone had seven metropolitan provinces and eighty bishoprics, all the way from Armenia to India. Christianity was winning favor in the eyes of the Persian Court. There was no thought that any reverses might interfere with the spread of Jesus' gospel of God's kingdom on earth.

Then, suddenly, a new movement appeared in Southwest Arabia. The claims of Christianity and the victorious Roman Empire were strenuously challenged. What at first appeared to the Christians as a despised heresy, espoused by a nomadic chief, assumed huge proportions and began to vanquish the Christian movement in the Near East. Schools of Christian learning were closed, monasteries were deserted, churches were converted into mosques, books that did not agree with Moslem teaching were burned and authors of new books were punished. Christian scholars were conscripted to translate works of Aramaic and Greek authors into Arabic. This was done to help propagate the new faith of Islam that was steadily ousting Christianity.

In some provinces writers of commentaries who even incidentally or unwittingly disagreed with the Koran were promptly exiled or put to death. Christian authorship was under a severe ban. These unhappy events, accompanied by constant persecutions, put an end to any further attempts to expound Holy Scripture from a Semitic point of view. In sheer destitution, Christians were ready to relinquish everything for a restricted freedom in which they could worship Jesus as their Lord and Savior. Although deprived of schools and learning, the teachings of Jesus were largely preserved through customs and practices, which Islam could not displace, and by copies of Scriptures that escaped destruction.

A PROVIDENTIAL INTERVENTION

However, the providence of God wrought an extraordinary miracle. A great deal of Christian literature suffered, but the Gospels stood unchallenged. Even though the Koran became the revered book of the Moslems, Mohammed (570-632 CE) accepted the Gospels as the veritable word of God, as also did his successors and all Moslems throughout the world.

The version of the Gospels honored by Moslems was not the Vulgate of the Western world, which they repudiated as second-hand

xvii

and as an unreliable translation. It was the Eastern Aramaic text of the Gospels, the *Peshitta*—meaning "clear, straight"—that they accepted. This name is justified by its clarity of style, directness of expression and simplicity of language. This was the text that the Semitic people of this region knew and used before they became Moslems. This is the authentic and official text of what once was the original Eastern Church, the Mother Church of Christianity.

Years later when other peoples accepted Christianity, the Peshitta was translated into Greek, Armenian, Arabic, Persian and other languages. Even the Christians of Malabar, India, who are known as the Christians of St. Thomas (one of the apostles of Jesus), adopted the Peshitta from the earliest centuries. It was the universally accepted text among all Christians in the Near and Middle East. And it has so continued to the present day. Semitic Christians never used the Vulgate translation.

THE PESHITTA TEXT AND OTHER ARAMAIC VERSIONS

Originally, the Eastern Aramaic text of the New Testament consisted of twenty-two books. The book of the Revelation and four epistles—2 Peter, 2 John, 3 John and Jude—were not included. The book of the Revelation was accepted after the Council of Nicaea, 325 CE, but many of the Eastern Bishops in Persia rejected it.

It would seem that the appearance of other Aramaic versions that differed from the Peshitta Aramaic text came about because of the defeat of Rome and the treaty made by the Emperor Jovian with the Persian King Sapor, 363 CE. By this pact Rome ceded five provinces in the Euphrates valley to Persia. Before this time, Christians of these provinces had been under Rome and subject to the ecclesiastic authority of Antioch. After the treaty, they automatically came under the jurisdiction of the Eastern patriarch, whose See was at Seleucia, the imperial capital of the Persian Kings of the Sassanian dynasty.

The patriarch of the East and his associates not only welcomed these Christian refugees but also permitted them to use their own versions. These versions included portions of the New Testament not found in the Peshitta. Undoubtedly, this was due to the fact that such parts originated in the Eastern Roman Empire after the compilation of the Peshitta and could not be sent to Persia because of the conflict that began soon after the death of Constantine and lasted for many years. It is unfortunate that these later versions and the fifth century Jacobite Christians' version should be confused with the ancient Peshitta text. This text was used in the native church of Persia centuries before and was quoted by Eastern writers of the second and third centuries.

TRANSLATING FROM ARAMAIC INTO GREEK

The following shows some of the difficulties in translating the Aramaic text into Greek. These differences also prove the originality of the Near Eastern Peshitta text of the New Testament.

1. The Aramaic word for "seed" is *zara* and the word for sower is *zarua*. The differences in the Aramaic formation of these words is so slight that the Greek translators overlooked and confused the word "seed" with the word "sower."[2] The Aramaic text reads, "Now listen to the parable of the seed" and not ". . . the parable of the sower," according to all Western versions of the gospel of Matthew. Such mistakes are unavoidable in a language like Aramaic, where a word has many meanings and a dot misplaced can altogether change the meaning of a word. This was especially true before vowel points were introduced and when punctuation was not observed. In addition to this there was no uniformity in writing and copying.

2. The Aramaic word *gamla* has three meanings: "camel, large rope, beam." Therefore, in Aramaic, Matthew 19:25 correctly

---

[2]See Mt. 13:18.

reads, "It is easier for a rope to go through a needle's eye" and not "It is easier for a camel. . ."

3. The Aramaic word for a certain large piece of money called *kakra*, "talent," is similar to the word "province." The difference is distinguished by a single dot and according to the letter over which it is placed. Thus *kakra* with the dot over the letter "k" means "talent coin," and *karka* with the dot placed above the "r" means "province." When reading this word with the Aramaic letters and not the transliteration into English characters, the "k" and the "r" look almost alike, especially with the dot placed above the letters.

    One sees this confusion in the parable of the nobleman who rewarded his servants not with coins but with cities, which is improbable.[3] This mistake was no doubt due to a copyist who placed the dot over the wrong letter. Such an error could not have occurred in the Greek version if it was the original, because Greek has different words for "coin" and for "city" or "province." If the Peshitta were a translation from a Greek text, the word would have been *medinata*, which means "cities." Also in the example of the parable of the seed, it would have been the parable of the sower going from Greek into Aramaic. This further proves that the Peshitta Aramaic text is consistent in its report of the teaching of Jesus that harmonized with contemporary customs.

4. In the Greek version of John's gospel, 12: 40, we read: "He hath blinded their eyes, and hardened their heart; that they should not see with their eyes, nor understand with their heart; and be converted, and I should heal them." The Aramaic Peshitta text reads: "Their eyes have become blind and their heart darkened, so that they cannot see with their eyes nor understand with their heart, let them return and I will heal them." In Aramaic the word

---

[3]See Lk. 19:13, 17, 24, King James Version.

avaro means "have become blind." The grammatical differences between "He made them blind" and "have become blind" is indicated by the final letter "o" which is the third person plural.

MEANING OF ARAMAIC WORDS

Furthermore, some Aramaic words were not translated into Greek because they were not clearly understood, such as *raqa,* "to spit," *mammon,* "wealth;" *ethpatakh,* "be opened." In other passages of the gospels Aramaic words have been retained and transliterated into the Greek and English versions, such as "eli, eli, lemana shabaktani." (There are approximately 44 Aramaic words left in the New Testament.)

Some Aramaic words were translated to agree with the usage of the languages into which they were put. For instance, the Aramaic word *towa,* "envied," expressing emulation, was translated as "blessed" in the Beatitudes for which the Aramaic word is *brekha.* The Aramaic word in the text is *toowayhon.* It would be difficult to literally translate the word because it would read as "Envied are the peacemakers, for they shall be called children of God." This word and a few other Aramaic words cannot be translated exactly because there really are no English equivalents for them or the meaning would be misunderstood. Some of the Aramaic colloquial and idiomatic expressions, as well, could hardly be translated into other languages without the loss of thought.

It is a well known fact that languages undergo changes. Many words become obsolete and lose their meaning, especially when translated into other languages expressing different cultures. These original meanings could often be obtained by examining the phraseology and thought conveyed by the words.

For instance, medical terms were unknown in the Near East, and even in some areas today they are not that well known. In northern Iraq, where Dr. Lamsa was born, the Assyrian people still used ancient terms when describing various diseases. A mentally unbalanced person is called *dewana,* which literally means he or she is possessed by a devil or has become wild. The King James Version of Mark 1:34 reads that Jesus "suffered not the devils to speak because they knew him." The meaning in Aramaic is that Jesus did now allow the mentally deranged to speak after he had healed them, because some of them were his acquaintances. Jesus did not want them praising him.

Mark 9:17 reads that a boy had a "dumb spirit." In Aramaic this means that the particular disease had caused dumbness in the boy and not that the spirit was dumb. The King James Version of Luke 11:14 reads that Jesus "was casting out a devil and it was dumb." The Peshitta text, which reflects Aramaic style of speech, reads that Jesus "was casting out a demon from a dumb man." Luke 4:41, in the Aramaic reads: "Demons also came out of many, who cried out saying, You are the Christ, The Son of God." The people who were sick cried out after they were healed. It is hardly credible that demons who were cast out would acknowledge Jesus as the Messiah/Christ.

Interestingly, Near Easterners still believe that every sickness is caused and controlled by spirits. Undoubtedly this primitive belief comes from the fact that the actual causes of diseases were not known. Such beliefs in evil spirits and demonology are found not only among Semites but among all peoples living even today under primitive conditions in Asia as well as in Europe and the United States. We are, however, grateful to science for demonstrating that diseases, including delusions and fears, are from physical, mental and environmental causes. These things have nothing to do with demons or evil spirits.

MORE CONFUSION AND MISUNDERSTANDING

There are other instances that create confusion when interpreting passages of scripture literally. For example, the Aramaic term *al* means "enter into, attack, wrestle, chase, intercourse" and a score of other meanings; however, it has been almost exclusively translated as "enter into." An outstanding example of this misunderstanding is Matthew 8:31, where it reads that the spirits or demons "entered into the swine." According to the context and the style of Aramaic speech, the word here means that after Jesus had healed them, the lunatics attacked the swine. These lunatics were Syrians or Gadarenes. Their people kept and herded swine, which were an abomination to the Jews. Jesus was a Jewish prophet. As a token of appreciation and gift to Jesus for what he did for them, and as proof of their conversion, they were willing to destroy the herd of swine that belonged to their people. This was one reason why the owners of the swine went into a panic and urged Jesus to leave their land, lest their business be completely destroyed by more conversions to the Jewish faith. We must also consider the fact that the evil spirits did not need Jesus' permission to enter into the swine any more than they needed permission to enter into the men who were supposedly possessed by them.[4]

This word *al* is still used when people say, "The oxen are entering into each other" or " the men are entering into each other," referencing the idea that the men are attacking each other—that is, fighting. So also when a wolf attacks a fold, Aramaic speaking people still say, "the wolf has entered into the sheep."

COLLOQUIALISMS

There are similar difficulties in the matter of colloquialisms in New Testament scriptural passages. In John 20:22, we read that Jesus blew his breath on his disciples: "He breathed on them." This means that he encouraged them. Again, John 2:17 reads, "The zeal of thy house hath eaten me up," meaning "the zeal for the temple has made me courageous." Such challenges are also evident in American colloquialisms that are difficult to translate into Near Eastern, Semitic

---

[4]See Errico & Lamsa, *Aramaic Light on the Gospel of Matthew,* "Lunatics and the Swine," pp. 132-134.

languages. An example would be the term "fire" with its various usages, such as "to set *fire* to a house, to *fire* a gun, to *fire* a worker." When English speaking people say that "a worker was *fired* from his job," a Near Easterner unfamiliar with American customs would believe that the worker was either burned or shot instead of being dismissed from his job.

A comparison between Aramaic and Greek texts, in the light of the above illustrations, brings us to the conclusion in favor of the Aramaic origin of all four Gospels. The strongest argument, however, is that Jesus and his disciples spoke Aramaic. It was also the language of the Church in Jerusalem, Syria and Mesopotamia. The "Hebrew tongue" in which Paul spoke to the people of Jerusalem and in which the ascended Christ spoke to Saul on his way to Damascus[5] refers to Aramaic. Indeed, this was the Apostle's mother tongue. He prayed and expressed his deepest emotions in this tongue. See Romans 8:15, Galatians 4:6, I Corinthians 16:22, where he uses such Aramaic words as *Abba,* "Father," *Awoon,* "our Father," *maranetha,* "Our Lord has come."

THE ARAMAIC LANGUAGE

As far back as the seventh century BCE, Aramaic was the language of communication for commerce and diplomacy between the nations in Mesopotamia, Asia Minor and Palestine.[6] The Greeks referred to this language as Syriac, because they confused Syria, which is in the north of Palestine, with Assyria, which is a totally different country between the Euphrates and Tigris rivers, east of Syria. This confusion exists even today in the United States. It is a historical fact that Aramaic was the colloquial and literary language of Palestine, Syria, Asia Minor and Mesopotamia, from the fourth century BCE to the ninth century CE.

---

[5]See Acts 21:40; 22:2; 26:14.
[6]See 2 Ki. 18:26.

After the Assyrian and Chaldean (Babylonian) exile, Hebrew ceased to be spoken and gave way to Aramaic. This Semitic tongue became the widely prevalent, popular language. From the days of Nehemiah and Ezra, Jewish writers wrote in Aramaic. This is further seen in the books of Daniel, the Psalms and in the composition of other Old Testament books. Attempts were made to restore Hebrew by some Jewish scholars, who warned the people that the angels do not understand prayers offered in Aramaic and would therefore be handicapped in acting as their mediators before God.

Other Jewish scholars defended Aramaic against such criticisms, adding that God himself spoke to Adam in Aramaic and that Abraham was an Aramean. Jacob's children were born and raised in Assyria and later sojourned in Canaan, after which they migrated with him to Egypt.

During the reigns of the Achaemenian dynasty in Persia, beginning with Cyrus, 528 BCE, Aramaic was used as the official language for correspondence between the kings and their provincial governors as far as Egypt. Jewish literature after the time of Christ was written mainly in Aramaic, and works in Hebrew were translated into Aramaic. Josephus, the Jewish historian, used Hebrew and Aramaic words indiscriminately. The reason for this is that Hebrew was an Aramaic dialect and the differences between them were largely in matters of pronunciation rather than meaning. After the destruction of the second temple, the Jews became wholly an Aramaic speaking people and Hebrew became the language of the scholars.

GREEK REFUSED BY PALESTINIAN JEWS

Greek was seldom spoken except by the cultured few and by government officials. The Jews obstinately resisted every attempt at Hellenization, as the Maccabean struggle clearly indicates. The brief Greek rule over Syria and Mesopotamia might be compared with British rule in India, Mesopotamia and Palestine. British officers, governors and soldiers invariably acquired the native languages, but only a few natives knew English.

Some natives who did not speak English nevertheless adopted English names, such as George, Victoria and Henry. Their purpose in doing so was to win favor with their rulers. The same was true during the Greek conquest. Jews and Syrians adopted Greek names without necessarily implying that they used the Greek language in daily intercourse. The same course was followed by the Jews during the Babylonian exile. The Jews adopted Chaldean names. Doubtlessly this custom is confusing to the Western mind that is unfamiliar with the characteristic temperament of Semites. The Assyrians, for many centuries, had been ruled by Turkey, but they still speak and write their own language. A few Assyrians speak Turkish when dealing with officials of the government.

GREEK TEXTS AND ARAMAIC TEXTS

It is very significant that the Aramaic Peshitta text contains not a single reference to the Greek people in the gospels. The Greek text of the gospel of John does mention that some "Greeks" wanted to see Jesus.[7] However, the Aramaic word in the Peshitta text of this verse is *ammeh*, "people," and the reference is to "Gentiles"—that is, Idumeans, Syrians and Assyrians.[8] This change in John's gospel was probably made by Greek translators who wished to introduce some references to their own people in the Gospel. The Aramaic word for "Greek" is *yonayah*, but it never occurs in the Gospels except in the single reference to the Greek language in the inscription on the cross. Nor is there any mention of Greek culture, philosophy or customs,

---

[7]See John 12:20 and the comment in this book, p.151, "Gentiles seeking Jesus."

[8]Also in Paul's letter to the Corinthians, the Greek text reads: "For the Jews require a sign and the Greeks seek after wisdom." But the same passage in the Aramaic Eastern Peshitta text contains the word *aramayeh*, "Arameans," and not *yonayeh*, "Greeks." The Greek version retains the term "Greeks" throughout this epistle.

proving that they did not influence Jesus and his disciples nor the early Christians.

The first Greek text of any importance was introduced by Erasmus to the Western world in 1516. In the preparation of this edition he had only ten manuscripts, the oldest of which belonged to the twelfth century. He did not know Aramaic nor had he access to any other manuscripts. At this time, the Near East was still practically unknown. It thus happened that Greek became known in Europe as the original language in which the Gospels and the rest of the New Testament were written. This much is implied by the translators of the King James version in their little known "Preface," which sets forth the circumstances that induced their undertaking.

It is important to know that the Aramaic Eastern text, the first compilation of the New Testament scriptures, was made in Edessa. This was the capital of the buffer state of Ur-Hai, near Harran, where Aramaic was the spoken language. This state changed hands during the conflicts between the Roman and Persian Empires. From the fourth century, however, it had a type of Christianity which was independent of Western influence. But Christianity was established here long before that time.

The Church in Edessa was founded by Addai or Thaddeus, one of the Twelve who was sent to that city as a missionary. St Thomas, another of Jesus' apostles, later went through that region. This city was the center of Aramaic learning and literature from earliest times so that it justifiably won the title of the "Athens of Syria." In the course of time it became the seat of Christian scholarship under the leadership of St. Epharim. It was there that he founded a school or great university. But even before his day the Gospels were well known in Mesopotamia and Persia. This fact is in accord with the testimony of Eusebius who made quotations from the Aramaic writings of Hegesippus, the defender of Christianity against Gnosticism. This is substantiated by the edition of the Gospels called the Diatessaron, prepared by Tatian, an Assyrian who lived in Mesopotamia about 172 CE. But this compilation by Tatian was repudiated and copies burned.

EDESSA

Unfortunately those who associate the Aramaic text of the Peshitta with Rabbulas, bishop of Edessa in 435 CE, overlook the fact that there were many bishops of the flourishing church at Edessa and Persia before he was born. How could these men have been elevated to the Episcopal See without written gospels? How could Christianity have been propagated and survived throughout the Near East without holy Scripture?

Rabbulas was anti-Nestorian. If he had translated the gospels from the Greek, he would surely have included the Revelation and the four omitted epistles—2 Peter, 2 and 3 John and Jude—and would have made the Eastern text correspond with the Vulgate. But such was not the case. The text which existed before his day is known in some places as the Old Syriac. This is another name for the Peshitta because at this time Peshitta had already become old. Its origin is lost in obscurity and references to the ancient text have doubtless been confused with another version called the *Damparshey*. This Aramaic word comes from the root *parash*, "to select," and was used as a lectionary.

The existence of the Edessene Church from apostolic times and the venerable age of its Scriptures leads to the conclusion that the Aramaic text was a spontaneous growth and that Edessa was the logical place for this growth. It might be said that this is merely tradition. But is not tradition another word for history? It is the living voice of the past conserving the values of its wisdom and experience, especially during persecutions when books were burned and destroyed. If we discount this voice then the past becomes a closed door and we are left with no key to open it in the East or the West.

ARAMAIC THE ORIGINAL LANGUAGE OF THE GOSPELS

The original language of the Gospels, therefore, is the native Galilean Aramaic, the vernacular of northern Palestine, and not the

Chaldean Aramaic that was spoken in southern Palestine. It was the same language that was spoken by the Assyrians who were brought to the cities of Samaria and Galilee by the Assyrian kings after the ten tribes were taken into captivity.[9]

The manner of speech, phraseology, idioms and orientation of the Gospel are vividly and distinctively northern Aramaic. Parables and allegories are all derived from Semitic customs and there is no reference to incidents from alien sources. The constant repetitions are characteristic of Semitic usage. Phrases as *Amen, amen amarna lkhon,* "Truly, truly, I say unto you," and expressions such as "in those days," "And it came to pass," "And he said to them," are peculiarly Aramaic. Then again, the original has fewer words because the thought is conceived in the native tongue and easily expressed to the people of the same language. This is not the case with a translation that of necessity must use more words to convey the meaning. Consider the first clause of the Lord's Prayer. The Aramaic uses two words—*Awoon dwashmaya*; the Greek uses six words—*Pater hemon ho en tois ouranois*—as also does English—"Our Father who art in heaven." If the Aramaic text were a translation from the Greek, then more words would have been used in the Peshitta text and the translation would have had obscure and confusing phrases. This is not the case with the Peshitta, which consistently sustains its title meaning "clear."

A translation frequently misses the real meaning of the original and often has to use synonyms to bring out shades of meaning. This was obvious to Dr. Lamsa because for years he had translated letters and documents for the United States government and for several institutions. Therefore it was easy for him, because of constant practice, to tell whether a writing was a translation or written in the original, especially in the case of his mother tongue, Aramaic.

Interestingly, the Aramaic Near Eastern text retains all the Semitic names in their original form and pronunciation that correspond with the Hebrew names. Compare the names Matthew,

---

[9]See 2 Ki. 17:24.

chapter 1 and Luke, chapter 3 in the original Aramaic text. Another interesting fact is that the Semitic Eastern text in referring to Peter always speaks of him as Simon and, at times, as Simon *Kepa* (Peter, meaning "stone"). It was natural for the Greek translator to use only the Greek term, thus translating the Aramaic word *Kepa* into the word *Petrus*. Contemporary issues that were present at the time were not considered during the writing of the Gospels because they were understood and needed no explanations.

The Gospels are only an outline of Jesus' teaching. If they were written outside the Semitic atmosphere and its related situations, the writers, doubtlessly, would have furnished explanations and the gospel narrative would have been much longer. A Greek writer, for instance, would have made comparisons between Semitic and Greek culture, making them clearer to Greek readers. But such a course was superfluous to Aramaic speaking people.

The Gospels were written much earlier than Western scholars suggest. If they were of a late date, the writers would not have been able to make direct and accurate quotations as was done in the so-called "Sermon on the Mount" (Matthew 5-7) and other sayings of Jesus. The nearest and shortest way to trace the authorship of the gospels and the place they were written is to rely upon internal evidence.

The writers must have been Semites, for they were familiar with the Hebrew Scriptures and with customs and manners, such as the Passover and other festivals, as well as with the topography of Palestine. These authors wrote to their contemporaries. This is why they did not stress the general issues, because the public knew them. Had the gospels been written at a later date, the writers would have undoubtedly explained such issues as head tax, messianic expectations and so forth.

The opening sentences in Luke's gospel clearly implies that there were many other gospels written on scrolls and extensively circulated, and that they were the work of eyewitnesses who were associated with and knew Jesus. The place where these writings were produced must have been either Palestine or Edessa, the two great centers where Aramaic was spoken. There is no reason why these Aramaic speaking countries should have their sacred scriptures written in a language that was alien to them. The evidence therefore is convincing for an Aramaic original and it is our contention that it is the Aramaic Peshitta text.

Jesus was born and reared in the Near East, speaking the Aramaic language and living under the influence of Semitic, Eastern customs, practices and habits. He spoke in terms that the people of his time understood. Nevertheless, his personality transcended his own culture and much of the religious teachings of that day. His life was a powerful demonstration of a spiritual presence, a living image of God for everyone to see. Jesus' gospel of God's kingdom, his practical teaching and his healing powers have transformed the lives of women, men, and children the world over, giving humanity a new hope.

This commentary reveals the human Jesus in his original setting, a son of the ancient Near East. He was an Aramaic speaking Semite. *Aramaic Light on the Gospel of John* completes the series on the four gospels based on the Aramaic Peshitta text, along with Semitic, Near Eastern customs, manners and background. The rich and abundant blessing that spiritual understanding brings to one's heart be upon the reader.

Rocco A. Errico and George M. Lamsa

ABBREVIATIONS

Old Testament

Gen.	Genesis
Ex	Exodus
Lev.	Leviticus
Num.	Numbers
Dt.	Deuteronomy
1 Sam.	1 Samuel
2 Sam.	2 Samuel
1 Ki.	1 Kings
2 Ki.	2 Kings
Ecc.	Ecclesiastes
Ps.	Psalms
Isa.	Isaiah
Jer.	Jeremiah
Ezk.	Ezekiel
Mal.	Malachi

New Testament

NT	New Testament
Mt.	Matthew
Mk.	Mark
Lk.	Luke
Jn.	John
Rom.	Romans
1 Cor.	1 Corinthians
Gal.	Galatians
Heb.	Hebrews
1 Pet.	1 Peter
Rev.	Revelation

Other Abbreviations

BCE	Before the common era, BC
CE	Common Era, AD
K.J.V.	King James Version

ܐܬܪ̈ܘܬܐ ܕܡܬܝܗܒܝܢ ܠܗܘܢ

ܒܝܕ ܗܿܝ

ܗܘܝܘ ܚܕܒܫܒܐ ܕܩܝܡܬܐ

ܒܪܝܟ̈ܘܗܝ

ܡܫܝܚܐ

INTRODUCTION
The Gospel According To John

JOHN THE APOSTLE

In Aramaic the title of the book is *karozootha dyohannan,* "The Preaching of John." John and Jacob[1] (James), the sons of Zebedee, were from the town of Bethsaida, Galilee. John[2] was one of the first disciples of Jesus, the Galilean prophet from Nazareth. Both he and his brother, Jacob (James), occupied prominent places among the disciples. According to Near Eastern tradition, John was the youngest of Jesus' disciples. Probably, this was the reason he survived during the reign of the Roman Emperor Trajan, 98 CE.

John was always closer to Jesus than any of the other disciples. He accompanied Jesus to the house of Jairus, to the Mount of Transfiguration, to Gethsemane, and was the only disciple who, with his mother Salome, stood near the cross. When Jesus was arrested, John did not desert his master although the other disciples had fled. He took a chance and remained with Jesus to the end. This is also why Jesus commended his mother, Mary, to John's care.[3]

After the crucifixion, John occupied a less important position at Jerusalem than that held by Jacob (James) and Simon Peter.[4] The reason might have been because of his young age or that he was engaged in some other work outside of Judea. Paul refers to him as

---

[1]Aramaic and Greek texts of the New Testament correctly maintain the name as Jacob and not James. A scribe incorrectly translated the name as James.

[2]The name John, the son of Zebedee, appears thirty times in the writings of Mt., Mk., Lk., the book of Acts and letter to the Galatians. These NT texts are the best sources for accurate information about this disciple of Jesus. John was a fisherman by trade.

[3]Jn. 19:25-27.

[4]Acts 3:1.

1

the pillar of the church.[5] He was in Jerusalem for quite some time.[6] Later he was sent with the apostle Simon Peter to Samaria; then he suddenly disappeared from the scene. We hear nothing further about him. Tradition places him at Ephesus in Asia Minor, but Paul, on his various journeys to Asia Minor, never mentioned meeting him. John might have gone to Ephesus after Paul's death to supervise the work in the area. At that time, the movement required the presence of an apostle in that region of the Near East.

AUTHORSHIP

Modern New Testament scholars greatly dispute John's authorship of the fourth gospel, Revelation and other writings attributed to him. Nevertheless, his authorship still has strong supporters, as is the case with the three canonical gospels, Matthew, Mark and Luke. Interestingly, Near Eastern Semitic Christians never disputed John's authorship of the fourth gospel. (However, they did reject the book of the Revelation. It was not accepted as canonical until the fourth century.)

This confusion is partially due to the fact that authorship in the Near East is totally different from Europe and America, where usually the author of a book is the actual writer.[7] In the Near East, the book is called by the name of the person about whom it is written or else bears the title of the subject matter. This is true for the gospel of John. The writing represents John's preaching about Jesus. Who exactly wrote the book or compiled it, no one can tell; but John was clearly responsible for the original account before Church scribes added more material and later edited it. Early Christian literature was written under extreme difficulties and such works were often condemned and destroyed by order of the government.

---

[5]Gal. 2:9.

[6]Acts 3:1; 4:13, 19.

[7]See Errico and Lamsa, *Aramaic Light on the Gospel of Matthew,* "Introduction to the Gospel of Matthew, Authorship," pp. 2-3.

Western biblical interpreters think that the "beloved disciple"[8] is responsible for the basic tradition behind the written form of the gospel. However, it cannot be adequately proved or disproved that the "beloved disciple" was the apostle John, the son of Zebedee. These authorities also suggest that an unknown disciple referred to as the "evangelist" wrote the gospel that the "beloved disciple" had dictated and that a third individual known as a redactor (editor) put the finishing touches to this appealing book.

Nevertheless, according to modern New Testament scholars, "weighty arguments" exist against John as author of the fourth gospel and as the "beloved disciple" mentioned in this writing. The strongest argument most scholars present is that John, being a Galilean fisherman, was unable to write.[9] But, like other disciples, John must have had written documents of Jesus' teaching. He had been with Jesus and with the disciples in Jerusalem when the Church was first organized.[10] He probably dictated his material and instructed a scribe to write his gospel in the most appropriate manner possible. This scribe was responsible for the editing, compilation, and perhaps the final form that we now have in the authorized canon of the New Testament. John also might have had some education, although the Jewish priests and elders called both him and Peter "unlearned men."[11]

The external evidence for the gospel of John is based on the testimony of his two disciples, Polycarp and Papias, as reported by Irenaeus. Nevertheless, there are those who believe that there is only one John to whom the authorship of the fourth gospel could possibly be attributed and that is John the apostle.

---

[8]See Jn. 19:26, 35; 21:20.

[9]See Acts 4:13.

[10]Again, the majority of today's NT experts and historians, both Roman Catholic and Protestant, believe that no writer of any of the gospels was an eyewitness.

[11]See footnote 7.

CONCERNING THE LATE DATING

For modern interpreters of the New Testament, establishing a firm date for the fourth gospel is most difficult. Dates now range from 40 CE to 110 CE. Among commentators today and according to so-called internal evidence, 85 CE appears as the most favored date, along with its final editing around 100 CE.

Dr. Lamsa believed that a late dating of this gospel by some scholars is difficult to accept. Why would John wait so long? There would be no reason to wait until the end of the first century to dictate his preaching about Jesus. Dr. Lamsa also suggests that the late date assumption was brought about because of confusing the date of the original writing with the time that its copy appeared.

In the Near East, even today, the copy of an original is always dated from the day and year in which the copyist completes his work. For example, a book written in 1600 CE and copied in 1900 would bear the date when the copy was finished. The copyist adds "This book was written in 1900" instead of "copied" in that year. The reason for this is that the same word is used to mean write or copy. A stranger, not familiar with the custom, will not only mistake the copyist for the author but will be led to believe that the book was actually written in 1900.

Most likely John had an early original manuscript of his material with him, and other copies and translations were later made from these scrolls. This might have happened during the conversion of the Greeks. (John, like the other disciples, at the beginning preached to the Jews and other Semites who were living among Gentiles.)

MODERN DIVISION OF THE GOSPEL

John's gospel contains 21 chapters. The entire Bible was divided into chapters in the 13th century CE, in Europe, and in the 15th century CE, chapters were further divided into verses. Our present version of John's writing, with its numbered chapters and verses, was executed only 600 years ago. Today, scholars usually divide this book into five sections:

1. The Prologue (1:1-18.)
2. John the Baptist and the First disciples (1:19-51.)
3. The Book of Signs (2:1-12:50.)
4. The Book of Glory (13:1-20:30.)
5. The Epilogue (21:1-25.)

ANTISEMITISM IN JOHN'S GOSPEL?

Now we come to another misunderstanding in the Gospel of John. Jesus was a Semite and his teaching is based on the Semitic writings of the Hebrew Bible, Genesis to Malachi. He also embraced the Jewish faith of his parents. All of his apostles and disciples were Semites. Most of the gospel writers and editors were Semites. Then, how could this gospel promote "antisemitism?" It does criticize certain Jewish leadership, religious teachers, ideas and teachings. But that does not make it anti-Semitic. This gospel is sympathetic to true and pious Jewish interest and teaching.[12]

CONCLUDING POINTS

The gospel of John was written for the community of believers in Asia Minor. The author omitted the genealogy and birth of Jesus because the Jewish people in this region did not maintain a strong sense of nationality and traditional theology. This is the reason they allowed Paul to speak in their synagogues in support of a Galilean prophet, a man whom the religious authorities in Judea had sent to the cross as a blasphemer and criminal. Also, the Jews in these northern regions were mostly descendants of the Ten Tribes of Israel

---

[12]See Rober Kysar, JOHN'S ANTI-JEWISH POLEMIC, pp. 26-27, Bible Review, February 1993.

and were not very friendly to the Jews in southern Palestine.

What is most interesting is that John's account used to be interpreted in terms of Greek or gnostic philosophical ideas and forms of thinking. Western New Testament experts thought that the fourth gospel was the least Semitic of all. However, the past 50 years of work on the Dead Sea Scrolls and other works have brought new understanding on many ideas and phrases expressed in this book. Now some scholarly deduction has it that John's writing is the most Semitic and Jewish of all the gospels.

> "Before the discovery of the Dead Sea Scrolls, many scholars considered the Fourth Gospel—The Gospel According to John—to be a mid-to-late-second century composition inspired by Greek philosophy. Today, 45 years later, a growing scholarly consensus finds John to be a first-century composition. More surprising still, it is perhaps the most Jewish of the Gospels. Elements that were once thought to be reflections of Greek philosophy were all there at the time in contemporaneous Palestine."[13]

---

[13]See the scholarly writings of James H. Charlesworth, *Reinterpreting John: How the Dead Sea Scrolls Have Revolutionized Our Understanding of the Gospel of John*, pp.19-25, 54, Bible Review, February 1993. A reminder: The goal of this commentary on the Gospel (Preaching) of John is to present the writings from a Semitic, Aramaic cultural and linguistic point of view. The translation of many scriptural passages in John and comments are based on the Aramaic tongue and customs of the Near East. However, I also include some of the latest biblical research findings, studies and suggestions when necessary.

CHAPTER 1

THE PROLOGUE

The first chapter integrates metaphoric poetry into its first 18 verses. Commentators do not agree as to which verses of the structure are poetic and which are prose. Regardless of the varying divisions concerning the introductory verses, undoubtedly verses 6-8 and 15 are separate segments within the poetic prologue. Some New Testament experts referred to this preface as a hymn. The opening verses are a summary of John's gospel. One cannot fully appreciate this until the entire gospel has been read and studied.

The following poetic form of the prologue is a direct translation from the Aramaic Peshitta text, verses 1-18. It provides the framework for the gospel's narratives and monologues. All themes are developed from this introduction. However, its major theme is the eternal, living Word in its various manifestations as creative power, life, truth, light and, finally, as human form—Jesus of Nazareth, the Messiah/Christ, who is the heavenly Messenger.

THE COSMIC MESSENGER

The Word was always in existence;
and He, the Word, was always with God
And God was always that very Word.

From the beginning, this one was with God.
Through him everything came to exist,
and without him not even a single thing
came into existence.

All life came to exist through him,
and that life is the light of humanity.
And He, the light, shines in darkness,
and the darkness could not overtake it

7

And it happened that there was a man who had been sent from God; his name was John. This one came as a testimony that he might testify about the light so that through him everyone might believe. He was not the light but only that he might testify concerning the light.

Undeniably, He [the Word] was the light of truth
who came into the world and enlightens
everyone.

He was in the world,
and the world existed because of him;
yet the world did not recognize him.

But those who accepted him,
he gave them
the right to become children of God
to those who believe in his name.

Those who are not of a special lineage,
and not of the desire of the flesh,
and not of the desire of a man,
but are born of God.

Now the Word took human form,
and dwelt among us;
and we saw his preciousness,
a preciousness like that of an only
beloved son of the Father
who is filled with
loving kindness and justice.

And John testified concerning him and cried out and said: This is the one of whom I said he is coming after me, yet he is ahead of me because he was before me.

And from his abundance
we have all received
loving kindness in the place of
loving kindness.

For the Torah was given by Moses;
but truth and loving kindness came by Jesus,
the Messiah/Christ.

God has never been seen by anyone;
except God the only beloved,
who is in the bosom of the Father,
he has spoken.[1]

Explanations of the poetic, metaphoric introduction will follow in the comments below.

THE ETERNAL WORD

In the beginning was the Word, and the Word was with God, and the Word was God. Jn. 1:1.

Part 1—IN THE BEGINNING. It takes three English words—"in the beginning"—to express the Aramaic term *brasheeth*. This opening phrase places the "Word" in a cosmological frame. John's gospel repeats the same opening as Genesis 1:1 that introduced the cosmological prose poem:[2] "In the beginning (*brasheeth*) God created the heavens and the earth."

According to the Aramaic and Hebrew texts of Genesis, the creator deity (*Alaha*-Aramaic, *Elohim*-Hebrew) is totally free of temporal and spatial dimensions. This is the reason the author uses "in the beginning." For that ancient time, it was a first in Near Eastern history and thinking. Now the writer of the gospel prologue

---

[1] Jn. 1:1-18, Aramaic Peshitta text, Errico. The poetic song is as close to a literal rendering as possible. Its style, structure and poetic way of writing using Semitic metaphors is typically Aramaic and not Greek. Mar Ephraim wrote his biblical commentary in the same style. The Semitic author uses the masculine pronoun "he" in describing the "Word" because he refers to the Messenger—Jesus of Nazareth, who is the manifestation and bearer of the eternal word.

[2] See Gen. 1:1-5 for a parallel comparison with Jn. 1:1-5.

also perceives the "Word" in the same way. The "Word" is beyond space and time just as God is beyond space and time. Thus, the phrase "in the beginning" simply means "before time was reckoned." It carries the idea "in the remotest past that the human mind can conceive." There actually was no beginning as we understand a beginning. It means "timeless and measureless."[3] Thus, the opening phrase may also be translated as "The Word always was."

Part 2—THE WORD. According to the Aramaic text, the emphasis is on "the Word." The writer uses the Semitic term *miltha*. It is equivalent to the Hebrew word *ha-davar,* "the word." In Aramaic it can mean "word, saying, sentence, precept, utterance, message, command, a communication." And depending on its usage, it can also denote the faculty of "speech, thought, reason, mind-energy."

Grammatically speaking, the Aramaic term *miltha* is feminine. However, here in the gospel it is masculine. The word *miltha* has become a title and therefore indicates a special usage of the term. It is the Word of God. The reference here is to the Messiah/Christ whom God had promised to Abraham, Isaac, Jacob, David and the prophets. "And in thee shall all families of the earth be blessed."[4] "The scepter shall not depart from Judah until Shiloh come."[5]

The author of this gospel reveals a hidden truth that the Word existed from the beginning and Jesus, as the messenger, was the embodiment of God's eternal Word. God has no beginning or ending; therefore, the divine promises are eternal. God and the Word were from the very beginning. It is the creative Word that God utters. According to Genesis chapter one, our present cosmic order came into being through this Word. It is through the Word that God is revealed. In summation, the term "Word" in this verse designates an individual—a personification of God's creative mind-energy (intelligence) that manifested through a human being, Jesus of Nazareth, the heavenly Messenger.

---

[3]See Errico, *The Mysteries of Creation:* The Genesis Story, " The Beginning," pp. 72-75.
[4]Gen. 12:3.
[5]Gen 49:10.

The last phrase of verse one, which we call 1c, says: "and God was that very word." In other words, God and the creative, spoken Word are one and the same. If we can free our minds from fixed theological notions and dogmas, we will have no difficulty in understanding this last section of the verse. Some biblical translators interpret this phrase as "and divine was the word" instead of "and God was that very word." But this is a poor rendering of the phrase. The following is a quote from a Roman Catholic scholar, Raymond E. Brown:

> The New Testament does not predicate "God" of Jesus with any frequency . . . .Most of the passages suggested (Jn. 1:1, 18, 20:28; Rom. 9:5; Heb. 1:8; 2 Peter 1:1) are in hymns or doxologies—an indication that the title "God" was applied to Jesus more quickly in liturgical formulae than in narrative or epistolary literature. . . . The reluctance to apply this designation to Jesus is understandable as part of the New Testament heritage from Judaism. For the Jews "God" meant the heavenly Father; and until a wider understanding of the term was reached, it could not be readily applied to Jesus. This is reflected in Mark 10:18 where Jesus refuses to be called good because only God is good; in John 20:17 where Jesus calls the Father "my God"; and in Eph. 4:5-6 where Jesus is spoken of as "one Lord," but the Father is "one God." . . . In verse 1c the Johannine hymn is bordering on the usage of "God" for the Son, but by omitting the article [in Greek] it avoids any suggestion of personal identification of the Word with the Father. And for Gentile readers of the line also avoids any suggestion that the Word was a second God in any Hellenistic sense.[6]

Nonetheless, one must approach the idea of the Word from a Semitic point of view. Angels and prophets proclaimed God's words when they said: "Thus saith the Lord." When these angels and prophets spoke for the Lord God of Israel, they used the first person

---

[6]Raymond E. Brown, *The Gospel According to John*, Volume 1, p. 24, Anchor Bible Series.

singular "I." Their words were accepted as God's directive because they spoke in the stead of God. They were representatives of God. The Word and God were one (God and Being are the same)

According to Near Eastern custom, messengers who carry specific communications from a ruler or king are received with the same honor as the king they represent. A king's word is to be respected and obeyed. Any negative remark about the messenger or the word he brings would be regarded as an offence against the king. The king, his messenger and word are considered one and the same. An old Near Eastern proverb says: "A man is valued by his words."

God sent the Messiah/Christ as the messenger; therefore, he, the envoy, represented God. Jesus was representative of God's eternal, creative word. The gospel author uses Semitic terms of speech in connecting Jesus with the messianic promises or utterances and not Greek terms of speech. It is inconceivable that John, a son of Zebedee and a fisherman, or any other Semitic author could have used a Greek term like *logos,* as most scholars believe, with a meaning alien to Semitic thought. It simply means that God and his Messenger are one and the same just as a king and his messenger are one and the same. This accords with ancient Near Eastern custom and understanding.

As we read further in the text, we see that this powerful "word of God" becomes human.[7] By becoming human, the word of God can be seen with human eyes and felt by human hands.[8] God, as some elusive, mysterious creator and power, will no longer be a total mystery. For God will be known through the messenger—*Miltha,* the Word.

In verse 2, "He [the Word] was throughout eternity with God," the writer reinforces the idea that the Word was with God. He was from the very beginning that creative Word behind all creation. The poetic writing clearly recognizes the close union and relationship between God and the Word. This is not polytheism. It is the same relationship as between a ruler and the messenger that he sends.

---

[7] See verse 12.
[8] See 1 Jn. 1:1.

LIFE AND LIGHT

In him was life; and the life was the light of men. And the light shineth in darkness; and the darkness comprehended it not. Jn. 1:4-5.

The Aramaic text reads: "All life came to exist through him; and that very life is the light of humanity. And he, the light shines in the darkness and the darkness could not overtake it."[9] One of the major themes in this gospel is eternal life. Thus, to prepare the hearer or reader for this theme, the composer of the prologue tells us that the Word is not only responsible for creation (verse 3) but this creative Word is also the source of life. Through Jesus' teaching, one comes to know God, and knowing God is life eternal.[10] Jesus, as the revelator of God, brings eternal life to light. His teaching is the source of God's knowledge, eternal life and light for all humankind.

The idea of "light" is very important in Hebrew Scripture. People of the ancient world greatly feared darkness and thought of it as chaos. They believed that those who were alive on earth lived in light but those who were deceased dwelled in darkness. About two or three hundred years before the time of Jesus, the concept of light began to change. Light was not only equated with good, but it was involved in combat with the powers of darkness—that is, evil. In apocalyptic Jewish literature, there were "the sons (children) of light" and "the sons of darkness."

Jesus' teaching was the light that shines in the midst of darkness (chaos and evil). Darkness could not conquer the light of the Christ. His teaching overcomes all ignorance and evil in the present and in the future.

THE WORLD

He was in the world, and the world was made by him, and the world

---

[9] Jn. 1:4-5, Aramaic Peshitta text, Errico.
[10] Jn. 17:3.

knew him not. Jn. 1:10.

The Aramaic word *alma*, "world," has two meanings: "the cosmic order"—that is, " the physical universe"—and "the world of humanity." In this verse, the author emphasizes the world of human beings. According to the writer, it is very difficult for humans to recognize the living word when it is personified, i.e., personalized. An idea or teaching can be reasoned, accepted, or rejected. But, in this case, the world did not recognize the emissary, who embodied God's word. Throughout biblical history, ancient Israel did not heed Yahweh's word. As a nation they would obey for a certain period and then revert to worshiping other deities. As far as the author is concerned, the basic failure of the world is not recognizing who Jesus really was—the eternal Word, God's Messenger.

BORN OF GOD

He came unto his own, and his own received him not. But as many as received him, to them gave he power to become the sons of God, even to them that believe on his name; Which were born, not of blood, nor of the will of the flesh, nor of the will of man, but of God. Jn. 1:11-13.

The Aramaic text reads: "He came to his own and his own did not accept him. But those who accepted him, he gave them the right [authority] to become children of God, to those who believe in his name. Those who are not of a blood line, nor of the desire of the flesh, nor of the desire of a man, but born of God."[11]

The evangelist expresses his own thoughts about Jesus as the manifestation of God's word in human form. The sad note for the writer was that many of Jesus' own people did not accept him as the Messiah/Christ; nor did they embrace his lord's gospel of the kingdom. Nonetheless, those of his own nation and those of the world who did accept his teaching came to realize their own potential as

---

[11]Jn. 1:11-13, Aramaic Peshitta text, Errico.

14

children (literally, "sons") of God.

"But as many as received him, to them gave he power to become sons of God." The Aramaic term *shultana* means "power, authority, right." It is not power in the sense of energy but rather the right or authority to acknowledge one's sonship with God. At that time, people did not fully realize what it meant to be a child of God. Through Jesus—that is, through his teaching—people come to a full realization of their relationship and oneness with God. The phrase "even to them that believe on his name" is an Aramaic way of speaking and means "to believe in his teaching." One must practice and put into action Jesus' gospel of the kingdom.

The evangelist saw that many of the people to whom the gospel was preached did not accept this new teaching. There were those who were subject to false teaching and would refuse to exchange the material for the spiritual and error for truth.

Those who would accept Jesus' preaching of the kingdom would be given power to become "sons of God," meaning "God-like." These people were not born of flesh and blood, nor of any man's will, but were born of God. They were called by God to become heirs of the kingdom of heaven.

It was difficult for many people who were born of flesh and blood—that is, subject to human reasoning alone and under the will of other men—to change to a teaching that was so strange to their way of thinking. Jesus' message of the kingdom was radical to the minds of people who had forgotten the true teaching of the Hebrew prophets and were guided by the doctrines of the elders. Nothing but a spiritual birth or realization could awaken them to their divine sonship which was their true identity.

THE FIRSTBORN MALE

And the word was made flesh, and dwelt among us, (and we beheld his glory, the glory, as the only begotten of the Father), full of grace and truth." Jn. 1:14.

15

The Aramaic text reads: "And the word took human form, and dwelt [tented or lived] among us; and we saw his preciousness, a preciousness like that of a unique beloved son[12] of the Father who is filled with loving kindness and justice."[13] Literally: "And the word [*miltha*] was [became] flesh and set up his tent [that is, pitched his tent] among us." This verse takes us back to the time of the Exodus when God tented (dwelt—set up the tabernacle) with Israel in the desert . "And let them make me a sanctuary; that I may dwell among them."[14]

The Aramaic word for "glory" is *shoowha*. It literally refers to a particular form of "glory," the glorious or precious presence of a beloved, firstborn son. This entire second part of the phrase deals with Near Eastern custom, and we need to understand it from that point of view. I translated the Aramaic word *shoowha* as "preciousness" instead of "glory" because of its Semitic context referencing a Near Eastern father and his firstborn son

Biblical authors often express spiritual ideas and truths in figurative and human terms of speech. Therefore, we can easily misunderstand the writer's meaning and intention. According to Semitic thinking, God is Spirit. God never begets nor is begotten. God is not subject to conditions of time, space or birth. Nonetheless, Near Easterners speak of God in poetic and metaphoric terms. They often describe God, the infinite presence, as having ears, hands, eyes and even wings.

In Aramaic, *yeheedaya*[15] does not mean "only-begotten." It means the "unique beloved son," "one of a kind," and refers to the firstborn son who becomes the sole heir. People who speak Aramaic understand this term when referring to their children and especially when distinguishing between the firstborn son and other children in the family. When using the term with God and Jesus, it is used

---

[12]Or "firstborn"–see the meaning of the Aramaic word "yeheedaya" further in the comment.

[13]Jn. 1:14, Aramaic Peshitta text, Errico.

[14]Ex. 25:8.

[15]The word is pronounced—*ee-hee-dye-yah*.

figuratively.

Interestingly, the Greek term *monogenes* in the New Testament does not mean "only begotten." How is it then that translators came to use "only begotten" for both the Aramaic and Greek terms? A Roman Catholic New Testament scholar clarifies this part of translation history for us:

> Literally the Greek means "of a single [*monos*] kind [*genos*]." Although *genos* is distantly related to *gennan*, " beget," there is little Greek justification for the translation of *monogenes* as "only begotten." The Old Latin version correctly translated it as *unicus*, "only," and so did Jerome where it was not applied to Jesus. But to answer the Arian claim that Jesus was not begotten but made, Jerome translated it as *unigenitus*, "only begotten," in passages like this one (also Jn. 1:18, 3:16, and 18.). The influence of the Vulgate on the King James made "only begotten" the standard English rendition. (Actually, as we have insisted, John does not use the term "begotten" of Jesus.) *Monogenes* describes a quality of Jesus, his uniqueness and not what is called in Trinitarian theology his "procession." It reflects Hebrew *yahid*, "only, precious," which is used in Genesis 22:2, 12, 16, of Abraham's son Isaac, as *monogenes* is used of Isaac in Hebrews 11:17. Isaac was Abraham's uniquely precious son, but not his only begotten.[16]

In the Near East, the firstborn son is the *yeheedaya*, "the sole heir" of all the father possesses. This "beloved son" is the glory and honor of his father. He is the one who will succeed his father, carry his name, and inherit his business. He will also be in charge of all his father's household and will give orders to his father's wife or wives. Other children do not inherit what the firstborn is to inherit. Nor do they have the responsibility that he will bear. In the parable of the Prodigal Son, Luke 15:11-32, the father says to the oldest son: "My son, you are always with me, and everything that is mine is yours."

---

[16]Raymond E. Brown, *The Gospel According to John*, I-XII, *A New Translation with Introduction and Commentary*, "Notes" and "Only Son," pp. 13-14.

The Aramaic word *bukhra*, "firstborn," is the same as the Hebrew word *bakhar*, which means "first fruits." In a family where there are many females but only one male child, more attention is paid to the male. The father and mother are wrapped up in him, and his sisters weave garments for him and wait on him. In the past, as late as the early 1900s, females of Semitic regions could not inherit property. A male child is always loved and needed so that he may preserve the family name and its possessions. When a father dies without leaving a male heir, his daughters and his property are divided among his nearest male relatives, and his own family may even be left destitute.

Jesus is the "beloved" because he is the firstborn of his father and the first one who thought of God as a loving Father. At that time, God was thought of as an overlord, who could be approached only by intermediaries and sacrificial offerings. Jesus unveiled the mystery of God and was thus recognized as the firstborn and beloved of the Father.

John uses the Aramaic term *yeheedaya* to mean that Jesus expressed a unique and beloved relationship with God as a father. Jesus' life was a vital and powerful manifestation of divine sonship. Therefore, he became known as the "sole heir"—that is, the "first-born" who inherits the Father's truth and shares with humanity—and as the "uniquely beloved son" of this universal and spiritual truth of divine sonship for the human family.

In his letter to the Romans, Paul says that Jesus is "the firstborn among many brethren."[17] According to the New Testament, through Jesus' teachings we come to understand that we and all nationalities are children of God. He constantly showed his sonship by his good works, teaching, various kinds of healing, and his spiritual presence after his ordeal of crucifixion and death. "And who came to be known as the Son of God with power and with the Holy Spirit, because he arose from the dead, and he is Jesus the Messiah our Lord."[18]

---

[17]Rom. 8:29.
[18]Rom. 1:4, Aramaic Peshitta text, Errico.

As the "firstborn son" brings joy to the hearts of his parents and glorifies them, so does Jesus, through his life and teaching, bring joy to all human beings. Humanity had lost this understanding of spiritual sonship. Jesus reinstates and reinforces the awareness that the human family is "the image and likeness of God."[19]

A Near Eastern father glories when he sees his "beloved son, the firstborn" because he sees himself re-created in his offspring. This is what John says about God as a father: "The glory as of the only beloved son of the Father." According to the author, it is only through Jesus' teaching that people learn of their spiritual sonship again.

"Full of grace and truth" means to be full of "goodness and justice." It is through the Christ that we see the favor of God (free salvation) to human beings and know the true justice (truth) of God. The Aramaic word *taybootha* means "favor, loving kindness, goodness." "Truth" here is the Aramaic word *qooshta*, and it refers to truth in the sense of "justice." God is just and, thus, the Word—that is, the Christ—is a manifestation of God's justice. God is faithful to the covenant and this truth is always just. In summation, the creative Word that was with God and is God now assumes human form and lives with humanity. This living, eternal Word is faithful and full of love that expresses kindness and truthfulness.

"And the word was made flesh" also expands the idea of the first verse: "In the beginning was the word and that very word was with God and God was that very word." God's word, the message, humanizes or incarnates itself in the messenger. Once a king makes his word known to a messenger, that messenger not only carries the word but it lives in him as well. Jesus is the living messenger that carries God's word. God's message humanized in Jesus of Nazareth. And as the messenger is (represents) the king, so is Jesus, as the messenger, God. This is not theology but Near Eastern custom.

---

[19]Gen. 1:26-27.

GRACE UPON GRACE

And of his fulness have all we received, and grace for grace. For the law was given by Moses, but grace and truth came by Jesus Christ. Jn. 1:16-17.

In verse 15, the gospel writer introduces John the Baptist again because he represents the last of the prophets under the former grace of the Mosaic law. But in the above verses, 16-17, the writer makes a contrast between the gift of the law given by God through Moses with the gifts of grace and truth (loving kindness and justice) given by God through Jesus as Messiah/Christ.

The phrase "grace for grace" means that a greater grace, favor and loving kindness brought through Jesus, surpasses the grace of the Mosaic law. In other words, "grace upon grace" or "grace in the stead of grace." We must not misunderstand the intention of the author. The contrast he makes between Moses and Jesus is not to denigrate Moses but to exalt the grace that came under Jesus. For it was Moses who testified that one greater than he was to come. This is the reason he writes "grace in place of grace." In other words, under the Messiah/Christ, his followers have received the fullness of divine grace.

GOD CANNOT BE SEEN

No man hath seen God at any time: the only begotten Son, which is in the bosom of the Father, he hath declared him. Jn.1:18.

Part 1—SEEING GOD. God can only be known—that is, felt—through intuition and being, rather than doing and thinking. In the book of Exodus we read: "And the Lord spoke to Moses face to face, as a man speaks to his friend."[20] In Semitic languages, "face to face" means that God conversed with Moses openly, not in metaphors

---

[20]Ex. 33:11, Aramaic Peshitta text, Lamsa translation.

20

and figurative speech. To the prophets and seers, he spoke in dreams and visions, using Semitic imagery and figurative speech, but to Moses God spoke directly. Moses felt the presence of God and heard the divine voice intuitively, for Moses had a great understanding of God and spiritual matters. Therefore, there was no need for figurative speech.

The Hebrew prophet Isaiah tells us that angels covered their faces when they approached God's presence. God has no face and no form; God is substance, essence, premise and intelligence that governs the universe. Thus, no one has seen God and no one can describe God. Scripture informs us that even Elijah could not see God's face.

God reveals itself in similitudes so that humans may come to understand what God is. God often appears as a human being in dreams, visions or when people are in a trance state. According to Jesus, God is spirit and not a human being.

God can only be seen in spirit and truth, just as the Christ is spirit, life and truth and can only be seen the same way. This is the reason that Jesus said "he that hath seen me hath seen the Father." In other words, he was good as God is good, for only good can reflect good, and evil reflects only evil. (See John. 4:23-24, 14:8-9.)

Part 2—IN THE BOSOM. The term "in the bosom" is an idiom that expresses someone who is "dear, close and beloved." When Near Eastern men express their love to their children, they hold them close to their chest. In other words, they are hugging their children close to their hearts. Shepherds also hold newly born lambs in their arms close to their chests.

God is the eternal Spirit and has no human form. Near Eastern Semites, when conveying a spiritual truth, always translate the idea in human terms of speech. They do this so that people may understand their spiritual ideas.

John the apostle and evangelist uses the term "bosom" to express the abundant love of God for the Messiah/Christ. By holding Christ in the divine bosom, God is declaring to the world that the Messiah/Christ is the godly, beloved son.

21

THE FORERUNNER

And this is the record of John, when the Jews sent priests and Levites from Jerusalem to ask him, Who art thou? And he confessed, and denied not; but confessed, I am not the Christ. And they asked him, What then, Art thou Elias? And he said, I am not. Art thou that prophet? And he answered, No. Then said they unto him, Who art thou? That we may give an answer to them that sent us. What sayest thou of thyself? He said, I am the voice of one crying in the wilderness, Make straight the way of the Lord, as said the prophet Esaias. Jn. 1:19-23.

The writer uses the term "Jews" throughout the gospel to indicate only certain groups of Jews who were opposed to Jesus, whether ecclesiastical or non-ecclesiastical authorities. It does not mean all Jewish people. It is supposed that the Pharisees sent their official delegation to inquire of John the Baptist. However, it is unlikely that the Pharisees would have done this. In the early first century, priests had greater authority than the Pharisees. It is more likely that the evangelist reflects conditions at the end of the first century, where the situation was reversed. In other words, at the end of the first century the Pharisees and not the priests had the greater authority. According to the gospels of Matthew, Mark and Luke, the Jewish people and many religious leaders favored John the Baptist. There was no open confrontation with him.

Levites were another branch of the priesthood but were not as powerful as the priests themselves. They were helpers whose primary duty was to assist in temple services, especially as musicians. (Rabbinic sources tell us that from time to time, the Levites functioned as temple guardians—that is, as police.)

John the Baptist clearly and emphatically denies his role as the Messiah or any other prophet. He says: "I am not the Messiah." "I am not Elijah nor a prophet." These statements show that the ministry of the Baptist is to decrease while the ministry of Jesus is to increase. He also denies being that special end-time prophet[21] or even the

---

[21] Dt. 18:18, Maccabees 4:46, 14:41.

fulfillment of the Malachi prophesy.[22] Malachi predicted that the prophet Elijah would come before the day of the Lord (Yahweh). The Baptist did not accept any title nor any special position. He claimed that he was only a clear, true voice as predicted by the Hebrew prophet Isaiah.[23]

"A voice crying out in the wilderness" is a Semitic idiom and refers to an unobstructed voice—that is, a message that is simple and straight to the point. John was to clear a path for the coming one who was greater than he. In the Near East, before any great leader or potentate entered a town, preparations were made to clean up the roads and, if necessary, to make a road ready to receive and celebrate the arriving dignitary. John the Baptist was simply the forerunner to prepare the way for the coming new world leader. He did so by preparing the hearts and minds of the people to receive the Messiah.[24]

THE LAMB OF GOD

The next day John seeth Jesus coming unto him, and saith, Behold the Lamb of God, which taketh away the sin of the world. Jn. 1:29.

When Near Easterners visit shrines and holy places they pledge a lamb or an ox to God. The worshipers, during their prayers, ask God to grant their requests, promising to offer a gift when the petition has been granted. In addition to this, Semites believe that God has a share in their sheep and other products because God is the source of all supply. They must give so that they may receive. They pledge to God the best lambs and oxen before they are born.

According to Near Eastern custom, families will choose a lamb that is the finest, fattest, and without any blemish among newly born

---

[22] Mal. 4:5-6.

[23] Isa. 40:3.

[24] See Errico and Lamsa, *Aramaic Light on the Gospel of Matthew*, "Mightier Than I," pp. 34-36 and *Aramaic Light on the Gospels of Mark and Luke*, "Part 2, The Voice in the Wilderness," pp. 6-7.

lambs. Then they will dedicate it to God for the sake of a particular member of the household. Families usually make their choice in early spring when farmers' livestock (oxen, sheep, cattle) begin giving birth to their offspring. Once they have chosen the one they want, they refer to it as "the lamb of God."

The shepherd in charge of this precious lamb will lavish a great deal of care and love upon this little animal. Then, either at the end of summer or in the early autumn, they will sacrifice the lamb, broil its meat, and share it with people who are attending the ceremony at the shrine. They will also rub the blood of the lamb on the person for whom the animal has been chosen and dedicated to God.

Jesus was as an innocent lamb without blemish. Humanity chose Jesus, a lamb, as an offering to God. Jesus' death, as a righteous man, would do away with the sacrifice of animals. He was to be the living, spiritual sacrifice of love that constantly remains on the altar. He was the suffering servant of God.[25]

The author tells us that Jesus, as the sacrificial lamb, delivers the world from sin's power. "To take away sin" means to destroy its power. This deliverance breaks the terrible grip that sin (grave error)[26] has upon the world of humanity. Through Jesus' death on the cross, a new reality was to be born for the world—an undivided, harmonious world of peace, joy and love.

JESUS GUIDED BY SPIRIT

And the two disciples heard him speak, and they followed Jesus. Then Jesus turned, and saw them following, and saith unto them, What seek ye? They said unto him, Rabbi, (which is to say, being interpreted, Master.) Where dwellest thou? He saith unto them, Come and see. They came and saw where he dwelt, and abode with him that day: for it was about the tenth hour. Jn. 1:37-39.

---

[25]See Isa. 52:13-15, 53:1-12.
[26]Sin in Aramaic means "to miss, to miss the mark," thus, an "error, mistake."

The Aramaic text reads: "And when he said it, two of his disciples heard it; and they went after Jesus. And Jesus turned around and saw them following him, and he said to them, What do you want? They said to him, Rabban, where do you live? He said to them, Come and you will see. And they came and saw where he stayed, and they remained with him that day; and it was about the tenth hour."[27]

John the Baptist had humbly declared to his disciples that he was not the Messiah. He told them that Jesus of Nazareth was the promised one and the lamb of God. John's declaration concerning Jesus made some of his disciples leave him and go after Jesus. When the two disciples saw Jesus beyond the Jordan, they addressed him as "Rabban." This is an Aramaic term meaning "our teacher, chief, or great one." It was an honorific term and, at that time, was the greatest title given to a teacher of religion.[28]

Jesus never remained at any one place for a long period of time. He was always on the go. This is the reason he told John's two disciples who were looking for him to come and find out for themselves where he was staying. Jesus, like John the Baptist, had no financial support. He went wherever he was invited and where the spirit guided him. Many times Jesus went hungry and lodged in caves and fields.

One of the first disciples was Andrew, who then informed his brother, Simon Peter, that he had found the Messiah. (See John 1:40-41.)

THE MESSIAH

He first findeth his own brother Simon, and saith unto him, We have found the Messias, which is, being interpreted, the Christ Jn. 1:41.

The word "Messiah" is *m'sheeha* in Aramaic and *m'shakh* in

---

[27] Jn. 1:37-39, Aramaic Peshitta text, Errico.

[28] See Errico and Lamsa, *Aramaic Light on the Gospel of Matthew*, "Rabbi and Father," p. 282, Part A "Rabbi."

Hebrew. It derives from the Semitic root *m'shakh*, meaning "to anoint with oil." The Aramaic word for "oil" is *misha*.

The Hebrew people also interpreted the term Messiah as one who is a mediator or intermediary. It is probable that Israel borrowed this Chaldean interpretation of the Messiah during the Babylonian (Chaldean) captivity. They used it concerning the promised one who was to bring reconciliation between God and his estranged people. In truth, the Messiah/Christ was to be a mediator between God and humanity.[29]

The Christ was ordained for this mission from the very beginning. All other efforts would fail. Truth must finally be revealed by the eternal word through the messenger, Jesus the Messiah/Christ. Reconciliation would come about through Jesus' teaching of the gospel of God's kingdom.[30]

SIMON KEPA

And he brought him to Jesus. And when Jesus beheld him, he said, Thou art Simon the son of Jona: thou shalt be called Cephas, which is by interpretation, a stone. Jn. 1:42.

In all Greek versions of the New Testament, the Greek word *Petros*, "stone," is a direct translation of the Aramaic word *Kepa* (pronounced *Kay-pah*), meaning "stone." However, the proper name of Andrew's brother is Simon. In Aramaic, it is *Shimon* and comes from the root *shma*, "to hear." As a proper name, it signifies "he who hears, one who is alert, sharp and perceptive." Simon is one of the most popular and common names among Semites. It is a sacred name that a mother bestows on her son when God has answered a prayer for a male child, signifying God has heard her voice.

Most Semitic names have religious meaning. Semites do not use names of common articles for human beings. Nonetheless, when they

---

[29] See Gal. 3:20.
[30] See Mt. 16:15-16; Mk. 8:29, Lk. 9:20.

are upset with each other, they will use nicknames that are disparaging. In the case of Simon, however, the term "stone" is not used disparagingly but for another reason.

For example, if a man's name happens to mean "sweet" but he always displays a grumpy disposition, the community would nickname him "sour." In Simon's situation, his nickname came about because he could not grasp or see through things easily. In reality, it would have been an insult to Simon if Jesus, who had just met him, called him "Stone." Jesus was merely repeating what was commonly known about him. The Aramaic text reads: "And he [Andrew] brought him to Jesus. And Jesus looked at him and said, You are Simon the son of Jonah; you are called [nicknamed] Kepa."[31]

Andrew was introducing his brother Simon to Jesus. While Jesus was greeting him, he mentions the fact that he knows Simon's nickname. People know of one another without being acquainted. Probably, Simon was a fisherman and hunter of notable reputation. These particular occupations give one much publicity in the Near East. The Aramaic text uses the names Simon or Simon Kepa and not Peter. The writers used the proper name and nickname together to distinguish him from Simon the Canaanite and other Simons.

THE PROPHET FROM NAZARETH

Philip findeth Nathanael, and saith unto him, We have found him, of whom Moses in the law, and the prophets, did write, Jesus of Nazareth, the son of Joseph. And Nathanael said unto him, Can there any good thing come out of Nazareth? Philip saith unto him, Come and see. Jn. 1:45-46.

Nazareth was a small town in Galilee. Some of the Jewish sects despised this town because it was inhabited by Gentiles—that is, other Semitic races who had become Jews by religion.

Centuries before, the King of Assyria had brought people from

---

[31]Aramaic Peshitta text, Lamsa translation. The phrase "which is by interpretation a stone" in the King James Version is not present in the Aramaic text.

27

the other side of the River Euphrates and settled them in Galilee after the ten northern tribes of Israel were taken captive in 722 BCE. Many Jewish leaders and religious authorities rejected the Galilean claim to the Jewish faith because these people were of mixed Semitic races. This is the reason that the Jewish officials told Nicodemus: "Examine the scriptures; no prophet shall rise from Galilee."[32]

When the Jews returned from the Chaldean exile (Babylonian captivity), the ancestors of the Galileans came to Zerubbabel and to the chiefs of the fathers and offered to help rebuild the temple. They said that since the captivity they had been worshiping the God of Israel. But the Jews refused their assistance.[33] So we see that even centuries before Jesus, the Jews had rejected the Galileans, who were referred to as the adversaries of Judah and Benjamin.

Jesus and his disciples were Galileans and spoke the Galilean northern dialect of Aramaic. The Hebrew prophet Isaiah calls Galilee "the land of the Gentiles, the people who dwell in darkness." This famous statesman predicted that a great light would shine from Galilee and that the Messiah would become a light unto the Gentiles.[34]

Nathaniel was to become a disciple of Jesus but not one of the twelve.[35] His reply to Philip was a mixture of scorn and mistrust. He was skeptical about anything good happening in Nazareth.

---

[32] See Jn. 7:52.

[33] See Ezra 4:1-4.

[34] See Isa. 9:1-2.

[35] Some NT interpreters believe that Nathaniel was just a symbolic figure representing Israel and not a real person. However, there is no proof to support such a notion although the gospel author may be using the real Nathaniel as a symbol for Israel. An Aramaic speaking Bishop, Ishodad of Merv, in the 9th century CE thought Nathaniel was one of the twelve apostles, i.e., Bartholomew. Again we lack any evidence for such an idea. This story of Nathaniel, as a faithful disciple, was a received tradition among the Johannine community.

UNDER THE FIG TREE

Nathanael said unto him, Whence knowest thou me? Jesus answered and said unto him, Before that Philip called thee, when thou wast under the fig tree, I saw thee. Jn. 1:48

The Aramaic text reads: "Then Jesus saw Nathaniel as he was coming toward him and he said concerning him: Look, truly, a son of Israel, there is no deceit in him! Nathaniel questioned him: How do you know what kind of person I am? Jesus replied: Even before Philip called you I knew about you. Nathaniel answered and said to him: My teacher (*rabbi*), You are God's son, you are the King of Israel!"[36]

Jesus traveling to Galilee and then meeting and calling Philip seems to be intentional. (It may be that the author's idea was to place the emphasis on Philip going after Nathaniel, who was from Jesus' region.) Philip's town was Bethsaida Julius, which was located on the northeastern shore of the Lake of Galilee. It was also the hometown of Simon and Andrew.

Philip had just informed Nathaniel that he had found the "prophet" whom Moses had predicted would come.[37] Although Nathaniel was doubtful and skeptical, he did decide to go and see what Philip was so excited about. He was willing to see for himself if what he was hearing were true. When Jesus saw Nathaniel approaching, he remarked that this one was truly an Israelite in whom there was no guile. Nathaniel was an outspoken man but honest and sincere. Jesus spoke out about Nathaniel's character and integrity.

Nathaniel was surprised by Jesus' remark and asked him: "How do you know about me?" Jesus answered him, using an Aramaic idiom: "I saw you under the fig tree." This idiomatic phrase means "I have known about you since you were a child or since you were in the cradle." To say "I have seen you under the fig tree" does not mean I have actually seen you under the tree, but that I know you

---

[36]Jn. 1: 47-49, Aramaic Peshitta text, Errico.
[37]Dt. 18:15-18.

29

very well. This idiom comes from an old custom.

During the hot summer months, fig trees serve as a protection from the scorching sun. While the women work in the fields, their babies lie under the shadow of the trees. There is also a tradition that says when Joseph and Mary fled to Egypt, Jesus saw Nathaniel under a fig tree. The problem with this tradition is that Jesus would not remember such a happening that occurred when he was a baby. Today, Aramaic speaking people say, "I saw you when you were in the yoke of an egg." These expressions are idiomatic terms of speech and must not be understood literally.

The writer was not telling us that Jesus saw a vision of Nathaniel under a fig tree, but that Jesus knew something of Nathaniel's character and good reputation. Nazareth is not very far from the Lake of Galilee. Semites speak and know about each other although they may have never met. Once Jesus acknowledged Nathaniel's good qualities, it created in Nathaniel a sense of awe and appreciation for the Nazarene teacher. He surrendered himself to Jesus as the son of God—that is, as God's messenger.

AN OPEN HEAVEN

Jesus answered and said unto him, Because I said unto thee, I saw thee under the fig tree, believest thou? Thou shalt see greater things than these. And he said unto him, Verily, verily, I say unto you, Hereafter ye shall see heaven open, and the angels of God ascending and descending upon the Son of man. Jn. 1:50-51.

Because Jesus had known about Nathaniel's traits and qualities, the young man was ready to believe in the teacher from Nazareth. It was a complete turn around for Nathaniel and the opposite to what he had said earlier to Philip: "Can anything good be found in Nazareth?" Jesus assured not only Nathaniel but all the other disciples who were present that they would see greater things. "Truly, truly, I say to all of you that from now on all of you will see the sky opened and God's messengers coming and going to this Human Being!"[38]

In the Near East when kings, princes, governors and high officials are on good terms with one another, there is always open communication passing back and forth between them. Governmental emissaries and court messengers carry ordinances and messages constantly to each other. When relationships become strained then all contacts come to a halt.

"Hereafter ye shall see heaven open, and the angels of God ascending and descending upon the Son of Man" is typical Aramaic speech. It means that from now on there will be constant messages and communication between heaven and Jesus. In other words, what had been a mystery would be revealed through Jesus. An "open heaven" refers to "mysteries unveiled or revelations made known." The term "angels" (messengers) means "God's counsel, thoughts." Messengers would be coming and going to Jesus as a "son of man," i.e., human being. Communication between heaven and earth would take place through the ministry of Jesus.

Jesus lived in an era when some religious teachers were telling people that God had distanced himself from this world. According to these men, God had nothing to do with humankind. This period in Jewish history is called Deism. Also, during this period no prophets or seers had appeared on the scene. Israel as a nation had been without them for many years. God had been silent, but now heaven was open and God's messages would be declared.

Many people at that time had acknowledged John the Baptist as a prophet. He was the last prophet of the old order and he had been a witness that Jesus was the Anointed. Now Jesus' teaching would bring open communication between heaven and earth. His teaching was the revelation of God to humanity. This revelation was to come through angelic powers—that is, through God's counsel and the Spirit of truth to men and women everywhere.

---

[38] Jn. 1:51, Aramaic Peshitta text, Errico.

31

CHAPTER 2

THE WEDDING AT CANA

And when they wanted wine, the mother of Jesus saith unto him, They have no wine. Jesus saith unto her, Woman, what have I to do with thee? Mine hour is not yet come. Jn. 2:3-4.

The Aramaic text reads: "What is it to me and to you, woman? My turn has not yet come." This rendering is more expressive of a Semitic, Near Eastern wedding custom. The phrasing indicates: "This is not our concern, mother. It is not my turn to buy the wine for the wedding feast." Jesus was not rebuking his mother nor did he speak harshly to her as the King James Version implies: "Woman, what have I to do with thee? Mine hour is not yet come." In Aramaic, the term *atta*, "woman," is a polite and respectful form of speech. It is equivalent to "madame."

The Aramaic word *shaa* means "hour, time, turn." However, in this passage it signifies "turn." Jesus' reply to his mother was referring to the custom that male celebrants attending the wedding keep the wine flowing to the guests. This is especially necessary for a poor man's wedding feast. At the celebration, men sit on the floor in a line in the order of their age and social standing. The rich, honorable and noble sit in high places. The poor and least important men sit in lower places. But both the poor and rich may drink and rejoice. Women also sit on the floor but on the opposite side in a circle. Musicians and servants occupy a position near the door. The bridegroom bears the major responsibility of supplying the food for the feast unless he is poor. Neighbors bring favorite prepared dishes as gifts to the bridal couple. One can see women coming with trays on their heads bearing these special foods. And, as we mentioned earlier, wine is provided by the male guests. Everything is done on a liberal scale.

Guests take their turns when assigning the servants to procure wine for the party. As the servants pour and serve the wine, they mention the name of the guest who has purchased the round of wine. It is then drunk by all to the health and happiness of the couple. Every guest must do his duty in this matter so that the wedding banquet may be merry and successful. Nevertheless, it is improper for any guest to call a server to bring the wine out of turn. It must follow the social protocol of the wedding feast. If such a circumstance were to happen, even by mistake, it would create resentment among the guests who had not yet had their proper turn. Such a departure from this traditional practice would also be regarded as an insult to the guests of higher standing. It is incumbent upon every celebrant at such a time to give proof of his friendship and loyalty to the bridegroom. If any guest fails in this duty, he is regarded as an enemy.

Generally, a Near Eastern wedding lasts from three to seven days. Although Near Easterners are usually sober, they drink heavily on these festive occasions. Men are almost compelled to become inebriated. If a man does not drink and become merry, others take this refusal as a sign of his disapproval of the wedding match or even as a sign of jealousy. It is considered a great honor to become drunk at a friend's wedding, thus assuring a successful party. Women, on the other hand, do not drink at weddings but sit and watch their husbands and sons enjoy themselves. Often they are engaged in conversation and gossip about the bride and, at the same time, they constantly keep an eye on their male relatives. These women would be hurt if the names of their husbands or sons were not mentioned as generous providers for the celebration.

At the wedding feast of Cana, Mary had her eyes fastened on her son as she sat with a group of women. Among the guests, Jesus was probably the only one who was sober. (Religious teachers and holy men do not have to drink.) It was also evident to Mary that her son had not yet taken his part in entertaining the guests with a round of drinks. It might have happened that there was a lull in the course of the festivities. Many of the servants were standing idle, for according to the Aramaic text, "the wine had decreased." Mary, supposing it was Jesus' turn to treat the guests, made a sign to him with her eyes. Her facial expressions and gestures were saying: "They have no wine. You must do your part now." Jesus responded to his mother by gesturing with his face and hands that his turn had not yet come. Mary then turned to the servants who were standing near her and whispered to them that they should do whatever Jesus might request of them. This also meant that when Jesus sent them to procure wine, she would pay for it.

Mary and Jesus had come a distance from Nazareth to Cana. In the Near East when a mother and son travel together, the mother usually holds the family purse. They do this because Near Eastern bandits regard it cowardly to rob a woman. Mary had not the least thought that Jesus would perform a miracle. Jesus, as a young man, had shown no signs or given any proof of messianic powers, nor had he done any miracles. Why should his mother expect him to perform a miracle at this time? She was really the most surprised and gratified when she heard the chief guest exclaim that the last round of drinks was the best. The guests had expected to be served water because they had seen Jesus command the servers to fill the earthen jars with water. They knew he was a prophet and religious teacher.

Religious men who attend banquets may not only decline to purchase wine for the guests but may also urge male guests to stop drinking. They know the danger that drunkenness poses during wedding feasts. As it often happens during this time, over indulgence in wine can result in quarrels and perhaps even lead to unintentional murder. Generally, religious men refrain from drinking at these banquets. They make every effort to help pacify the guests who keep insisting on having more wine. It would be scandalous for a holy man to order more wine and instead he will often suggest water.

When the wine began to decrease, Jesus did not order more wine nor did he pray over the jars to change the water into wine. He simply ordered the servants to give the guests water which, according to the chief guest (master of ceremonies), tasted best of all. Jesus never claimed during his ministry that he changed water into an intoxicant. When John the Baptist sent messengers to question Jesus to see if he was the Messiah or not, Jesus answered: "Go and describe to John the things which you see and hear. The blind see and the lame walk and lepers are cleansed and the deaf hear and the dead rise up and the poor are given hope."[1] Jesus did not tell these men that he was a miracle worker who could change water into wine.

We need to realize that the gospel writer recorded this incident at least 40 to 45 years after Jesus' death. The writer's statements, "And when the chief guest tasted the water that had become wine. . . .This is the first miracle which Jesus performed in Cana of Galilee and thus he showed his glory,"[2] are based solely on the remark made by the chief guest. "Then the chief guest called the bridegroom and said to him, Every man at first brings the best wine; and when they have drunk then that which is weak; but you have kept the best wine until now." These words from the chief guest to the bridegroom were meant as a compliment to Jesus as a prophet and teacher. Undoubtedly, Jesus served the best drink of all. Water is the most precious liquid in the world. People can live without wine but no living creature can survive without water. Jesus had divine power but did he serve more wine to those who already had been drinking too much? Holy Scripture condemns drunkenness: ". . . nor drunkards. . . shall inherit the kingdom of God."[3]

(Some churches in the Near East use unfermented wine for Communion. Others dilute fermented wine by adding two parts water to one part wine. In either case, fermented or unfermented, in ancient days as well as today, both kinds of drinks are called wine.)

Symbolically speaking, water represents life, light and truth. In addition, the term "wine," metaphorically, means "joy, teaching, inspiration." Interestingly, and depending on how it is used in speech, wine can also be symbolic of teaching that is polluted with traditions.

This incident has a spiritual significance. Jesus' teaching was the best the Galileans had ever heard. Jesus solved the shortage of wine

---

[1]Mt. 11:4-5, Aramaic Peshitta text, Lamsa translation.
[2]Jn. 2:9,11, Aramaic Peshitta text, Lamsa translation.
[3]1 Cor. 6:10, K. J. V.

35

by offering the guests water and quenching their thirst with a spiritual wine which represented his pure teaching. Prior to this time, the people of Galilee had been governed by man-made traditions, but from now on the teaching of Jesus would govern them.[4] Jesus' wine was truth and inspiration. The master of ceremonies spoke in figurative speech that was typical of Near Easterners on such occasions. Nevertheless, he spoke the truth concerning Jesus. He commended the wine of God—that is, the new insights and knowledge that the prophet from Nazareth was teaching throughout Galilee.

Some of the ancient Aramaic speaking writers and commentators on Scripture say: "The wine that Jesus gave was a spiritual wine, the earth was not its mother, the water was not its father, nor was it nourished by the air. It was the wine of God."

The change that Jesus wrought was a miracle, not just because the guests drank a better wine—a spiritual wine—but because the need was met with a wine that satisfies the soul. The wine that God made was the presence of his messenger who gives true teaching. God's wine intoxicates the soul and spirit with joy and inspiration, filling the heart with truth and the knowledge that comes to know life everlasting.

DEALERS AND MONEY CHANGERS

And found in the temple those that sold oxen and sheep and doves, and the changers of money sitting: And when he had made a scourge of small cords, he drove them all out of the temple, and the sheep, and the oxen; and poured out the changers' money, and overthrew their tables; Jn. 2:14-15.

Streets of Near Eastern cities are very narrow and one may only

---

[4]Many modern NT scholars, both Protestant and Roman Catholic, believe that this narrative is the invention of the gospel storyteller. Others suggest that the story comes from common lore. Regardless of whether one takes this episode as a historical happening or not, the story follows Near Eastern custom. The narrative also suggests depths of symbolic meaning. Semitic scribes did write in a symbolic style.

walk in single file in either direction. Even today crowds that gather before the shops in Jerusalem are often dispersed so that the flow of pedestrian traffic can become easier. Peddlers and small traders follow prospective buyers for hours, offering bargains so that they may induce them to purchase their goods.

Jesus made a whip of small cords twisted together and tied at both ends. Cord is always found in the market places. It is used to tie burdens on the backs of men and animals. Jesus did not put out the regular merchants. He only threw out the money changers and those who were buying animals in advance of the Passover to hold for large profits. He overturned the trays of money changers who were not there legally.[5] Money changers sit on the ground close to the walls of the houses. There were no tables, and in many areas of the Near East, they are still unknown.

The Aramaic text, verse 14, reads: "And he found in the temple those who were buying oxen and sheep and doves, and the money changers sitting." Notice that the Aramaic text reads that these men were "buying," but the King James Version reads that the men were "selling." One can easily see how this mistranslation occurred. In Aramaic the same word is used for buying and selling. A point placed over the second letter means "selling," but a dot placed under the same letter denotes "buying."

It would be more reasonable to understand that Jesus dispersed the tumultuous crowd that was bargaining, swearing, expectorating and conducting dishonest business. This kind of dealing should not be carried out on temple grounds. He did not interfere with legitimate temple business that was permitted during festivals. Thousands of people had come from other towns and far countries. They had to purchase oxen, sheep and doves for their sacrifices. They had to exchange their money for temple money, which was the only kind that could be offered to God in the temple. It was the dishonesty that provoked Jesus.

---

[5]See Errico and Lamsa, *Aramaic Light on the Gospel of Matthew*, "House of Prayer, p. 259.

DEFENDING THE HOUSE OF PRAYER

And his disciples remembered that it was written, The zeal of thine house hath eaten me up. Jn. 2:17.

"The zeal of thine house has eaten me up" is a northern Aramaic idiom. Assyrians today still use this idiom, which means: "The zeal of your house has made me courageous." Another way to put it would be: "Zeal has strengthened me to fight and defend your house." The term "eaten" in this verse means "to defend." There are several other idiomatic sayings like this one, but they are not easily rendered into western thought.

For example, an Assyrian says to another: "I have come to heal your head." This means, "I have come to comfort you over the loss of your family member." Assyrians also say "He has eaten wrath," meaning "he is enraged." Another saying is: "Eat the care of my family." This can be challenging if not understood. It means, "Look after the interest of my family."

Jesus felt grieved when he saw that the temple area, which was to be a place of prayer, had become a center of business and corruption. The zeal for his Father's house made him so courageous that he could drive out the peddlers and rebuke temple authorities for allowing such things to happen.

DESTROY THIS TEMPLE

Jesus answered and said unto them, Destroy this temple, and in three days I will raise it up. Jn. 2:19.

The phrase "destroy this temple" is another northern Aramaic idiom. This phrase does not refer to the actual structure of the temple but to Jewish traditions and rituals. The temple was the center of Jewish worship, the abode of the God of Israel. When the temple was first built, worship became centralized in the state of Judea. In other words, God also became localized in the Jewish temple. The

38

inference of Jesus' statement is that by destroying his body he would rise in power and the Jewish temple—that is, what the temple represented—would be destroyed. Jesus' teaching would totally dismantle all false notions, doctrines and beliefs that were built around the temple. His powerful gospel of the kingdom would build a new temple not made with human hands.[6]

According to the writer, Jesus was referring to his body, his death and to his resurrection that would occur after three days. When all these things happened, Jesus would build a true religion of humanity and an understanding of genuine worship. After three days a new, faithful and authentic high priest would function for his followers not from earth but from a spiritual plane.

The Jews who were listening to Jesus took his sayings literally. This style of speaking symbolically was foreign to those in Judea who spoke southern, Chaldean Aramaic. They thought that he would literally tear down the temple and rebuild it in three days. To them, this all sounded insane and blasphemous. Indeed, the chief accusation against Jesus was based on this assertion that they had misunderstood. Even today Semites believe that it is a blasphemy to say such words about a church building or any holy structure. When a church wall falls down or is destroyed, they say: "The wall is resting." It would be sacrilegious to plainly say that the wall was destroyed. A wall is a part of God's house and everything belonging to it is sacred.

A SPIRITUAL NOT A STRUCTURAL TEMPLE

Then said the Jews, Forty and six years was this temple in building, and wilt thou rear it up in three days? Jn. 2:20.

The temple in Jerusalem was the center of the Jewish state and religion in Judea. It was the most precious symbol and structure of Israel's then present and former glory. All Jewish sacred institutions were built around this magnificent temple. Tradition and law

---

[6]See following comment "A spiritual not a structural temple."

supported its powerful authority. The temple had also become a matrix of pride, craft and corruption. Revolutions and wars were proclaimed in the name of God and in defense of God's temple. For centuries spoils and offerings of silver and gold were accumulated in this holy place. Its opulent wealth was coveted by foreign rulers. Whenever these foreign powers invaded Jerusalem, they would carry away its treasures. A structure that was once built and established for the pure worship of God and for a blessing to its people had become a curse.

But now, Jesus' gospel of the kingdom was to establish a religion of humanity, founded on justice and love rather than on a temple embellished with silver and gold. In his infinite understanding of God, he realized that the priesthood and its autocratic power were unnecessary The temple, its sacrifices and traditions were to disappear in the light and proclamation of the kingdom of God. A new temple was to be built in the hearts of every man, woman and child. The God who, until this time, was worshiped by sacrifices was now to be worshiped in spirit. Yahweh, the Lord of hosts, whom the priests and prophets could not see or approach, was soon to be known as the loving Father of all nations and races.

Jesus' assault on the temple was an attack on the priestly institution. The priesthood had become a hierarchy and it was to come to an end forever. It was not an attack on the structure made of stones, which had often been destroyed and was soon to suffer that fate again. Through his teaching, Jesus was building a different kind of temple. He was to inaugurate a new, simple religion through his death and resurrection. It was to be a spiritual temple and a religion that did not need Aaronic descendants and high priests. Jesus himself would become like the ancient spiritual leaders of the past, a priest-king after the order of Melchizedek. This type of leadership represented spiritual and political powers during the time of the Hebrew patriarchs. Abraham paid tithes to Melchizedek when passing through his territory. There would be no special blood line or genealogy to carry out. Humanity was soon to realize that everyone is the temple of God. "And I heard a great voice from heaven saying,

40

Behold, the tabernacle of God is with humankind and God will dwell with them, and they will be the people of God and God will be with them and be their God."[7] "Do you not know that you are the temple of God, and that the Spirit of God dwells in you?"[8] "Or do you not know that your body is the temple of the Holy Spirit that dwells within you, which you have of God, and you are not your own?"[9]

[7]Rev. 21:3, Aramaic Peshitta text, Errico.
[8]1Cor. 3:16, Aramaic Peshitta text, Lamsa translation.
[9]1Cor. 6:19, Aramaic Peshitta text, Lamsa translation.

CHAPTER 3

BORN AGAIN

Jesus answered and said unto him, Verily, verily, I say unto thee, Except a man be born again, he cannot see the kingdom of God. Jn. 3:3.

"Born again," *mitheelidh min dresh,* is a Galilean, northern Aramaic expression of speech. One may translate it as "born anew, born from above," or simply "reborn." It means one has to change one's thoughts and habits and become like a child. "Born again" also refers to the experience of divesting one's self of all past learning and notions and beginning to learn anew. Interestingly, the Aramaic word for "born" is *yalad* and the word for "boy" or child is *yalda*. Semites often say: "he is simple, pure and harmless like a child."

Children have nothing in their hearts against anyone. They know no creed and have no racial hatred. Usually little children love and trust everybody. They are friendly to people of all races and religions. A child is free from man-made teaching and has not yet developed the human pride that separates and divides people. An open, free young mind accepts anything that is taught and what it finds reasonable.

According to the writer, Nicodemus was an elderly man and a great leader of the Pharisees. He had a good reputation as a learned teacher of religion and tradition. Undoubtedly, it would be a tremendous challenge for him to change his teaching for something that would endanger his reputation. This was especially true because he did not understand this new teaching nor could he change at his age.

Nicodemus came to see Jesus at night, hoping to persuade the Galilean prophet to reverse his attitude toward the religious teaching and traditions and to be more conciliatory toward the priestly system. He probably told Jesus that it was useless to build on a strange foundation and that it would be better to build on the Jewish religion that the prophets of old had laid down.

42

Nonetheless, Jesus knew that much of the teachings were supplemented by the tradition of the elders. Doctrines of men had substituted the teaching of Scripture. How could blind guides lead the people to God? Jesus knew that the system had to collapse. It was of no use to build on a structure that needed to be changed and rebuilt. Religious teachers had first to free themselves from dogmatic traditions so that they could understand the meaning of the new law and principles that he was teaching. These principles were to be engraved on human hearts and not on tablets of stone.

Nicodemus could not understand the term "born again" because Jesus spoke Galilean Aramaic and the Jews of Judea spoke Chaldean Aramaic. Nicodemus took the expression "born again" literally. However, Jesus meant that not a physical but a spiritual experience was necessary to perceive God's kingdom. God's sovereignty is not discerned with earthly eyes but only through a new spirit and insight.

This kingdom is present everywhere, but only a transformed human being can perceive and enter into the activity of God's presence. In modern terminology we would refer to this as an altered state of consciousness. The alteration of one's heart and mind brings about the ability to see and participate in God's rule.

BORN OF WATER AND SPIRIT

Jesus answered, Verily, verily, I say unto thee, Except a man be born of water and the spirit he cannot enter into the kingdom of God. That which is born of the flesh is flesh; and that which is born of the spirit is spirit.
Jn. 3:5-6.

"Born of water and the spirit" means "to be completely cleansed within and without." Water is symbolic of outward cleansing. Spirit is symbolic of inner purification. The term "born of water" refers to water baptism that cleanses the body. However, Jesus uses this expression as a metaphor and combines it with spirit. An inner cleansing can only happen through a baptism of spirit. It washes away sin and purifies the heart, mind and soul. Spirit regenerates and transforms. By using the expression "born of water and spirit," Jesus meant that a total change needs to happen to a person before he can enter (participate in) God's kingdom. This was meant as a further clarification of "born again." John's gospel gives us a parallel teaching of Jesus that is in harmony with the synoptic gospels (Matthew, Mark and Luke) concerning the kingdom. John places a new angle on Jesus' teaching about God's kingdom. He expands the idea of "seeing and entering" by using the term "born again."

At that time, Jews baptized to cleanse their bodies. When there was enough water available, they would wash their hands before they prayed or ate. Near Easterners still practice this custom today. Nomad Arabs, because of the lack of water, cleanse themselves with sand. These ceremonies only affect the body. Water baptism carried different meanings. For John the Baptist it was an outward sign of cleansing through repentance (turning to God). For the apostle Paul, it was to share in the burial with Christ and rising in a new life. For the gospel writer, it was a total transformation—water and spirit—a brand new beginning.

"That which is born of the flesh is flesh; and that which is born of the spirit is spirit." Jesus distinguishes flesh and spirit. "Born of the flesh" refers to those who are only physically and materially minded—that is, those who are subject just to bodily desire. "Born of the spirit" refers to those who have freed themselves from destructive forces and have transcended the material world. They do not judge by outward appearances. These people become heirs of God's kingdom.

THE WIND AND THE SPIRIT

The wind bloweth where it listeth, and thou hearset the sound thereof, but canst not tell whence it cometh, and whither it goeth: so is every one that is born of the spirit. Jn. 3:8.

Part 1—THE WAY OF THE WIND. Although the wind is made manifest by the movement of air, no one knows where it begins and where it will end. This verse does not refer just to the direction of the wind. For even in those days, they understood about southerly or westerly winds. It was the source of the wind that was a mystery to them. They did not know how it was formed and how it died.

This saying denotes the mysterious birth of the spirit. It is just like the wind. It is strange and mysterious to those who only think in terms of natural birth. A spiritual nature rules those born of the spirit. "As you do not know the path of the wind, and the manner of a woman who is with child; even so you do not know the works of the Lord who makes all."[1]

Now if we cannot fully understand the way of the wind, how then would we understand the ways of the Spirit? How can we understand spirit, which is the finest essence in nature? This is the reason God is called "Spirit." Like electricity, spirit can be felt but cannot be seen by human eyes or discerned by any other means. We can contact spirit and understand it only through God's spirit that is in us. Things of the spirit can only be discerned spiritually. Unfortunately, Nicodemus took everything at face value and did not understand what Jesus had just told him.

Part 2—BORN OF THE SPIRIT. In Aramaic, the phrase "born of the spirit" means "to be regenerated, reborn and restored to the image of the original humans that God had created."[2]

A human mind that has not awakened to its spiritual nature does not understand the ways of those who are born of the spirit. It does not know what kind of forces govern a spiritual man or woman and what motivates them to act so differently. Those who have not embraced spiritual principles cannot comprehend those who are born of the spirit.

"For the things which we discuss are not dependent on the knowledge of words and man's wisdom, but on the teaching of the Spirit; thus explaining spiritual things to the spiritually minded. For the material man rejects spiritual things; they are foolishness to him; neither can he know them, because they are spiritually discerned. But

---

[1]Ecc. 11:5, Aramaic Peshitta text, Lamsa translation.
[2]See Gen. 1:26-27.

the spiritual man discerns everything, and yet no man can discern him."[3]

Both Jesus' opponents and his disciples were puzzled by his teaching of God's kingdom, especially turning the other cheek, going the second mile, not resisting evil and loving one's enemies. They questioned how meekness could replace force and the sword? How can nonviolence win the hearts of the violent? How could such teaching bring peace and understanding?

Jesus' teaching and the power of his gospel of the kingdom have been a mystery to many philosophers, prophets, political leaders and religious men for centuries. Jesus' principles and ethics are mysterious like the wind. The reason for this is that his teaching is based on invisible spiritual forces and powers. The followers of Christ must rely on God. Their faith must rest in the spiritual energies—the eternal truths—that can guide all humankind to its true destiny.

NO ONE HAS ASCENDED TO HEAVEN

And no man hath ascended up to heaven, but he that came down from heaven, even the Son of man which is in heaven. Jn. 3:13.

According to Jesus, no man had ascended into heaven except Jesus himself, who came down from heaven. Christ, in Jesus, existed with God from the very beginning (see John 1:1-3). The Messiah/Christ was promised to Eve, Abraham and King David.

Jesus, in this instance, speaks of his spiritual oneness with God. And, according to Jesus' teaching, heaven and earth are one. In the realm of the spirit, the whole universe is one and has no divisions. The kingdom of heaven begins right now, on earth.

Jesus tells Nicodemus that the mysteries of heaven are known only to those who are in heaven. Therefore, he was the only one who could explain these mysteries. He had the power to reveal spiritual truth that had been hidden from the eyes of the human family.

---

[3] 1 Cor. 2:13-15, Aramaic Peshitta text, Lamsa translation.

A modern way to put this would be: "I have just come from Washington DC; no one here has been there. I know how the government functions there. If you wish to know how it functions, you must ask me because I am carrying out these functions while I am here."

LIFTED ON THE CROSS

And as Moses lifted up the serpent in the wilderness, even so must the Son of man be lifted up. That whosoever believeth in him should not perish, but have eternal life. Jn. 3:14-15.

Part 1—THE SERPENT AND JESUS. The Aramaic text reads: "Just as Moses raised the serpent in the desert, so is this *bar-nasha,* ["human being," literally:"son of man"], ready to be raised up so that anyone who believes in him may not perish but have everlasting life."[4] These verses point back to an event that involved the Hebrew prophet Moses and the Israelites when they were traveling in the desert. "And the Lord [Yahweh] said to Moses, Make a fiery brass serpent, and set it on a pole; and it will happen that anyone who is bitten by a serpent, when he looks at it, will live. So Moses made a brass serpent and put it on a pole, and it happened that if a serpent had bitten anyone, when he looked at the brass serpent, he recovered."[5]

The tribes of Israel had been complaining and murmuring against Moses and his leadership while journeying through the desert. They had passed through an area that was filled with fiery serpents. These awful and frightful looking creatures had bitten many of the people and they had died. The snakes were a shiny, reddish color, hence the name fiery serpents. (The Hebrew word is *seraph* from the Semitic root *saraf* and means "to burn.") The Israelites were horrified and filled with fear when they saw these slithering creatures.

---

[4]Jn. 3:14-15, Aramaic Peshitta text, Errico
[5]Num. 21:8-9, Aramaic Peshitta text, Errico

47

Jacob Milgrom, a Jewish biblical scholar, says that the seraph figure was:

> A winged snake similar to the winged Egyptian uraeus (cobra). Its image, engraved on a bronze bowl inscribed with a Hebrew name, was found in the excavation of the royal palace of Nineveh, dating to the end of the eighth century. It was believed that looking at it would generate its homeopathic healing.[6]

When the Israelites were bitten by the fiery serpents in the Sinai desert, the Lord God commanded Moses to make a brass replica of the snake. He was to set it up on a pole so that everyone who was bitten might look at it and be healed. Most of the people who were bitten died from fear. So great was their fear of the fiery snakes that the healing forces in the bitten bodies of the victims became paralyzed.

But now those who were bitten and looked at the brass serpent hanging on the pole were healed; their fear was gone and the healing energies overcame the venom of the serpent. Raising the serpent on the pole symbolized the conquest of fear and plague.

The raising of Jesus on the cross symbolized the destruction of the fear of death, the grave and the power of evil forces. Through the cross, sin, sickness and death were dealt a deadly blow. It also revealed God's love for his children. What was once a symbol of death became a symbol of life to those who believed in Jesus and his teaching. The cross became the acknowledgment of life everlasting.

Now the cross of Jesus would heal humanity of its sin of violence. All humanity is bitten with the desire for retaliation and vengeance. There are those who still forcibly take personal property, land and human life to obtain what they want. Nations and political powers are not free of this sin against humanity. When people and nations become infected with envy, strife, jealousy, covetousness and hatred, the serpent's bite is working in their hearts and minds. All this brings suffering and death for humankind. According to John's

---

[6]Jacob Milgrom, *The JPS Torah Commentary*, "Numbers," p. 174.

gospel, the cross of Jesus cures the poisonous venom of hatred and violence (biblically speaking—sin) and brings an end to acting out rage, hostility and revenge. But one has to comprehend the meaning of the cross and the reason for Jesus' death. One has to look upon the raised and crucified lamb that humanity had chosen to sacrifice—an innocent victim—to find the cure and recover from death.

Just as Moses raised the fiery brass serpent in the desert for the salvation of his people, so Jesus being raised on the cross brings life (salvation) to all humanity. Moses said: "Anyone who looks at the serpent will live." The gospel writer links the story of the raised serpent and its life-restoring image with the cross of Jesus and its life-restoring image—"life eternal."

Part 2—ETERNAL LIFE. In Aramaic *haye dalaalam* literally translates as "life of the eternal age, everlasting life." The Aramaic term *laalam* (Hebrew—*Olam*) means a period of time without visible beginning or termination. This Semitic expression can refer to several things depending on how and where it is used: 1) Life that surpasses death. 2) Life—resurrection from the dead. 3) The continuance of the soul after physical death or simply "eternal presence" rather than time.

However, when reading all the passages in John's gospel, we may conclude that the writer refers to a specific quality of life that begins here and now for those who have embraced Jesus' teaching. Death cannot affect or destroy this quality of life, neither can anything now present in this world touch or hurt it. This is divine life and not just natural life. It has the quality of endurance (unending) and imbues one with life now and forever. "O death where is your sting? O *sheol* [grave] where is your victory?" [7]

The question is: Did Jesus teach eternal life or did John add this idea to Jesus' teaching? In the mind of the gospel writer the term "kingdom of God" equates with "eternal life." Jesus' conversation with Nicodemus, the Jewish teacher, is about God's kingdom, but now eternal life is carried into their dialog. Luke's gospel reports

---

[7] 1 Cor. 15:55, Aramaic Peshitta text, Lamsa translation.

49

Jesus as saying: ". . . Be assured of what I am telling you that there is no one who leaves houses, parents, brothers, wife or children for the sake of God's kingdom who will not receive many times more at this time and in the world to come, life eternal."[8]

Although this may be a paraphrase of what Jesus actually said and probably not in this context, Jesus undoubtedly did teach about eternal life. Jesus also considered eternal life and God's kingdom as synonymous. Not only is "eternal life" a theme connected with Jesus' message of the kingdom but "love" is also. Love and life are inseparable and are a part of God's kingdom (presence).

DID GOD PAY A RANSOM?

For God so loved the world, that he gave his only begotten son, that whosoever believeth in him should not perish, but have everlasting life. For God sent not his son into the world to condemn the world: but that the world through him might be saved. Jn. 3:16.

Part 1—A MISUNDERSTOOD VERSE. No passage of scripture is quoted more than this one and yet, theologically, it is probably the most misunderstood verse in John's gospel. The reason for this is that Western readers are not familiar with Near Eastern customs and mannerisms of speech.

Many biblical teachers and gospel preachers sincerely believe that God sacrificed Jesus of Nazareth to pay the debt of sin. These religious teachers use the term "redemption" meaning that God paid a ransom or a price to redeem the human family from sin and evil. But, in order to redeem something, a price has to be paid to someone. To whom did God pay a price? Is there someone greater than God? Is sin or evil greater than God that God would have to pay a price to purchase his people back from evil? The payment, of course, was Jesus' blood, shed on the cross. There are others who say that God reconciled himself to humanity by Jesus' death or that God appeased

---

[8]Lk. 18:29-30, Aramaic Peshitta text, Errico.

his own wrath against humanity through the shed blood of his beloved son.

Interestingly, nearly all passages of scripture that are in the King James version read "redemption," but in the ancient Aramaic text the word is *porkana*, meaning "salvation" and not "redemption." As we have said, redemption is made effective by means of a payment or a ransom to someone else.

It is often said that "Jesus died for our sins" and that our sins could never have been forgiven without his death. The primary meaning of the Aramaic word *mittol* is "because of" or "on account of" and lastly "for." We understand this to mean that Jesus died *because* of our sins and not *for* them. (For further explanation see part 2 of this comment.)

Greed, hatred and domination in Jesus' day, were prevalent even as they are in our century. But today they are more pervasive and dangerous because with our weapons of mass destruction, we can annihilate with the touch of a button or the release of invisible airborne poisonous chemicals. The world has been inundated with evil since creation. Wars, hatred, murder, lies, false accusations, fear, envy and jealousy still prevail in human history. Jesus died for his gospel of the kingdom that was to destroy the power of hatred, fear, prejudice, murder and mistreatment of the human family.

At that time, sinful men sacrificed Jesus as the lamb of God. Jesus told his disciples that he would be delivered into the hands of sinful men and put to death. God, being a loving Father, does not need to be appeased by his children with sacrifices. No caring, kindly, human father would try to appease his wrath by putting one of his sons to death.

Now, if we assume that Jesus died to appease the forces of evil, then the seeming evil is stronger than good—God. Furthermore, it is usually the weaker who pays the stronger, the vanquished who pays tribute to the victor. Therefore, such an act would not only prove that Satan or the Devil is an entity, but that it is also a power equal to or greater than God.

Again, if God delivered Jesus to sinful men just to appease his own wrath and thus reconcile himself with humanity, his children, then God could hardly be equated with love or known as a loving Father. Customarily, only unenlightened people killed their sons in honor of kings and princes. They also offered their sons as sacrifices so that they could appease the wrath of these kings and redeem captives by payment of blood ransom. In Scripture there is the story of the King of Moab, who sacrificed his son, the crown prince, who was to reign in his place, to appease the wrath of the kings who fought against him. (See 2 Kings 3:27.)

Feudal chieftains settled blood feuds and brought reconciliation among the clans by sacrificing a member of their tribe. Baal worship was founded on this idea of appeasing the gods through human sacrifices and other offerings. But Israel, having been admonished through the Mosaic laws, inaugurated the practice of animal rather than human sacrifice.

Some theologians teach that Jesus took our sins upon himself and offered them to God; others say that God forsook Jesus while he was on the cross because God could not look at the sins that Jesus was bearing. In the Bible, we read that God sees every evil thing that humans do and nothing is hidden from the eyes of God. So God did not turn away from Jesus on the cross because he was bearing the sins of humanity.[9] According to these scholars, God made Jesus a sin offering for humanity. Yet in John's gospel we read that when Jesus forgave sinners, all he said was: "Go and sin no more." He did not say: "Offer something to appease God's wrath." Jesus taught forgiveness of sin differently. Luke's gospel reports the risen Christ saying: "And he said to them, Thus it is written, and it was right, that Christ should suffer and rise from the dead on the third day; and that **repentance should be preached in his name for the forgiveness of sins among all nations;** and the beginning will be from Jerusalem."[10]

---

[9]See Errico and Lamsa, *Aramaic Light on the Gospel of Matthew*, "Jesus' Triumphant Cry," pp. 346-352 and *Aramaic Light on the Gospels of Mark and Luke*, "Part 2—Jesus not Forsaken," pp. 92-96.

[10]Lk. 24:46-47, Aramaic Peshitta text, Lamsa translation.

Forgiveness was to come about through repentance—that is,turning to God—and not by blood sacrifice. This was a shocking teaching that contradicted Hebrew belief. "Because nearly everything, according to the law, is purified with the blood; and without the shedding of blood there is no forgiveness."[11] Of course, the Hebrews, just like other nations, often tried to appease God by means of sacrifice and offerings, at times even offering their children.

Assuredly, Jesus' death on the cross was predicted by the prophet Isaiah.[12] He knew that anyone who would venture to challenge the temple system and the corrupt political systems of this world would meet with death. Not at any time did Isaiah say that Jesus' death would reconcile God with humanity or pay a debt to anyone or anything.

In his teaching, Jesus condemned hypocrisy, injustice, exploitation, and the misuse of religion. All Hebrew prophets who had spoken out against evil kings, princes and the wicked order of their days had met with the same fate. It was because of their outspokenness that they were all killed.

The death of Jesus was different in that he was willing to die, knowing that he would rise from death. Therefore, his death was a triumph and it revealed the depth of God's love for humanity. Scripture reads that "God is love." Love does not demand human sacrifice because there is nothing in love to be appeased. Jesus died on the cross not to appease God or to pay a debt to sin but to reveal that life is indestructible and everlasting, for God is life. Jesus, through his death on the cross, inaugurated a new world order, an order of meekness, loving kindness and a nonviolent way of living for all nations.

Part 2—HUMAN SACRIFICE. The Aramaic text reads: "For in this manner God so loved the world that he even gave [sacrificed] his beloved son so that anyone who believes in him may not perish but have eternal life. Because God did not send his son into the world

---

[11]Heb. 9:22, Aramaic Peshitta text, Lamsa translation.
[12]See Isaiah chapter 53.

that he might condemn the world; but that the world might live through him."[13] You will notice that the text no longer mentions Nicodemus. He simply fades out of the picture. The gospel writer shares his thoughts by emphasizing his own ideas about Jesus' person and teaching and the effect it will make in the world if one accepts his master's message. Almost all New Testament scholars agree that these words (John 3:16) were put on Jesus' lips. We need to change our understanding about this scripture. We normally interpret it as an atonement passage. But it can be read and understood non-sacrificially.

First, let us look into human sacrifice. "Human sacrifice" or, in particular, *child sacrifice* was one of the appalling abuses in the ancient world. The horrifying truth is that the history of religions attests to human sacrifice in a number of places. The Phoenicians, Ammonites, Moabites, the peoples of Egypt, Canaan and Greece all practiced child sacrifice. However, historians inform us that it scarcely ever occurs in primitive religions, but almost exclusively in the higher and more developed.[14] Evidently, human sacrifice prevailed only for limited periods; animal sacrifice replaced human oblation. Exodus 22:29 commands the sacrifice of the firstborn male (child sacrifice). Yet, the Torah abolishes the sacrifice of the firstborn son by offering an animal in his place (Exodus 34:20; 13:13). The law sanctioned animals as a substitution. Nonetheless, animal sacrifice is also an abuse.

In the books of the prophets we find strong condemnation against animal sacrifice. The prophet Jeremiah has penned one of the most vigorous criticisms and denunciations of this practice as a means for atonement. He denies that God ever commanded Moses, as described in elaborate detail in the Torah, to slaughter animals for offerings to God.

---

[13]Jn. 3:15-16, Aramaic Peshitta text, Errico.

[14]For an understanding of the notion of human sacrifice, I recommend reading James G. Williams, *The Bible, Violence and the Sacred: Liberation from the Myth of Sanctioned Violence*, San Francisco, Harper & Row, 1991.

Thus says the Lord of hosts, the God of Israel: Add your burnt offerings to your sacrifices and eat meat which I did not command your fathers to eat. Neither did I command them concerning either burnt offerings or sacrifices in the day when I brought them out of the land of Egypt; But this thing I commanded them, saying, Obey my voice, and I will be your God and you will be my people; and walk in all the ways that I have commanded you, that it may be well with you.[15]

Shedding of blood, animal or human, for reconciliation among people or between God and humanity is a cruel and barbaric human idea. Ancient biblical scribes placed this command for blood sacrifice on the lips of God. Other prophets besides Jeremiah knew this truth and cried out against the shedding of animal blood. Isaiah, the great Hebrew statesman and prophet, declared:

Of what purpose is the multitude of your sacrifices to me? Says the Lord; I am full of the burnt offerings of rams, and the fat of fed beasts; and I do not delight in the blood of bullocks or of lambs or of he-goats. When you come to appear before me, who has required this at your hand, to tread my courts? Bring no more vain offerings to me; their savour is an abomination to me; in the new moons and sabbaths, you call an assembly; I do not eat that which is obtained wrongfully and taken by force. Your new moons and your appointed feasts my soul hates; they are a burden to me; I am weary to bear them. And when you spread forth your hands, I will hide my eyes from you; even though you make many prayers, I will not hear; your hands are full of blood.[16]

Thus says the Lord: Heaven is my throne and the earth my footstool; what is the house that you build for me? And what is the place of my rest? For all those things has my own hand made, and all those things belong to me, says the Lord. And to whom shall I look, and where shall I dwell? But to him who is calm and

---

[15]Jer. 7:21-23, Aramaic Peshitta text, Lamsa translation.
[16]Isa. 1:11-15, Aramaic Peshitta text, Lamsa translation.

humble, and trembles at my word. He who kills an ox is like him who slays a man; he who sacrifices a lamb is like him who kills a dog; he who offers a meal offering is like him who offers swine's blood; he who burns incense is like him who blesses an idol. Yea they have chosen their own ways, and their soul delights in their idols.[17]

According to the prophets, no killing of animals can atone for sin. God would rather we stop the evil and find forgiveness through repentance—turning to God. By taking this step, we are empowered to end the evil we may be practicing. Hosea, another prophet, says in the name of the Lord of Hosts: "For I wanted compassion and not sacrifice; and the knowledge of God and not burnt offerings."[18] A Hebrew prophet by the name of Micah cried out against the notion of offering his own son as a sacrifice:

With what will I come before the Lord, and how will I be pleasing before the high God? Will I come before him with burnt offerings, or with calves of a year old? The Lord will not be pleased with thousands of rams, nor with ten thousands of heifers; **if I should offer my firstborn it is an iniquity to myself and the fruit of my body, it is a sin against my soul**. He has showed you, O man, what is good and what the Lord requires of you, that you will do justice and love compassion and be ready to walk after the Lord your God.[19]

God never required animal or human sacrifice. Even Micah says: "If I should offer my firstborn, it is an iniquity to myself, and the fruit of my body, it is a sin against my soul." Then how could God require Jesus—the beloved son—to sacrifice himself to appease God's judgment against human sin? Does God demand a violent act in order to become a forgiving, compassionate, loving being? If this is not true then what does the cross truly represent? Can we understand it

---

[17]Isa. 66:1-3, Aramaic Peshitta text, Lamsa translation.
[18]Hosea 6:6, Aramaic Peshitta text, Errico
[19]Micah 6:6-8, Aramaic Peshitta text, Lamsa translation.

from a non-sacrificial perspective?

Jesus' commitment to endure the cross was a voluntary act of love and self-sacrifice on his part. He said that he was willing to lay down his life. He also did not want his followers to avenge his death. This is the reason for his cry on the cross: "Father forgive them for they know not what they do." The cross becomes a symbol of love and forgiveness because Jesus showed a new way of life that was nonviolent and non-retaliatory.

God did not require Jesus' death for the forgiveness of sins. According to the gospel, Jesus was delivered into the hands of sinful men and these men crucified him. He died on account of humanity's sinfulness. In ancient religions, atonement and freedom from guilt and blame could only come about through the sacrifice of some innocent person or animal. This was done to bring about reconciliation between people or between people and their gods and goddesses. Jesus in his teaching of the kingdom abandons this primitive understanding of God. Jesus called God "Father," which in Aramaic means "Beloved."

Love does not require the blood of an innocent to be shed for those who do evil. By simply turning to God—that is, by turning to good—one turns from evil and finds life and forgiveness. This is Jesus' teaching.[20]

CONDEMNED ALREADY

He that believeth on him is not condemned: but he that believeth not is condemned already, because he hath not believed in the name of the only begotten son of God. Jn.3:18

John continues to inform the reader that Jesus did not come into the world to condemn the world. The world already lives under condemnation because of its own penchant and propensity for

---

[20]For an in depth study of a non-sacrificial approach to the cross of Jesus and of sacred violence see bibliography under the heading "Sacred Violence."

violence and hateful crimes. Most nations and societies use force and violence to maintain peace. Most of the history of humanity, both politically and religiously, is a cruel and bloody one. Crime is everywhere. The world wallows in its own condemnation. What it needs is deliverance from the vicious cycle of violence and inhumane acts. Jesus' gospel of the kingdom brings life—that is, abundant living. Therefore anyone who believes in him, who adheres to the principles of the kingdom, finds a new way of living and does not exist in a state of condemnation.

Jesus practiced nonviolence, yet he died a violent death. Apparently, this is the way of the world, be it religious or nonreligious. Jesus' teaching introduces a new order of life, perhaps with a price of losing one's life in a world living under the reign of hate and racial and ideological superiority. "To believe in his name" is to follow a nonviolent way of living. Meekness, truth, justice and compassion reign in God's kingdom. Not to believe is to live under the old system of fear, violence and condemnation.

This condemnation has nothing to do with God's judgment or what is referred to in the Bible as "the day of judgment." The reference here is to the rejection of Jesus' kingdom message. For example, Peter denied Jesus but later repented and followed him. It was difficult for many of the Jewish people to understand this new teaching. It was strange to their way of thinking. Some of these people were sincerely seeking truth but could not grasp the mysteries of the kingdom as taught by Jesus. However, some of them did understand Jesus' teaching but deliberately rejected it because they loved their evil deeds. They did not want to change their ways and therefore would have to answer for their behavior. (See the following comment.)

DARKNESS

And this is the condemnation, that light is come into the world, and men loved darkness rather than light, because their deeds were evil. Jn. 3:19

Until the 1900s, in most parts of the Near East, nearly all robbery, banditry and crime were committed during the dark hours of the night. Strange as it may seem, a man might hold a noble position during the day, but at night he might go out on the road to rob travelers. In some cases religious men, after performing their daily services, engaged in robbery at night, stealing sheep and oxen. These acts were committed in the dark in order to keep their identities a secret.

Immoral deeds were also practiced in the dark so that the act might not be brought to light. In the Near East, it used to be difficult to do evil by daylight without revealing the culprit's identity. No perpetrator wants to face the severe punishment that is carried out if he is caught. One reason for this is that many families lived under the same roof. There was no privacy. Those who did good deeds were not afraid of light for they wanted their deeds to be seen by people. Evildoers were ashamed when their works were brought to light. "There is nothing covered, that shall not be revealed; and hidden, that shall not be known."

BAPTIZING BEYOND JORDAN

And John also was baptizing in Aenon, near to Salim, because there was much water there: and they came and were baptized. Jn. 3:23

This was a place well known to travelers. It was where the caravans met and crossed on either side of the river Jordan.(The Aramaic word *awra* derives from the root *abar* "to cross."*Awra* means a "crossing place.") John was baptizing there because he could easily meet people going in both directions.

Shaleem and another small town, Bethabara, were on the western banks of the Jordan, probably near Jericho. John could not have baptized in the desert beyond Jordan. There would have been no water there. Besides, why should he go so far from Jerusalem and other populous cities that were situated west of Jordan. *Ainyon* (Aenon) is an Aramaic word of Chaldean origin meaning "springs."

The other city, *Bethabara,* is a compound noun. *Beth* means "house," *abara,* "fords."

Most Near Eastern religions practiced water baptism. It was a form of ablution and a sign of initiation of new members. A convert was washed, signifying that he was cleansed from all doctrines, dogmas and evils of the faith in which he had been participating. He becomes reborn in the new faith.

Baptism was practiced by John, although it is not mentioned in Jewish practices. They did perform some ablutions, such as washing of hands and parts of their bodies before they ate meals. Baptism as an immersion originated in southern Mesopotamia. Even today there is a sect called Essenes or people of St. John, who are the followers of John the Baptist. They continue to practice baptism as a token of cleansing.

TRUE AUTHORITY

John answered and said, A man can receive nothing, except it be given him from above. Jn. 3:27.

The Aramaic text reads: "John answered, saying to them: No man can receive anything of his own will, except it is given to him from heaven."[21] Jesus' rapid success and the spread of his teaching was puzzling to some of John the Baptist's disciples. They thought their master had the plan of salvation and that he was a great prophet. They could not understand why the people were flocking to Jesus.

John told his disciples the truth. He tried to convince them that Jesus was popular not because of his knowledge or cleverness but because it was God's will. God's approval was on Jesus and this was the secret of his growing popularity. John, himself, had proclaimed Jesus as the lamb of God.

At this time, John the Baptist had begun relinquishing honors and glory that had been bestowed on him. After all, he was a

---

[21]Jn. 3:27, Aramaic Peshitta text, Lamsa translation.

messenger who had come just to prepare the way for the promised one. A messenger's mission is of limited duration. This is the reason many of John's disciples began turning to Jesus. John's mission was drawing to a close and, in a short while, he would be imprisoned by Herod.

THE BEST MAN

He that hath the bride is the bridegroom: but the friend of the bridegroom which standeth and heareth him, rejoiceth greatly because of the bridegroom's voice; this my joy therefore is fulfilled. Jn. 3:29.

Social meetings for men and women are very rare. In the Near East, marriage is not an easy accomplishment. Although men eagerly look forward to their wedding day, marriage is a strenuous affair for the bridegroom. The man, who before this time had not even dared speak to a woman, is kissed and teased by all women on his wedding day.

Generally, bridegrooms are bashful and retiring. They are so overwhelmed by the change and excitement that they hardly say a word. The bride escapes all this confusion because her face is veiled. During this time, the best man acts as spokesman for the groom anytime he wishes to say something. He sits by his side and is joyful when the groom whispers something into his ear. He is watchful and observes every move and act he may make. The best man is the happiest one at the wedding.

John the Baptist was acting as the best man for Jesus, who was the groom. He was glad to hear the good news about the works, wonders and popularity of the Galilean prophet. John had already recognized the greatness of this teacher and was content with his mission as that of a messenger and spokesman for Jesus.

FROM ABOVE

He that cometh from above is above all: he that is of the earth is earthly, and speaketh of the earth: he that cometh from heaven is above all. And what he hath seen and heard, that he testifieth and no man receiveth his testimony. Jn. 3:31-32.

The Messiah/Christ was with God from the very beginning. Therefore, he was above all prophets and men of God. Christ in Jesus knew the things of heaven (spiritual matters), but those who were of the earth only knew and understood earthly things.

John the Baptist confesses that Jesus as the Christ is greater than he. John admits that Jesus had a greater understanding of God. The Baptist was a humble man to testify this way about himself and the Galilean prophet. Genuine teachers who practice truth lose their sense of self-importance and vanity.

John's teaching was just for the keeping of the law of Moses and other ordinances, but Jesus had come to reveal things that were hidden even from the eyes of Moses and the Hebrew prophets. He had come to declare all men equal and to give the world a universal spiritual religion with a new understanding of God as the Beloved (Father). Jesus had to come to teach people to love one another and their enemies, to bless those who cursed them and not to resist evil. All these teachings were heavenly—that is, had a universal aspect.

John the Baptist came for the Jews only, but Jesus came for all people. There was no comparison between Jesus' teaching and that which John taught. However, Jesus' teaching was difficult and challenging to understand and implement two thousand years ago and it is still the same today. One has to be born again, to become like a child, to comprehend such profound universal teaching.

THE SEAL OF APPROVAL

He that hath received his testimony hath set to his seal that God is true. Jn. 3:33.

"Set to his seal" is an Aramaic colloquialism meaning "the approval of an act." During a conversation, Semites often say: "I will set my seal on all that you have said." This means: "I believe all you have said is true."

In the Near East letters and documents are always stamped with a seal because many people cannot read or write. Noblemen, princes and government officials carry a seal with them, attached to their belts, and are always ready for emergencies. A man's seal is his word of honor and power. Once it is affixed to a document, the conditions must be sacredly kept.

The reference here is to Jesus' works. He who accepts the testimony of Jesus sets his seal that God is true because he believes that Jesus is true.

FATHER LOVES THE SON

The Father loveth the Son, and hath given all things into his hand. He that believeth on the Son hath everlasting life: and he that believeth not the Son shall not see life; but the wrath of God abideth on him. Jn. 3:35-36.

According to common Near Eastern custom, a father will turn everything over to his firstborn son.[22] The firstborn son receives absolute authority over everything the father possesses. This is a special relationship between the father and the son. This theme will run throughout the gospel of John. If one wishes to know the father, then one must come to the son to understand him.

This is the reason for the following verse: "Anyone who believes in the son has everlasting life and anyone who does not obey the son will not see life, but God's anger will remain on him."[23] Since everything has been given to the son, all those who have confidence in the son will see life. Those who disobey will not see life but God's wrath. According to the text, these are the words of John the Baptist.

---

[22]See Jn. 1:14, "The Firstborn Male," pp. 16-19 of this commentary.
[23]Jn. 3:36, Aramaic Peshitta text, Errico

The wrath of God is what John the Baptist, some prophets of old, and apocalyptic writers anticipated if people disobeyed God. This was their style of language and preaching. Actually, God does not reward or punish anyone.

This kind of language concerning wrath and judgment was prevalent for several centuries before the ministry of Jesus, during the formation of the early Church and continues to this very day. Nonetheless, it was never the gospel or language style of Jesus and was never a part of his ministry. He came to save those who had lost their way. According to Jesus, God restores and not destroys people.

What is meant here is very simple. Anyone participating in Jesus' teaching would see and find life. However, if one chooses to live life practicing evil, then that very evil itself has its own wrathful and harmful results. At that time, everything was attributed to God. When someone suffered a catastrophe, that calamity was attributed to God and known as God's wrath. "Believing in the son" means practicing the teachings of the son. "Not believing the son" refers to those who do not follow or practice the teaching of the son. Jesus' gospel teaches love, truth, justice, kindness, compassion, forgiveness to mention a few. When we practice these things we have life and not death.[24]

---

[24]According to some modern NT scholars, these words were put on John's lips by early church scribes.

CHAPTER 4

JESUS SUSPECTED

When therefore the Lord knew how the Pharisees had heard that Jesus made and baptized more disciples than John. (Though Jesus himself baptized not, but his disciples.) He left Judea and departed again into Galilee. Jn. 4:1-2.

The translator or copyist inadvertently changed the name "Jesus" in the beginning of the sentence into the word "Lord." "When therefore the *Lord* knew...." Then, in the relative clause, he inserted the name "Jesus." This is the reason the King James Version reads: "When therefore the *Lord* knew how the Pharisees had heard that *Jesus* made and baptized more disciples than John." Because of this mistake the sentence seems to refer to the Lord God and not to Jesus. This means that God knew that the Pharisees had heard that Jesus had baptized and so forth. However, the Aramaic text reads correctly: "When *Jesus* knew that the Pharisees had heard that *he* made many disciples and was baptizing more people than John . . ."[1]

Many of the Pharisees were jealous of Jesus. They had been watching his movements from the onset of his ministry and were beginning to suspect his intentions. It was becoming more dangerous for Jesus to remain in the same place for a long period of time; therefore, he had to keep on the move.

A SAMARITAN WOMAN

There cometh a woman of Samaria to draw water: Jesus saith unto her, Give me to drink. (For his disciples were gone away unto the city to buy meat.) Then saith the woman of Samaria unto him, How is it that thou, being a Jew, asketh drink of me, which am a woman of Samaria? for the Jews have no dealing with the Samaritans. Jn. 4:7-9.

---

[1]Jn. 4:1, Aramaic Peshitta text, Lamsa translation.

Part 1—SAMARITANS. The Samaritans and the Jews had long been enemies. This history goes back to the time of the rebuilding of Solomon's temple and the return of the Jewish exiles from Chaldea (Babylon). It begins with Samaria, the capital of the kingdom of Israel—the ten (northern) tribes. This does not include the southern kingdom of Judah whose capital was Jerusalem. About 880 BCE King Omri founded Samaria. In 721 BCE the Assyrians captured the entire northern kingdom of Israel, deported its people and resettled the territory with pagans from other parts of their empire.[2]

According to Jewish tradition, the Samaritans were the descendants of these settlers. We do not know the exact date when the Samaritans became a separate religious sect with a temple of their own on Mt. Gerizim. However, most scholars favor the fourth century BCE. Evidently, Jesus had sympathy for this group of people. This is shown through his parable of the so-called "Good Samaritan" and the story of the "Ten Lepers."[3] Nevertheless, Jesus himself instructed the twelve apostles not to enter any town of the Samaritans but rather to go to the lost sheep of the house of Israel.[4]

The Samaritans do not derive their name from any geographical designation but rather from the term *samerim,* "keeper [of the law]." John 4:9 informs us that the Jews had no dealings with them. These Samaritans felt they were a special chosen group and called themselves "the sons of light." They criticized the Jerusalem temple and did not celebrate Purim or Hanukkah.

Samaritans also adopted their own peculiar edited Torah but did not accept the books of the prophets. They were a religious community that developed independently of the spiritual leadership of Jerusalem—a people who were, for cultural and historical reasons, alienated from the Jews and could not maintain friendly relations with them. There is a proverbial saying about this hostility between Jew and Samaritan: "He that eats the bread of the Samaritans is like

---

[2]See 2 Kings.18:9-12 and chapter 17.
[3]See Lk. 17:11-19.
[4]Mt. 10:5-6.

to one who eats the flesh of swine."[5]

Part 2—A WOMAN OF SAMARIA. The Samaritan woman was startled to hear a Jew asking her to give him a drink of water. The Samaritans were the descendants of the races whom the King of Assyria had brought from the other side of the River Euphrates and placed throughout Samaria and Galilee in the eighth century BCE. As we said in Part 1 of this comment, these lands originally belonged to the ten tribes of Israel who were taken captive and placed east of the River Euphrates in Assyria, Babylon, Afghanistan and Persia. There was a great deal of racial and religious animosity between the Jews and Samaritans. Jesus, however, refused to accept any racial differences or to acknowledge any barriers between these people. For Jesus, everyone belonged to God and all races were God's children. Jesus always looked for the good that was in people. He had compassion on Syrians and all others of Gentile races whom he found ready to accept the truth and live under the principles of God's kingdom.

Jesus was thirsty. He and his disciples had traveled many miles without seeing a well. He must have a drink. Therefore, he, a Jew, asked a Samaritan woman for a drink of water. He was able to ignore the boundaries that religious notions invent and cross over the lines of social separation created by false traditions and racial biases.

LIVING WATER

Jesus answered and said unto her, If thou knewest the gift of God, and who it is that saith to thee, Give me to drink; thou wouldest have asked of him and he would have given thee living water. The woman saith unto him, Sir, thou hast nothing to draw with, and the well is deep: from whence then hast thou that living water? Jn. 4:10-11

Water shortage is always a challenge and problem in Palestine

---

[5]Bernard Brandon Scott, *Hear Then the Parable: A Commentary on the Parables of Jesus*, p. 197.

and Syria. Droughts occur periodically and cause brooks, springs and wells to dry up. Then water has to be carried from a distance on the backs of men, women and animals. One of the most difficult tasks for a housewife is to provide water for the family. Until the advent of Western technology in the Near East, Semites constantly dreamed of having abundant water flowing near their homes. It was one of their strongest desires. Reservoirs and piping systems were practically unknown. People were totally dependent on rivers, brooks and wells. In some areas of the Near East this problem still exists. Up until the 1950s water was so scarce that at times people suffered from thirst and often had to retire at night literally dying of thirst. Water was coveted more than food.

In Scripture the term "water," *maya,* means "life-giving, sustaining truth." However, the Samaritan woman understood Jesus literally. She thought she would be relieved of the burdensome task of carrying water. But she wondered from where Jesus would obtain living water. (In Aramaic, "living water" refers to water that constantly flows and never becomes stagnant or polluted.)

She said to him: "My lord, you have no bucket and no deep well. Where do you get this living water?" The well from which the Samaritan woman was drawing was dug by the patriarch Jacob. She did not realize that Jesus was greater than the Hebrew patriarch, nor did she know anything about the kind of water Jesus could give her. The "living water" that Jesus offered was truth and life; he knew that the Samaritans would be more thirsty for truth than just for water.

A PROPHET

The woman saith unto him, Sir, I perceive that thou art a prophet. Jn. 4:19.

The Aramaic word for "prophet" is *nbia* deriving from *nba,* "to foretell, predict, prophesy." It also suggests something that "springs forth." In both the Aramaic noun and verb the letter "b" is pronounced as a "v" or "w." *Nabia* also means a "gusher." A prophet is a teller of future events and one who reveals hidden secrets. People also consider him a seer and fortune teller. When animals are lost, Semites consult a prophet just as Saul had done with the prophet Samuel when his father's donkey was lost.[6] Unmarried girls also seek advice about matrimony from such individuals. Women whose husbands are in foreign lands enquire as to their return and safety. In ancient times prophets also acted as statesmen and reformers to whom people looked for guidance to peace and prosperity.

When Jesus told the Samaritan woman "You have had five husbands," she immediately thought he was a prophet or a seer. In the Near East, a prophet is recognized as a man of God. People judge him not by what he says but by what he does and if his predictions come true. Jesus also knew that the one with whom she was now living was not her legal husband. She was secretly living with him as a concubine. Jesus had never met this woman before and meeting her at the well of Jacob was not accidental but providential. The woman was about to become instrumental in spreading the news of the gospel in Samaria. She was the first Samaritan convert to the new message of the kingdom. This gospel of God's kingdom sprang from the teaching of the *Torah* and Jewish prophets.

THE TERM "JEWS"

Ye worship ye know not what: we know what we worship: for salvation is of the Jews. Jn. 4:22.

The word "Jews" comes from the Hebrew word *Yehuda,* meaning "glory." This is the name that Jacob gave to his son Judah. It is the name by which the tribe of Judah was known in Egypt, in the desert wanderings, and after the conquest of Palestine.

When the ten tribes were taken captive to Assyria in 721 BCE, the remaining tribes of Judah, Benjamin, and a remnant of the people in the south, were known as Jews. Even before this time, the tribe of

---

[6]See 1 Sam. 9:6.

Judah had attained prominence and power through the house of David. After the division between the north and the south, all people who followed the house of David were called Jews. The ten tribes were later amalgamated with Assyrians, and an Assyrian colony was established in Samaria and Galilee. These people were called Galileans. (Interestingly, there is a tribe of people in Afghanistan known as the *Pashtun* who claim to be descendants of ancient northern Israel. The Assyrians had also scattered some of the ten northern tribes in northern Iraq and Afghanistan.)

During the time of Jesus, a man was either a Galilean or a Jew. The Galileans were also Jews by faith, but racially they were different. Thus the term "Jews" from that time until today has a religious and not just a racial significance. An Egyptian or a Turk who embraces the Jewish faith is known as a Jew. Herod was a Jew by religion but an Idumean by race. Jesus was a Jew by faith, but the scribes and Pharisees rejected him on the grounds that he was a Galilean. The apostle Paul was a Jew by faith and was of the tribe of Benjamin. (In other words, he was a Benjamite and not literally a Jew by blood—that is, from the tribe of Judah.) "For I was circumcised when I was eight days old, being an Israelite by race, of the tribe of Benjamin, a Hebrew son of Hebrews, and according to the law, a Pharisee."[7]

In the Near East, even today, when a man changes his religion, he also changes his nationality. Thus, when an Assyrian who is a Christian becomes a convert to Islam, he is no longer called an Assyrian but a Moslem, Turk or Kurd. So, also, when an Assyrian accepts the Protestant faith, he is called by the nation to which the missionary belongs—English, French or American.

TRUE WORSHIP

Jesus saith unto her: Woman, believe me, the hour cometh, when ye shall neither in this mountain nor yet at Jerusalem worship the Father. Ye

---

[7]Philippians 3:5, Aramaic Peshitta text, Lamsa translation.

worship ye know not what: we know what we worship for salvation is of the Jews. But the hour cometh, and now is, when the true worshippers shall worship the Father in spirit and in truth: for the Father seeketh such to worship him. God is a spirit and they that worship him must worship him in spirit and in truth. Jn. 4:21-24.

Samaritans worshiped on Mt. Gerizim, the place where Joshua, during the conquest of Palestine, gathered the people together and had them pledge loyalty to God. Because of this historic event, the mountain became a holy place, first to the Israelites and later to Samaritans who inhabited the region during the captivity of the Israelites. Jerusalem, the city where the temple was built and where the Jews worshiped, was declared a holy place about four hundred years later.

But the day was soon coming when true worship of God's way would supplant both the worship of the Samaritans and also that of the Jews. Religion would no longer be restricted to damp and dark shrines and temples. This would not only hold true for the Jews and Samaritans but for people of all races. Nevertheless, salvation came from the Jews and their *Torah*. The Messiah was promised first to the Jews and the lost tribes of Israel, then to the Samaritans and the rest of the world.

The Aramaic text reads: "But the time is coming, and it is here, when the true worshipers shall worship the Father in spirit and in truth; for the Father also desires worshipers such as these. For God is Spirit; and those who worship him must worship him in spirit and truth."[8]

Ruha, "spirit," in Aramaic also implies "universal." God's presence is everywhere and God's spirit fills the entire universe. There is no place in the universe where God is not present. If God had a physical form, then God would be limited and subject to space and time. God, being spirit, embraces all. Spirit is indivisible and the finest substance in all the universe.

In those days, the Jews worshiped God as one would worship a

---

[8] Jn. 4:23-24, Aramaic Peshitta text, Lamsa translation.

great human ruler and potentate. They no longer understood the simple, ancient Abrahamic concept and teachings of the prophets. Abraham worshiped God anywhere regardless of time or place.

Moses had erected the tabernacle in the desert and founded the priestly organization of worship. He also systematized animal sacrifice for offerings to the God of Israel. After King David died, his son Solomon built the colossal and elaborate temple in Jerusalem. All these structures and institutions served to distract people's thoughts away from the spirituality and universality of God. During this time the Jewish God became like other gods, needing meat, cereal and gift offerings. This centralized worship, with its complex rituals, gave the people a misleading, incorrect concept of God. They thought that God dwelt in the temple and could only be worshiped in the holy structure.

Jesus knew that God, being *ruha,* "spirit,"—all-encompassing and all-embracing—is the only essence of all life and, hence, the Father of all creation. Only faithful worshipers of God would understand the true meaning of the Lord God of Israel. These people would worship God in a universal and spiritual sense. They would learn that God does not need worshipers nor sacrifices but rather that humanity needs God.

The ancient Hebrew concept of a local, tribal God was alien to the concept that God is Spirit. The hour had come! Truth had to triumph over error. Israel's God had to be taken out of the dark, dimly lit temple and understood universally.

JESUS REVEALS WHO HE IS

Jesus saith unto her, I that speak unto thee am he. And upon this came his disciples, and marveled that he talked with the woman: yet no man said, What seekest thou? Or, Why talkest thou with her? Jn. 4:26-27.

Part 1—JESUS AS MESSIAH. Apparently this is the first time that Jesus revealed himself to non-Jews. John the Baptist had called him the Messiah. Simon Peter had declared his master as "the Christ

(Messiah), son of the living God." But Jesus had never spoken of this great title openly. It was easier to convince this simple and unlearned Samaritan woman than his own people and especially the Jews in the south.

Now the seeds of the new gospel would be sown among the Samaritans. The work of the gospel was like white, ripened wheat fields, ready to be harvested. Samaritans, Arameans (Syrians), Assyrians, other Semitic clans and Gentile races were about to hear and receive the light of God—that is, Jewish Scripture and the new covenant. Not only these people but the entire world was waiting and ready for a change. Salvation, which is spiritual and mental freedom, would burst forth, relieving the people from want, oppression and injustice. This gospel of the kingdom would give birth to peace of mind, love, and understanding.

Part 2—TALKING TO A WOMAN. In the Near East, talking to women is not tolerated. It is against Eastern etiquette and seen as scandalous. However, it is proper to ask for a drink of water from a woman coming from a well or spring. Relatives, friends and even strangers will often stop a woman on her way back from the well and request a drink from the jar that she carries on her shoulder. Without uttering a word and in a gracious manner, the woman will hand over the jar to the man and wait until he has had his fill.

In the Near East, women usually carry water. It is embarrassing for a man to carry water. Men who have no women at home often stop their female neighbors passing their homes and request water. Semites believe that giving a thirsty man a drink of cold water is a sacred duty that carries a good reward in the hereafter. But to ask a woman for a drink at a well or spring is an entirely different matter. This is considered a breach of proper conduct and a reflection on one's moral character.

Most springs and wells are situated outside the towns and are meeting places for men and women, especially lovers. (Many Semitic poets speak of lovers meeting at a well or spring.) Social relations between men and women are not permitted. The only time a man can see his fiancee or even a woman he admires is when she goes to the well. Water is carried during the afternoons and most men know the hour when certain women come for water. Some men go in advance and wait at the well to see their sweethearts uncovering their faces and filling their jars with water. If no one is present, some lovers would not hesitate to carry on a short conversation.

Speaking to a woman at a well is resented by most Near Easterners, who suspect the motives of those who do this. This is the reason that the disciples were surprised when they saw Jesus conversing with a woman at the well. They judged him by their own cultural standards. However, they did not dare say a word to him.

SPIRITUAL FOOD

In the meanwhile his disciples prayed him, saying, Master, eat. But he said unto them, I have meat to eat that ye know not of. Therefore said the disciples one to another, Hath any man brought him ought to eat? Jesus saith unto them, My meat is to do the will of him that sent me, and to finish his work. Jn. 4:31-34.

Jesus had totally disregarded the ancient cultural custom concerning talking to a woman at a well. He knew that most lovers would do such a thing and that men, generally, pretend they are thirsty just so they can converse with a woman. Nonetheless, he was not ashamed to converse with the woman at the well of Jacob, despite the fact that she was also a member of a rival religion. Jesus knew that the woman needed a drink of living water, the truth that he was teaching.

His disciples had already bought bread in Samaria and now they begged him to eat, but Jesus was not hungry. The conversation with the Samaritan woman and the reception of his gospel in Samaria were to him greater than food. He also knew that she would herald the new gospel among her people, which would remove the animosity between Jew and Samaritan and heal the old wound. His teaching would create a better understanding between the two rival faiths.

When one does God's work and prospers in it, one does not have

74

time to think about food. The joy that comes from the success of the teaching relieves hunger. Jesus felt deeply satisfied and joyful. A human being lives not just from bread alone but from spiritual food that satisfies heart and soul.

HARVEST TIME

Say not ye, There are yet four months, and then cometh harvest? behold, I say unto you, Lift up your eyes, and look on the fields; for they are white already to harvest. Jn. 4:35.

Part 1—FOUR MONTHS TO HARVEST. In Palestine it takes about four months from the time the wheat is sown until it is harvested. The sowing is done early in the spring and requires only a few weeks because each family raises just enough for its own needs. Then, they wait patiently for the harvest season. During this waiting time, there is scarcely any work for the men to do; however, women are busy making rugs and doing housework.

Part 2—THE FIELDS ARE WHITE. In the Holy Land there are two harvest seasons. The barley harvest falls in April and the wheat harvest follows several months later. Barley is one of the chief grain supplies. Since it is planted early, the harvest falls early. It is greeted with much joy because it comes at a time when the farmer's entire supply of wheat is exhausted. People count the days and eagerly await the new crop. The grain grows very low and in most places it is pulled by hand instead of being cut with a sickle.

When the barley is gathered the wheat fields are becoming white because the grain is ripening. Men prepare their sickles and hire extra laborers for the wheat crop.

Jesus' disciples first worked among the Jews, then among the Gentiles. The Jews were like the barley harvest, but the greater harvest of wheat was to follow. While the disciples were teaching among the Jewish people, Gentiles were preparing to accept the new gospel. The disciples need not be idle; there was plenty of work to be done. Jesus' disciples would teach the gospel of the kingdom and demonstrate its power throughout the world.

SOWER AND REAPER

And he that reapeth receiveth wages and gathereth fruit unto life eternal: that both he that soweth and he that reapeth may rejoice together. And herein is that saying true, One soweth, and another reapeth. Jn. 4:36-37.

Part 1—SOWER AND REAPER REJOICING. Generally, an owner of a field does the sowing, but the wheat is cut by hired reapers. When the fields are ready for harvest, every farmer hastens to hire laborers so that he can gather and store his crops before the rainy season begins. It is not safe to leave the fields of ripened grain uncut. The wheat that is raised represents the sole means of livelihood for the family. If anything should happen to it, the family would be reduced to poverty. While the field is ripening, the owner suffers from anxiety. Often, older men spend sleepless nights fearing that an enemy might burn their crops.

Harvest is an exciting season. There is great joy in every home because the new wheat furnishes bread, and the storehouses will be replenished. An owner of a field supervises the work, and his wife and daughters bring cooked food to the reapers. The laborers are just as happy as the owner because they also depend on the wheat for their wages. Usually, this will take care of the needed supply for the reaper's family. Thus the owner (sower) and the reaper rejoice together.

Part 2—SOWING AND REAPING. "One sows and another reaps" is an Aramaic expression referring to men who profit from the labors of others. One who sows may die before the crop is ripe; then the wheat is harvested by a relative or even a stranger who did not labor in the sowing. Or the ripened grain might be confiscated by enemies or suffer from some other disaster.

As we have said in the above comment, in many areas of the Near East, sowing is done by the owner of the land, but the harvest

76

is gathered by hired laborers. In the Spring, farmers find plenty of time to plant. In the Summer, the crops of wheat have to be gathered hastily for fear that they may be destroyed by fire or stolen. Additional laborers are therefore hired and their wages are paid in wheat.[9]

The field represents the Jewish religion. The sowers were the prophets who proclaimed God's word and announced the coming of the Messiah. The disciples are the laborers who are ready to harvest what they had not sown. Jesus taught his disciples that in their work they were completing what the prophets had previously begun. His gospel of the kingdom was not the beginning of a new religion but the fulfillment of the promises that God had made to Abraham, Isaac and Jacob.

THE FAITH OF THE KING'S SERVANT

Then said Jesus unto him, Except ye see signs and wonders, ye will not believe. The nobleman saith unto him, Sir, come down ere my child die. Jn. 4:48-49.

The Aramaic text reads: "Jesus said to him: Unless you see miracles and wonders, you will not believe. The king's servant said to him, My Lord, come down before the boy is dead." The term "king" in the Aramaic text refers to a petty ruler. The servant came to ask Jesus to heal the ruler's boy.

Many of the Pharisees and priests had rejected Jesus because he had not wrought a miracle great enough to convince them that he was the Messiah/Christ. Moses had said that the Messiah would perform greater miracles than he had done. However, this was not the only reason for their rejection. On many occasions the Jews were deceived by false messiahs and were led into deadly struggles against Rome. Now they were cautious about accepting a man who claimed that he was the Messiah.

When Jesus made this statement to the king's servant, he used

---

[9]See James 5:4.

the plural pronoun "you," meaning "you people" or "you Jews." The entire statement that Jesus made was not directed to the servant but to people in general.

When he spoke these words, however, Jesus was also testing the servant's faith: "Unless you see miracles and wonders, you will not believe." The servant understood what Jesus meant by this remark and instead of arguing, he begged him to come before the boy died. This proves that the servant was not looking for miracles, but that he believed in Jesus and in his power as a healer. He knew Jesus could heal the boy.

CHAPTER 5

JESUS QUESTIONS AND HEALS A SICK MAN

When Jesus saw him lie, and knew that he had been now a long time in that case, he saith unto him, Wilt thou be made whole? The impotent man answered him, Sir, I have no man, when the water is troubled, to put me in the pool: but while I am coming, another steppeth down before me. Jesus saith unto him, Rise, take up thy bed and walk, And immediately the man was made whole, and took up his bed, and walked. . . . Afterward Jesus findeth him in the temple, and said unto him, Behold thou art made whole: sin no more, lest a worse thing come unto thee. Jn. 5:6-9, 14.

According to the text, a certain man had been sick for 38 years. He had been sitting among many who were blind and lame. He was waiting to be healed by the mysterious movement of the water, at a place called *Bethesda* in Hebrew, "the house of mercy." Jesus asked him if he wanted to be healed. The man replied that he did but that he could not get into the pool in time when the angel stirred the waters.[1]

Jesus knew that this man, who had spent so many years in the temple grounds, had been helpless to get into the water before others. But he also knew that the man made a good living by begging for alms and was probably better off financially than many healthy laborers who had employment. This is why Jesus questioned him about wanting to be healed. He also understood that there were many lame and ill men in that place who preferred to make an easy living by begging. They would rather keep their illness than be healed and have to face an uncertain future and perhaps even starvation.

In these lands begging alms can be a lucrative business, especially in the precinct of holy places. Some beggars are even placed there by politicians and religious authorities who share the gains. But this man sincerely desired to be healed. He believed in the

---

[1]At that time people believed that when the water stirred, an angel had descended and disturbed the water. Then anyone entering the pool would be healed.

story of the supposed healing waters. He wanted to begin a new life and to trust God for his daily sustenance. Jesus felt this positive attitude from the man and commanded him: "Take up your quilt and walk." The man was healed instantly and picked up his quilt and carried it around in the temple. But because this was the Sabbath, some of the Jews became angry with Jesus and wanted to kill him. (See verse 16.)

When Jesus saw this man again in another area of the temple, he warned him not to sin again. We can see from this that some illnesses come from sin—that is, the breaking of God's laws. Illness does not originate in God but from the misjudgment of people; hence, men of God have power to heal the sick and cast out unclean spirits, i.e., mental and emotional illnesses.

Some religious teachers believed that God strikes people down with illnesses as a punishment for their sins. The religion of Zoroaster held the notion of two gods, the god of good and the god of evil. This religion also taught that sin and suffering were created by the god of evil.

Jesus knew that there was only one power in the universe— God, who is omnipresent, omniscient and omnipotent. He also knew that God was not the author of sin or sickness. When Jesus saw the man he had healed, he warned him to abstain from any evil acts that would create physical illness. Sometimes when people turn from their errors and are healed, they may return to their former habits, ways and erroneous deeds; then greater troubles come upon them.

Even today there are religious leaders who believe that God is the originator of sickness as punishment for sin. They do not realize that God cannot be the author both of good and of evil. No spring issues both sweet and bitter water at the same time. If God were the source of illness, then he would not have granted power to the prophets, Jesus or his disciples to heal these diseases. Sickness, then, being the work of God, would be indestructible.

STRICT SABBATH OBSERVANCE

But Jesus answered them, My Father worketh hitherto, and I work. Therefore the Jews sought the more to kill him, because he not only had broken the sabbath, but said also that God was his Father, making himself equal with God. Jn. 5:17-18.

Much of the religious ideas during the time of Jesus had become very dogmatic. Religious authorities had written vast commentaries trying to explain the law and ordinances of Moses. They had forgotten the simple religion of their prophets.

Any act done on the Sabbath was considered a violation of the Sabbath, but this was not the case before the Babylonian captivity. Prior to that time the Jews were a pastoral people, needing to take care of their sheep and cattle every day. Moses instituted the Sabbath so that the people could have a day of rest. He did not mean for it to become a burden.

Some of these strict religious Jews were angry with Jesus because he said, "My Father does the work and so I do it too." This implied that God did not rest on the Sabbath but was healing through Jesus. The people had forgotten that God cared for them and met their needs every day of the week. Additionally, they felt that God's name was so holy that they hesitated to utter it. God was no longer like a caring shepherd looking after his sheep but had become dependent on their sacrificial offerings and gifts for the temple.

Jesus wanted these Jews to realize that his healing work was done with the consent of God. God, as a Father, healed and cared for his people even on the Sabbath. Jesus had told them that of himself he could not do anything, but God was working and teaching through him, just as a human father teaches everything to his son.

God is the author of goodness, health and perfection; therefore, all healing comes from God. If Jesus had been working against God, how then could he heal the sick and restore sight to the blind? The Father had given him power over everything. God was his witness because he was doing good works. The sick, blind and insane were healed with the power God had granted him. The good works that

Jesus did were the proof that God was with him and had sent him to do these things.

FATHER AND SON

Then answered Jesus and said unto them, Verily, verily, I say unto you, The Son can do nothing of himself, but what he seeth the Father do: for what things soever he doeth, these also doeth the Son likewise. For the Father loveth the Son, and sheweth him all things that himself doeth: and he will shew him greater works than these, that ye may marvel. Jn. 5:19-20.

Arts and handicrafts have been kept secret for long ages in most Near Eastern countries where the machine has not made its appearance. Special arts and crafts have been handed down from father to son. This is how secrets of blacksmiths, coppersmiths and silversmiths are carried on from one generation to another.

Typically in the Near East, when individuals desire to learn a trade or an art, they have to work for years without pay in order to acquire skill in their workmanship. A master does not reveal the secrets of his trade to apprentices until they have served out their full time and proved themselves deserving of his confidence and favor. Some apprentices who have not been loyal to their masters leave their trades without learning the secrets that give distinction to the art or craft and make it saleable. These men cannot start a business for themselves but must secure employment in other places in hope of gaining trade secrets that they lack.

However, this is not the case when a master has a son. From childhood, a son is brought up under the careful guidance of his father. He eats with his father and works with him in the field and at the shop. The father and son share their lives together constantly. A daughter imitates her mother and learns her ways. If a mother has special skills making things, then her daughter will learn those secrets.

In a shop, one sees a father and his little boy working together. A father mixes formulas and finishes objects in the presence of his son. Apprentices and other workers are not allowed to see these processes. But the father teaches his son everything he knows and lets him practice on objects that an apprentice is not allowed to touch. Usually, a father teaches his son with gentleness and patience, hoping some day to hand over the family trade to him so that it may continue in every detail in the coming generation. "Everything has been delivered to me by my Father, and no man knows the Son except the Father, nor does any man know the Father but the Son and he to whom the Son wishes to reveal him."[2]

Jesus, as a provincial teacher and healer, did not gain his knowledge and skill from schools or priests but from his heavenly Father. Teachers and priests were like apprentices. They were selected and trained to learn the secrets of God's kingdom, which they did not understand. Jesus was like a Near Eastern son and understood the secrets of the kingdom because God, like a father, revealed everything to him. Jesus constantly communed with his Father, so his knowledge was not gained from books but from a continual relationship with God. Nothing was withheld from Jesus. As a son he was doing the works that the Father intended to be done. Jesus and his Father were always working in harmony and accord.

THE PIOUS NOT CONDEMNED

Verily, verily, I say unto you, He that heareth my word, and believeth on him that sent me, hath everlasting life, and shall not come into condemnation, but is passed from death unto life. Jn. 5:24.

People believed at that time that judgment was to come in the future. But the presence of Jesus and his gospel of the kingdom had brought that day upon the nation and world. Judgment day had come—that is, light had dawned in the world, exposing the darkness.

God, who is the heavenly father, has turned over the power of judgment to the son; therefore, Jesus has become a true judge. This

---

[2]Mt. 11:27, Aramaic Peshitta text, Lamsa translation.

judgment vindicates the pious who truly believe in God and hear the message of the son, but is, at the same time, a condemnation of those who refuse this message of the kingdom. They would be condemned because their evil works would condemn them. Jesus' teaching brought the light of God to humanity.

Those pious who received the son—that is, his teaching—pass from death unto life without any hindrance. They now had the opportunity to receive life. Jesus words are the fountain of life even for those who are spiritually dead. (See verses 25 and 26.)

THE DEAD WILL HEAR THE SON

Verily, verily, I say unto you, The hour is coming, and now is, when the dead shall hear the voice of the Son of God; and they that hear shall live. For as the Father hath life in himself; so hath he given to the Son to have life in himself. And hath given him authority to execute judgment also, because he is the Son of man. Jn. 5:25-27.

Part 1—HEARING JESUS. The hour was coming for the judgment day when even the dead would hear Jesus' voice, but it was already here. Now is the time for those who are living but are dead spiritually. They have the opportunity to accept the light of truth. Those who receive this teaching find life everlasting.

Since God is eternal and indestructible, humankind is also eternal and indestructible. Humanity was created in the image and likeness of God. But, God had placed all power in the hands of Jesus, who had the authority to grant the realization of everlasting life to those who would accept his teaching.

Part 2—HUMAN BEING. Jesus, as a human being (son of man), was endowed by God with power and authority. In this instance, Jesus speaks of his humanity. God had anointed Jesus just as the Hebrew prophets had been anointed. God had given him power to work wonders and miracles, heal the sick, restore the mentally and emotionally ill, raise the dead and execute judgment. The expression "execute judgment" refers to his authority to point out those who hear and see truth demonstrated but reject it. Their rejection of the light condemned them.

The term "son of man" is an Aramaic form of speech that means a "human being." Jesus, as a human, was anointed by God and came to be the temple in which the Christ—that is, the spirit—dwelt. It is through this sonship that we also come to realize that we are children of God. Jesus, in his humanity, was wholly dependent upon God. He said: "I can do nothing of myself; but as I hear I judge, and my judgment is just; for I do not seek my own will but of him who sent me." This entire argument was aimed at those who were ready to kill Jesus because he made himself equal to God.

DEAD WILL RISE

Marvel not at this: for the hour is coming in the which all that are in the graves shall hear his voice, And shall come forth: they that have done good unto the resurrection of life; and they that have done evil, unto the resurrection of damnation. Jn. 5:28-29.

At that time, the Jewish concept of the resurrection was naive and rudimentary. Prior to the Babylonian exile of the Jews, there was little or no mention of the resurrection. The Hebrews, like the Egyptians, Assyrians, Syrians and Chaldeans, had a small glimpse of the life hereafter. They provided the deceased with food, furniture, utensils, seeds and even servants. In many cases in the ancient world, if a man died, his wives would be buried with him. It was the prophet Daniel who first aired the doctrine of the resurrection. Daniel prophesied: "And many of those who sleep in the dust of the earth shall awake, some to everlasting life and some to shame and everlasting contempt."[3]

The Jews had been persecuted and deprived of their homes and heritage by wicked kings. Daniel, through his prophecy, gave hope to those who suffered in this life. In another life, those who had

---

[3]Dan. 12:2, Aramaic Peshitta text, Lamsa translation.

suffered would rejoice when they would see their persecutors put to shame and suffering.

The teaching of the resurrection had not yet crystallized at the time of Jesus. A powerful group known as the Sadducees rejected this teaching. They believed in one life and adhered to the old concept that God had no control or dominion over the grave—that is, *sheol*.

Now the hour had come when the teaching of the resurrection would be revealed and proclaimed by the prophet from Galilee. Jesus, through his death and resurrection, would prove that life is continuous and indestructible and that God did have power over *sheol*. Even those who were in their graves would hear this voice and rejoice in the new hope that was given to them. They could now be free from *sheol,* whose bars would be broken once and for all. Then, the dead would become one with all life. Jesus brought the full realization that life is a continuous and endless stream.

SEARCH THE SCRIPTURES

Search the scriptures; for in them ye think ye have eternal life: and they are they which testify of me. Jn. 5:39.

The Aramaic text reads: " Examine the scriptures; in them you trust that you have eternal life; and even they testify concerning me."[4] Holy Scripture is the highest standard of truth and ethics because scriptures are the Word of God. Treaties between nations, written or oral agreements between individuals might be disregarded and come under suspicion, but the Word of Scripture is true and everlasting. Cases that courts and judges cannot settle are decided by taking oaths on Holy Scripture. People are also blessed or cursed with the words from Scripture.

The reference here is to the messianic promises made to Abraham, Isaac, and Jacob. Jewish sacred literature is built upon this holy covenant that is the highest court of law in the Near East. Jesus

---

[4]Jn. 5:39, Aramaic Peshitta text, Lamsa translation.

reminded the Jews of these promises that clearly bore witness to his mission. He knew that from Genesis to Malachi, scriptures recounted the divine promise of the coming of the Messiah, his rejection and suffering. It was a promise made by God that the son of a woman, Eve, was destined to crush the head of the serpent, evil.[5]

Moses said: "The Lord will raise unto you a prophet from the midst of you, of your own brethren like unto me. Unto him you shall hearken."[6] The prophet Isaiah called him "Wonderful Counselor, the Mighty God, the Everlasting Father, the Prince of Peace."[7] He also called him "the suffering servant."

Nearly all of the Hebrew prophets had some glimpse of the Messiah, his mission and the salvation of the world that was to come through him. These messianic prophecies in Scripture are like a golden thread woven in a costly tapestry. Invariably, all Hebrew prophets longed to see this day happen, but they did not live to see it.

The scribes and Pharisees had forgotten the writings of Moses and the teachings of their prophets. This is part of the reason these religious authorities rejected the Galilean prophet as the Messiah. Jesus told the Jews that if they doubted his words they were to examine Holy Scripture. As far as Jesus was concerned, Scripture would finally decide the issue.

AN AMBASSADOR OF GOD

I am come in my Father's name, and ye receive me not: if another shall come in his own name, him ye will receive. Jn. 5:43.

"I come in my Father's name" means "God has recommended me" or "I am God's messenger." In the Near East, all messengers or ambassadors of a ruler are received in the name of their king. No ambassador would be accepted without royal credentials. The theme

---

[5]See Gen. 3:14-15.
[6]Deut. 18:15.
[7]See Isa. 9:6.

of the Gospel of John is the "Word"; therefore, Jesus is the messenger, the one who represents God.

Jesus came in the name of God. He was sent to teach nothing but God's truth and his Father's way of life, but he was rejected by religious leaders. However, when other men came with their own credentials, proving their qualifications as teachers of religion and loyal to the doctrine of the elders, they were well received. These so-called teachers wore long robes and were highly honored and accepted. But, having authority only from God to teach the true doctrine of salvation, Jesus needed no credentials. He did not require long robes as an authority symbol to teach that God is a loving Father who cares for his people. Truth alone was sufficient to those who could hear the voice of God and accept his messenger.

It seems that people always welcomed false prophets and leaders simply because they were allured by misleading promises and an easy way of life. Again and again, the Jews were led astray by false prophets and were made to worship Baal. The worship of Baal offered a sensual way of life. Jesus' teaching upset the current system of worship and beliefs.

CHAPTER 6

THE MULTIPLICATION OF THE LOAVES AND FISH

There is a lad here, which hath five barley loaves, and two small fishes: but what are they among so many? Jn. 6:9.

When bread dough is made, a Near Eastern woman makes the sign of the cross over it and in the dough with her finger as a token of blessing. She then says, "God increase it and let it be shared with strangers and the hungry." Aramaic speaking women call it *borktha*, "blessing." Bread baked by pious and sincere women who devote themselves to prayer and fasting is considered especially blessed. People believe that the blessings of certain holy men and the pious hand cause good leaven to multiply. Families of bad reputation are known as having bad leaven and bread.

Some pious women are forehanded and always provide a sufficient food supply. They are known for their ability to satisfy many unexpected guests. When food is handled, God's name is invoked and his abundant blessings are sought. Sheep likewise are blessed and are expected to multiply. People ask for God's protection over the flocks. Semites often say God has increased their substance; he has given them sheep and other wealth.

Restaurants and hotels were unknown at that time. When men traveled, they had to carry sufficient bread with them in bags. Their supply had to last for the entire journey because bread could not be procured on the road. This habit is so inborn that immigrants often carry bread with them from Turkey and Persia to the United States. On a short journey travelers carry as many as fifteen loaves between garments. Fish, cheese and other food stuffs are also carried. Practically nowhere today can a group of Semites be found on a journey without bread and food supplies.

While a caravan is on the road, every man tries to conserve his supply of bread. Some men pretend they are short of bread and blame the shortage on their wives. They use this pretense because, while Semites are generous in sharing their food at home or on a journey, their supply is limited and they try to conserve what they have by seeking to eat with others. Invitations to share, however, are given reluctantly. This all changes on the return journey. Now everyone becomes generous because it is contrary to Near Eastern custom to bring back stale bread that would have to be thrown to the birds or given to strangers. Those who had hidden their bread are now ready to share it with others. The men who had previously said that they did not have enough suddenly display many loaves that they produce from their garments and bags. This looks like magic or even a miracle to the hungry.

Jesus was looking for a quiet, solitary place, but he was constantly followed by large crowds of people. In accordance with custom, these travelers surely carried hidden loaves of bread and fish. They did not know how long Jesus would stay nor how long they would be away from home. From the very beginning, some men must have generously shared their bread. Others, less generous, saved their food supplies by seeking to eat with friends. They were afraid Jesus might prolong his stay in the desert and they would not have sufficient to last the time spent with the Galilean teacher. If they did not have food, they would not be able to remain as long as Jesus.

When Jesus decided to dismiss the crowds, some of those who had previously shared their bread generously had exhausted their supply and were almost famished. The disciples feared that some of these people might faint by the wayside. Jesus instructed his disciples to feed them. There was a boy present who had five loaves of bread and two fish in his clothing. He was willing to share with the crowd. When he did this, others who had concealed their bread, now realizing that they were about to return home, produced the hidden foods. They began offering their hidden supply of food to the hungry crowd. Jesus blessed them and his blessing no doubt increased the sharing of bread so that they were all satisfied. There was not only enough to go around but an abundance remained. The gospel writer does not tell us the details of how the bread was produced or multiplied, but satisfying the hunger of this huge crowd with the means at hand was a miracle.

Semites believe that men of God can increase supplies of bread. They assign the cause to God from whom everything comes and in whose mind everything exists before it is accomplished. They consider it a miracle when selfish people are converted into unselfish givers. A Near Easterner who is poor prays that God may grant him food and some wealth. He expects God to do this by increasing what he has. God may also soften the hearts of the rich so that they might contribute to his relief. No doubt Jesus had the power to increase the bread; he was a holy man.

The teaching of the gospel of Jesus Christ throughout the centuries has wrought miracles and wonders. Men and women have been willing not only to share and to give liberally but to sacrifice even their lives for the sake of the kingdom of God on earth.[1]

BASKETS

When they were filled, he said unto his disciples, Gather up the fragments that remain, that nothing be lost. Therefore they gathered them together, and filled twelve baskets with the fragments of the five barley loaves, which remained over and above unto them that had eaten. Jn. 6:12-13.

Semites weave baskets from straw or willow. They are about twelve inches in diameter and four inches deep. People carry their food supplies and gifts in them. Baskets as bread containers were also used for outings. The crumbs are gathered because bread is scarce and never wasted. Semites consider bread to be sacred. It is always eaten, given to the poor or thrown to hungry dogs, birds, and even fish.

There is an ancient Near Eastern custom that is still practiced today in many areas of the Near East. When people visit a healer,

---

[1]See Mt. 14:17; Mk. 6:38; Lk. 9:13.

prophet or holy man, they bring him baskets full of food—such as bread, cheese, baked fish—or other gifts. One never goes empty handed to see a man of God. They do this because money is scarce in these lands.[2]

Bread is baked very thin and round, about twelve to fifteen inches in diameter. At times fish and cheese are wrapped in it. Fish are baked and left to cool before they are eaten. People usually take fish on a short trip because it will keep fresh for several days. Cheese and other food stuffs keep much longer and are carried on lengthy journeys.

There are many biblical examples of this custom. For instance, Jesus and his disciples carried bread when traveling. On one occasion, his disciples told him that they had forgotten to take bread with them.[3] When the angel of the Lord visited Gideon and gave him a message from God, Gideon asked the angel to wait there for him until he returned. The messenger of God agreed. Immediately, Gideon went home and prepared goat meat, unleavened cakes and a small pot of broth. Then he quickly returned to the messenger and presented the food.[4]

When Saul was searching for his father's donkeys, he told his servant that they had no bread left to take as an offering to the seer, Samuel. They wanted to consult with him concerning the lost donkeys. Since they had no bread to present to Samuel, they took a coin that was in the possession of the servant.[5] When Abijah, the son of King Jeroboam, fell sick, the king told his wife to visit Ahijah, the prophet, who was a healer. He instructed her to take a gift of ten loaves of bread, cakes and honey. (Cakes are bread baked with butter

---

[2]Interestingly, when Dr. Lamsa and I were traveling in the States and were lecturing in Houston, Texas, several Assyrian people brought bread and other gifts to him at the lecture hall. This occurred in many cities where there were Assyrian people.

[3]See Mk. 8:14.

[4]Judges 6:11-19.

[5]1 Sam. 9:7-8.

and milk.)[6] Also, we encounter another episode in the book of Kings: "There came a certain man from the city of giants, and brought the prophet of God bread of the first fruits, twenty loaves of barley, and new wheat rubbed from the ears in a cloth. . . ."[7]

When David fled from Absalom, Ziba brought him two hundred loaves of bread.[8] Naaman, the Syrian general, brought abundant gifts to the prophet Elisha when he healed him of leprosy.[9] When Ben-hadad, King of Syria, was sick, he sent Hazall with forty camels laden with presents to inquire of Elisha.[10]

Jesus fed the crowd on the mountain, which was near Tiberias. People had gathered from all the surrounding country, bringing with them the sick, lame, blind and the mentally and emotionally ill. They had also brought with them baskets containing food. This is how the baskets were also multiplied. Jesus blessed the bread and fish and his faith in the power of God increased the supply so that the hungry were fed and satisfied. There was such an abundance of sharing that there were twelve baskets left over, filled with fragments of bread.

Jesus had infinite knowledge of God's wisdom. He was always ready and able to face any situation and meet any need. He had raised the dead and opened the eyes of the blind. Jesus wanted the hungry crowds fed, and God supplied what was needed.

WALKING ON THE SEA

So when they had rowed about five and twenty or thirty furlongs, they see Jesus walking on the Sea, and drawing nigh unto the ship: and they were afraid. But he saith unto them, It is I; be not afraid. Jn. 6:19-20.

According to Aramaic style of speech, the expression "walking

---

[6] 1 Ki. 14:3.
[7] 2 Ki. 4:42, Aramaic Peshitta text, Lamsa translation.
[8] 2 Sam. 16:1.
[9] 2 Ki. 5:15-16.
[10] 2 Ki. 8:8-9.

on the sea" means "walking *by* the sea" or "*along* the seashore." The Aramaic word *al* has many meanings, such as "by, on, over, above, alongside, against, enter, attack, rape, chase, because." Its usage as a noun, preposition, verb or adverb is very confusing when translating into other languages. For example, the psalmist says, "*al nahrawatha d-Babel, taman etewen, wawkhen.*" Literally translated it reads, "*on* the rivers of Babylon, there we sat down and wept." It is correctly rendered in the King James version as, "*By* the rivers of Babylon, there we sat down. . . ." When one writes in Aramaic and wishes to reference the surface of the water, the writer must use *apey*, meaning "face." Therefore, when saying one was walking on top of the water, the writer uses the expression *al apey maya*, meaning "on the surface of the water." A*pey* does not occur in any of the Aramaic gospels when describing this event. Conversely, Genesis 1:2 reads, "*wruha dalaha mrahpa al apey maya,*" "And the spirit of God moved on the face [surface] of the water." In Hebrew the word for "face" or "surface" is *paney*.

John's gospel text just uses the preposition *al*. Therefore, it means "on" or "by," which implies that Jesus was walking by the sea or along the shore of the lake of Galilee. To this very day Assyrians say *ezal al yama*, "He has gone to the sea," or *khader al yama*, "walking along the shore." But, if we translate these phrases literally, we would say "on the sea." When an individual crosses a river or sea, one says in Aramaic, "He flew to the other side." Assyrians also say, "He took the sheep on the water," meaning "He took the sheep to the water so that they may drink."

Jesus' disciples were going from the port of Tiberias to Capernaum. Both cities are on the western shore of the lake of Galilee. They were not crossing over to the eastern side of the lake. Most translations of John 6:17 use the words "cross over to Capernaum." This misunderstanding came about because the Aramaic word *evra,* "landing place," is similar to the root of the word *avar*, "to cross." A proper rendering is "port or docking place."

Prior to this time, Jesus and his disciples had left Capernaum in their boat for the port of Tiberias. Then, after Jesus had increased the

94

bread supply and fed the people near the port, he instructed his disciples to return by boat to Capernaum while he retired to the mountain. Had Jesus been at Gadara on the opposite shore, he would doubtless have had to walk on the water to get to the boat. This question has nothing to do with Jesus' miraculous power. The issue is not whether he could walk on water but whether he actually did.

The boat was headed toward Capernaum. When the disciples had rowed about three or four miles, they saw Jesus "walking on the sea" (literally translated *al yama*, but when properly rendered, "by the sea."). When he drew nearer to the water, they became afraid, thinking he might be an angel or a spirit. Semites believe that angels attack men at night if they are by a body of water. Today no one crosses a stream or a river after nightfall without saying a prayer or calling on God's name. Jesus promptly spoke to them: "It is I, be not afraid." Verse 21 clearly indicates they wanted to receive Jesus into their boat, but it reached the docking place before they could take him in.

To explain this comment, one needs a map that shows the position of the boat and the location of the two cities. It is easier and quicker to walk from Tiberias to Capernaum than to take a boat and have to row. Jesus did not go with his disciples by boat because he wished to avoid the excited crowds that were waiting for him at Capernaum. These people wanted to make him their leader and king by force.

The gospels of Matthew and Mark tell a different story of Jesus walking on the water. (See Matthew 14:22-33 and Mark 6:45-51.) Symbolically speaking, clear and still water represents light and happiness; troubled water denotes doubt, fear and disaster to come. Jesus' disciples were disturbed. They wondered how Jesus could be proclaimed king without a revolution. Jesus, through his appearance, strengthened them. No doubt the disciples were in some difficulty that was solved by his presence. Christ's spirit could reveal itself on land, sea and in rooms with closed doors. Jesus manifested himself to his disciples not to perform a stunt but to take care of a need. Wherever there is a need, God's presence is there to aid. Therefore, the importance of this episode is not "walking on the water" but Jesus' appearance to his disciples.

The Church of the East teaches that Christ's spirit appeared to his disciples just as he appeared in the upper room when the doors were closed. (This ancient, Semitic, Near Eastern Church differentiates between Jesus as a man and the Christ that abided in him.) In view of this translation of the Aramaic Peshitta text and the geographical location of Tiberias, there was no need for Jesus to cross the lake.

Jesus walking on water is not a greater miracle than his healing the sick, opening the eyes of the blind, raising the dead or changing human hearts. Jesus promised his followers that they would do greater things.

SEEKING BREAD ONLY—SEALED BY GOD

Labor not for the meat which perisheth, but for that meat which endureth unto everlasting life, which the Son of man shall give unto you: for him hath God the Father sealed. Jn. 6:27.

The Aramaic term *htam* means "to seal." It also means "to attest, confirm, determine." God had determined from the very beginning that Jesus would come into the world to feed people with the bread of life, which is truth. God knew that humanity would stray from the way of truth, following after its own devices and laboring only for material things that perish.

However, when people are fed spiritual food—the true understanding of a spiritual life—then peace and harmony reign and material things abound. Many hungry and poverty stricken people sought after Jesus simply because of the food they were given while attending his talks. Some of them were interested only in bread and not the bread of life.

Others, after they had seen him feeding thousands of hungry people with a few loaves of bread and fish that were at hand, challenged him and asked him to show them a sign. They said to him:

"What sign do you show then, that we may see and believe in you? What have you performed?"[11] Clearly, these people did not consider the increase of bread that fed five thousand people as a miracle. They discounted it completely.

But Jesus refused to give them a sign because truth cannot be proved or supported by signs and magical performances. Truth needs no defense nor support because truth itself is the mother of miracles and wonders.

MANNA

Our fathers did eat manna in the desert: as it is written, He gave them bread from heaven to eat. Jn. 6:31.

Manna derives from the Aramaic term *mann-ho*, meaning "what is it?" This name was given to a desert food that the twelve tribes of Israel found in the wilderness and had never before seen. They found that it was edible and sweet to the taste like honey, but they wondered from where it came and what was its name. Israel named the food *manna*, "what is it?"

Manna falls on the ground in the early morning like dew. It rests on the leaves of the tamarisk plant that is still found in the Arabian desert and other areas of the Near East. Native people of the area gather and eat this substance. It is also a standard food for travelers.

God supplied manna and quail for the Israelites during their wanderings in the desert.[12] Scripture says that the quail were found lying high on the ground. This is an Aramaic way of saying that the quail were found in abundance, as they still are today. They are easily caught in the Arabian desert and used by the bedouins for food and also sold in the cities.

When anything in the Near East is easily accomplished, people say, "it is cooked, ready to be eaten." When food is abundant, they

---

[11] See Jn. 6:30.
[12] See Ex. 16:13; Num. 11:31.

also say, "the food is knee-deep." The Semitic writers of the books of Moses used Aramaic terms in describing the incidents that took place while the Israelites were traveling in the desert. Interestingly, people in the desert continue to speak pure Aramaic, the language that their fathers brought from Assyria and spoke until after their return to Palestine from Egypt. The word *mann-ho* is still used by the Assyrians and *manna* is still gathered and eaten.

THE BREAD OF LIFE

And Jesus said unto them, I am the bread of life; he that cometh to me shall never hunger; and he that believeth on me shall never thirst. Jn. 6:35.

In the Near East, bread is the main and most essential food no matter what else may be offered. Even if a family has an abundance of all kinds of food but has no bread, people consider that family to be poor. Men gain fame and are highly spoken of if their families are noted for their plentiful bread. In certain areas where old customs and manners are still carried out, very little is known about growing vegetables. When wheat crops fail, people face starvation.

To Near Easterners bread is sacred. They take oaths by touching and kissing it. Bread becomes a sacred bond between friends and the sign of intimate relationship. Friends often say, "I have eaten his bread. I will die for him." People who have become enemies to each other will reconcile by breaking bread together. Bread is also the bond of protection. Once an individual takes refuge in another's home and eats bread with him, the owner of that house must defend his guest at any cost, even with his life.

Jesus understood very well the attitude of his people regarding bread. That's why he said, "I am the bread of life." His listeners could immediately identify with his saying because of their feelings about the sacredness of bread.

Semites often say, "There is bread and salt between us," meaning "we are one by a solemn agreement." The phrase "bread and salt" is binding and holy. A person who breaks the covenant of "bread and salt" is considered a base person and one not worthy of trust. People will say about this offender that "he knows not the meaning of bread and salt." This is a stigma that holds forever.

Certain desert bedouins will treat even their greatest enemies with profound courtesy. They will serve them food and protect them with sword and shelter—for three days only—if they made a bread and salt covenant. (After three days, however, if their enemies are smart, they will flee for their lives.)

Normally, true Semites will not tell a lie while bread is present on the table. They believe that bread has a mystical sacredness because it is God's provision for humankind's basic need. From where else could daily bread come but from the caring, providing, loving hand of God. Dr. Rihbany says in his book *The Syrian Christ*:

> As the son of a Syrian family I was brought up to think of bread as possessing a mystic sacred significance. I never would step on a piece of bread fallen in the road, I would pick it up, press it to my lips for reverence, and place it in a wall or on some other place where it would not be trodden upon.
> What always seemed to me to be one of the noblest traditions of my people was their reverence for the *'aish* (bread; literally, "the life-giver"). While breaking bread together we would not rise to salute an arriving guest, whatever his social rank. Whether spoken or not, our excuse for not rising and engaging in the cordial Oriental [Semitic] salutation before the meal was ended, was our reverence for the food *(hir-metel-'aish)*. We could, however, and always did, invite the newcomer most urgently to partake of the repast.
> .... The *'aish* was something more than mere matter. Inasmuch as it sustained life, it was God's own life made tangible for his child, man, to feed upon. The Most High Himself fed our hunger. Does not the psalmist say, "Thou openest thine hand, and satisfieth the desire of every living thing.[13]

Bread is often used in Scripture figuratively, meaning "truth." It

---

[13]Abraham M. Rihbany, *The Syrian Christ*, pp. 193-195.

is truth that satisfies one's soul and grants everlasting life. Just as bread feeds and sustains a human body, truth nourishes and sustains one's spiritual life.

Jesus, because of his teaching, became the sacred bond between God and humanity. What he taught was the true bread, the bread of the spirit. He offered his life as spiritual food and for an everlasting covenant. No earthly bread is holier than his spiritual food, which he gives to all nations. Those who eat of his teaching never hunger or lack in understanding. His message nourishes the hearts and souls of the human family. His word brings peace, prosperity and a clear, loving understanding of God, who is life itself.

JESUS TO SAVE ALL HUMANITY

And this is the Father's will which hath sent me, that of all which he hath given me, I should lose nothing, but should raise it up again at the last day. Jn. 6:39.

Many of the Jewish leaders during this time were more concerned with the righteous than with anyone else. They did not want to bother with those who had gone astray from the way of God. Jesus came to awaken all people. He came to call not only the righteous but those who were lost, sick and fallen from the path of life. Jesus' plan of salvation was universal and all-inclusive because it embraced all humanity.

In the book of Ezekiel, we are told that shepherds of Israel had been careless and negligent; therefore, the sheep (Israelites) had scattered and some were lost. Ezekiel goes on to tell us that God would appoint a new shepherd who would heal those who were bruised and gather the lost sheep. This was the will of God—that all Israel and the entire world should be rescued and nothing or no one lost. In the Near East, when a shepherd loses one sheep, he also loses his honor and reputation as a good shepherd.

We are told that after his crucifixion and death, Jesus spent three days in *sheol* preaching to the imprisoned souls. Before this time,

100

there had been little hope of the resurrection. Jesus, through his own resurrection, demonstrated that life continued after death. He destroyed the fear of death and revealed life eternal. Those who believed in him would also be saved and raised in the last day.

TRUE RELIGION IS SIMPLE

No man can come to me, except the Father which hath sent me draw him: and I will raise him up at the last day. It is written in the prophets, And they shall be all taught of God. Every man therefore that hath heard, and hath learned of the Father, cometh unto me. Jn. 6:44-45.

In this instance, Jesus means that some men, no matter how learned they are, will not follow him. Only those whom God would draw to him would be ready to accept him and his new message. It was very difficult for the wise and the prudent to receive a humble teacher and accept simple words of life. They would have to surrender what they had worked years to acquire.

God's truth is so simple and direct it seems too good to be believed. Only those who are simple and pure in heart are drawn to Jesus' teaching. Those who are taught by God's spirit also understand and receive the Galilean's gospel of the kingdom.[14]

JESUS' FLESH AND BLOOD

Then Jesus said unto them, Verily, verily, I say unto you, Except ye eat the flesh of the Son of Man and drink his blood, ye have no life in you. Jn. 6:53.

Among Semitic people who speak northern Aramaic, one often hears, "I have eaten my body and drunk my blood." This means the speaker has worked to the point of exhaustion. Another common

---

[14] See Isa. 54:13

101

saying is, "I have eaten the body of my dead people," meaning, "I have labored under extreme difficulties." Yet another expression, "While working, I saw my dead folk," refers to the suffering and danger to which the speaker was exposed.

Such idiomatic sayings were not common in Chaldean Aramaic, which the people of Judea spoke. These expressions can not be understood when taken literally, as those who were listening to Jesus at that time did not understand them. There was a similar problem when Nicodemus could not understand the idiomatic expression "born again."[15]

Galilean Jews used these expressions when they referred to the historic struggles of their people for the temple and sacred traditions that Jesus vigorously attacked. Jesus insisted that the struggles and achievements were in vain because these people were not spiritually and politically liberated. The Jews could secure this liberty only when they would identify themselves with him in the martyrdom that his teaching would bring. This is what he meant by "eating his flesh and drinking his blood." They would be taking on his sufferings and responsibilities to bring about not only their own salvation but that of the entire world. Besides, it was against the Torah for a Jew to drink blood.[16] They misunderstood Jesus and thought that he was literally speaking of his own flesh. They had no knowledge of the spiritual food that never perishes or the teaching of God that was revealed to their prophets.

"Eating Jesus' flesh" means to make his truth a part of one's daily life. He called on the people to work hard and suffer as he had been working and suffering. The Aramaic phrase "Eat the book" means "Make this book a part of your life" or "memorize the book." Friends often say to one another, "I will eat you," meaning "I love you."

Jesus' words were the spiritual food that the world has always needed because they contain life and light. The flesh of the lamb that

---

[15] See Jn. 3:3.
[16] See Lev. 3:17; Deut. 12:16.

was eaten in Egypt and the water that Moses supplied by striking the rock had not helped to regenerate Israel. Jesus' teaching was to displace ceremonies and doctrines. Hungry humanity was offered a new and lasting food.

QUALITY OF SPIRIT

It is the spirit that quickeneth; the flesh profiteth nothing: these words that I speak unto you, they are spirit and they are life. Jn. 6:63.

"It is the spirit that gives life; the body is of no account; the words which I have spoken to you are spirit and life."[17] Jesus' words were spirit, and the spirit is life because spirit is eternal. The body is of no account because it is a manifestation of matter which is changeable and temporal. If the earth should move toward the sun, nature and form would undergo radical change.

The body is organized material substance. Life is the divine spark of God in the body. Human value is not estimated by physical appearance such as beauty, strength or the minerals of which it is composed. Human value is judged by the quality of spirit one possesses, because it is the spirit that gives life.

This does not mean that one should not take care of the physical form, for it is the temple of the spirit. Jesus means that we should be more concerned about our spiritual life because it is more important.

Jesus used figurative terms of speech. Some of his disciples who took his saying literally were weak and disloyal. They were offended at his remarks and a great many of them left him because of these challenging and difficult sayings. Jesus knew that they misunderstood him.

Often, when he attempted to explain some of his sayings to the twelve, Jesus told them that the words he spoke were spirit and life That is the core of his teaching. Spirit is what counts.

---

[17] Jn. 6:63, Aramaic Peshitta text, Lamsa translation.

SATAN

Jesus answered them, Have not I chosen you twelve, and one of you is a devil? Jn. 6:70.

The Aramaic text reads: "Jesus said to them, Did I not chose you, the twelve, and yet one of you is Satan?"[18] The term *satana* is a Chaldean Aramaic expression and derives from the root *sta,* meaning "to slide, slip, deceive, mislead, miss the mark, cause one to go astray." Usually this word is applied to one who causes these results. The Torah and the prophets very seldom used the term "Satan." It crept into Jewish literature during the Jewish exile and post-exile.

When Jesus spoke of Judas as a Satan, he meant that Judas was insincere, deceptive and crooked. Such terms are common in Aramaic and Arabic speech. People often call one another *satana,* "you Satan." In Arabic, *shytan* means "you deceiver." In colloquial speech, an ingenious person is also called *satana.* Jesus told his disciples "to be as wise as serpents" because serpents are clever.

Jesus made this same remark when Simon Peter offended him and tried to persuade him not to speak about his death. Jesus told Peter: "Get behind me Satan; you are a stumbling block to me; for you are not thinking of the things of God, but of men."[19] Later on, Simon Peter denied Jesus and yet he did not lose the spark of truth that was in him. Peter repented and became one of Jesus' loyal disciples.

At the outset, Judas apparently was a good man. But when he saw that Jesus was not a militant and political Messiah, he attempted to dissociate himself from his master. Jesus was not the kind of leader that he and the people had expected. Judas, being disillusioned, deserted his master and betrayed him. Later, he repented but suffered from a deep and painful sorrow for his impious act. He was so remorseful, in fact, that he took his own life.

---

[18] Jn. 6:70, Aramaic Peshitta text, Lamsa translation.
[19] Mt. 16:23.

CHAPTER 7

THE TERM "JEWS"

After these things Jesus walked in Galilee: for he would not walk in Jewry, because the Jews sought to kill him. Jn. 7:1.

Racially, the twelve sons of the patriarch Jacob were known as Hebrews.[1] The Hebrew patriarchs Abraham, Isaac and Jacob were not referred to as Jews. The reason for this is that the term "Jew" derives from one of the sons of Jacob whose name was Judah.

The Hebrews never called themselves "Jews" in the days of the patriarchs, when they were in Egypt, during the conquest of Palestine under Joshua, or in the early times of the monarchy. (Usually, Near Easterners are known by their religion rather than by their race.)

Until the time of the Chaldean (Babylonian) captivity, 586 BCE, the Jews were known as Hebrews or Israelites. After the fall of Jerusalem and the captivity of the tribes of Judah and Benjamin, the southern kingdom collapsed and the political nation was destroyed. (Earlier, the northern kingdom of Israel fell to the Assyrians. The Assyrian king scattered the ten tribes throughout the Near and Middle East.)

The remnants of the tribes that survived were identified by their religion. They were referred to as "Jews" because the temple that was their national shrine and center of worship was in Judea (Judah). Then, after the restoration and rebuilding of the second temple under Ezra and Nehemiah, the term "Jews" was frequently used and gradually replaced the name of the race, Hebrew.

During the time of Jesus, there was quite a difference between Jews, Galileans and Samaritans. Galileans were members of the Jewish religion, but their ancestors were Assyrians, Chaldeans,

---

[1]There is much scholarly controversy surrounding the term "Hebrew." Is the designation ethnic or geographic? According to Jewish scholars, it weighs in favor of the ethnic nature of the term.

Persians and other mixed races that the Assyrian King Shalmaneser had settled in Galilee.[2] They adhered to their own ancient customs and traditions but, at the same time, worshiped the God of Israel.

Southern Jews had no social relations with Samaritans. They also despised the Galileans because they did not rigidly follow the traditions of the Jewish elders, such as washing of hands before meals, fasting, and the strict observance of the Sabbath. The prophet from Galilee was attacked largely on these grounds.

Jesus was generally known as a Galilean.[3] On one occasion, he was wrongly called a Samaritan.[4] Galileans were closer in their religious affiliation with the Jews than were the Samaritans. All of Jesus' disciples, with the exception of Judas of Iscariot, who was of Judea, were Galileans.

JESUS' BROTHERS CHALLENGE HIM

Then Jesus said unto them, My time is not yet come: but your time is always ready. The world cannot hate you; but me it hateth, because I testify of it, that the works thereof are evil. Go ye up unto this feast: I go not up yet unto this feast; for my time is not yet full come. Jn. 7:6-8.

The Jewish feast of tabernacles in Jerusalem was approaching, and Jesus' stepbrothers began challenging him. They told him that he needed to go to Judea so that his Judean disciples and followers could see the works that he was doing. They also wanted him to perform wonders and miracles there in order to impress the high priests and other religious authorities who opposed him. They thought that he was wasting his time preaching and teaching to the simple townsfolk in Galilee.

Jesus' brothers did not believe in him and felt ashamed of him, his teaching, actions and mission. They thought he was a strange

---

[2]See 2 Ki. 17:24.
[3]Jn. 7:41, 52.
[4]Jn. 8:48.

person with odd ideas about religion. But Jesus was not ready just yet to go to Jerusalem and attend the feast. There was considerable work to be done in Galilee; until he was finished with his work, he would postpone going to the feast.

There were other reasons for Jesus not to go the feast at that time. Rumors had spread throughout Galilee and Judea that he would be arrested. Some of the religious authorities, elders, scribes, Pharisees and Herodians were determined to put him to death. Nevertheless, not one of them dared to speak openly against him because many of the Jews in the south believed in him. These Jews were tired of the Romans, Herodians and their cohorts—the priests who had crushed them under heavy foreign burdens for their own worldly gains. Jesus would attend the feast when he knew the time was right.

JESUS' EDUCATION

Now about the midst of the feast Jesus went up into the temple, and taught. And the Jews marveled, saying, How knoweth this man letters, having never learned? Jn. 7:14-15.

Public schools, colleges and universities in the Near East were unknown until the arrival of Christian missionaries. About ninety percent of the education was the study of sacred literature. In synagogues, churches and mosques, men and boys sit around the holy book and read in turn.

A few of the boys or men who are exceptional in their perception merit more tutoring by the priests, rabbis and teachers. Some of them acquire an education by constant attendance at religious services, where they commit to memory passages of Scripture and liturgy. Some men can quote the entire book of Psalms or dozens of passages from the gospels but cannot read them.

Similarly, even today, there are some bishops and priests who can read but cannot write. The fact is that in the Near Eastern world, until the early part of the 1900s, writing was an art by itself, and the

107

labor of it was done by professional scribes who were recruited from the ranks of the poor.

Reading and writing skills were unpopular among the rich. Missionaries, in the early days, had difficulty gaining consent of wealthy parents to send their boys to school. Until the turn of the 20th century, education was of no value for business and other purposes. Banks and commercial houses as we know them today were unknown.

Undoubtedly, Jesus had acquired an oral education, but he also knew how to read his native tongue of Aramaic and also Hebrew. This does not imply that he was educated for any priesthood. The Jews were surprised by his teaching because they could not understand how someone with a limited education had such a grasp of holy Scripture.

Jesus had an inner understanding of sacred literature because he understood it from a spiritual point of view. He did not take what he read and heard about Scripture literally. His mind was free from the traditions of the elders and other dogmatic approaches because he had not studied under the strict tutelage of "letter of the law" priests and religious educators.

JESUS' TEACHING QUESTIONED

Jesus answered them, and said, My doctrine is not mine, but his that sent me. If any man will do his will, he shall know of the doctrine whether it be of God, or whether I speak of myself. He that speaketh of himself seeketh his own glory: but he that seeketh his glory that sent him, the same is true, and no unrighteousness is in him. Did not Moses give you the law, and yet none of you keepeth the law? Why go ye about to kill me? Jn. 7:16-19.

Jesus' doctrine was questioned by the scribes, elders and teachers of the Torah. When they began questioning him about his teaching, his answer was that what he taught was not his own, nor was it alien to the teaching of the Torah or prophets. He taught from

108

God, from the books of the holy prophets that were read in the temple and synagogues. There was nothing foreign that these teachers could find to use against him.

In reality, many of the scribes and elders had supplanted the word of God with their own teachings. That was the reason they could not understand what Jesus taught. They all marveled at the miracle that he performed; yet they still wanted to kill him because he healed a man on the Sabbath.

Jesus' rebuttal to these teachers was that even the ritual of circumcision was permitted on the Sabbath. He knew that the scribes and elders were not consistent in their teaching or judgment, for if the Sabbath cannot be broken by circumcision, how then could it be broken by an act of mercy and compassion? (See verses 21-24.) And if God had not sent him, why was he given so much power that he could heal the sick and raise the dead?

These teachers knew well that Jesus was endowed with power from God and that he gave glory and honor to God who did the good works through him. But Jesus had no one to testify concerning him; therefore, these teachers would not accept his testimony.

SOME JEWS KNEW JESUS

Howbeit we know this man whence he is: but when Christ cometh, no man knoweth whence he is. Jn. 7:27.

Some of the Jews who were present knew Jesus and that he was the son of Joseph and Mary. They had seen him in the streets, marketplaces and in the fields. They also had heard him teach in the synagogue. To them he was just another citizen of Nazareth. They did not know him as the Messiah/Christ.

Jewish people were taught that when the Messiah comes, no one would know from where he came or whose son he would be. Jesus, Joseph and Mary were well known to the people of Nazareth and other neighboring towns in Galilee. This was one reason it was extremely difficult for some of these Jews to accept him as the

109

promised one. How could this meek and lowly man be the coming King of Kings? Should not the Messiah be a man of great power and strength? Even today, most people throughout the world look for mighty and wealthy leaders. This saying held true for Jesus: "No prophet is without honor except in his own town and among his own people."

TIME TOO SHORT

Then Jesus said unto them, Yet a little while am I with you, and then I go unto him that sent me. Ye shall seek me, and shall not find me: and where I am, thither ye cannot come. Then said the Jews among themselves, Whither will he go, that we shall not find him? Will he go unto the dispersed among the Gentiles, and teach the Gentiles? Jn 7:33-35.

Jesus spoke of his approaching death, which he knew was not far off. When he was crucified and departed this world, many would regret his demise. They would have missed their opportunity to hear his words of life and to sit at the feet of a teacher who came from a spiritual understanding of religion, the world and God.

Nonetheless, this saying was aimed at the disbelieving Pharisees who were never to see Jesus or find him again. They did not understand that Jesus was to leave this life. After the resurrection, Jesus appeared only to his disciples and followers; when they saw him again they rejoiced. But those who did not believe in him did not see him.

These unbelievers could not see where Jesus was going. They could not go to the cross for the sake of God's truth. But his disciples and followers were to see him again and were ready to die the same kind of death for the sake of his teaching.

These doubting Jewish teachers thought Jesus was going to the lost tribes from the house of Israel, who were now dispersed among the Gentiles. Earlier, Jesus had sent out seventy of his disciples with instructions to go to no one but the lost sheep of Israel. Most of the descendants of the ten tribes were now in Assyria, Iran, Afghanistan and other adjacent lands. These tribes had been taken captive by the Assyrian kings in 722 BCE.[5]

THIRSTY FOR TRUTH

In the last day, that great day of the feast, Jesus stood and cried, saying, If any man thirst, let him come unto me, and drink. Jn. 7:37.

"Let him come unto me and drink" is an Aramaic idiom meaning, "Let him come to me and learn from me." Semites often say "I ate the book" denoting "I committed the book to memory." They also say, "I drank knowledge like water." When wishing to show affection to a child, they say, "I eat you." Expressions such as these are very common in the Bible.

People were thirsty for the knowledge of God more than for water.[6] Although water was scarce in Palestine, people could obtain sufficient amounts for drinking from wells and brooks; however, the knowledge of God was even more precious.

The Israelites in the past had gone astray from the God of their forefathers and had transgressed the laws and ordinances. But now the doctrines of the elders had replaced the precious truth taught by the prophets. Jesus quenched the thirst of anyone who desired the knowledge of God.

WATER FLOWING FROM THE BELLY

He that believeth on me, as the scripture hath said, out of his belly shall flow rivers of living water. Jn. 7:38.

Water is abundant in Europe and America, but it used to be extremely scarce in the Holy Land. In ancient times, during the arid

---

[5]See 2 Ki. chapters 17-18; Jn. 8:21.
[6]See Isa. 55:1.

summer months, most of the brooks dried up and the water supply diminished; the land became parched with heat and looked like a desert. Many villages depended on wells for their water, but during droughts they, too, dried up and people had to carry water from long distances. Women walked miles carrying scanty supplies of water in earthen vessels on their heads and backs. This is the reason Near Easterners coveted water and why the Bible refers to it so often.

At times, water had to be rationed in small quantities in many areas of the Near East. People often went to bed thirsty and dreamt of drinking water from springs. To say that "water will flow from one's belly" means "one will never thirst again." Semites often say, "I am so thirsty, I can drink a river dry" or "My thirst is so quenched that I feel as if a river of water is flowing within me."

Jesus used the term "living water" symbolically to refer to his teaching—truth that sets people free from want and difficulties of life. This truth would be revealed so clearly that people would no longer seek the wisdom of the Pharisees, scribes and priests whose knowledge was limited. These teachers often became just like the dried out wells and springs during the summer months. The gospel of the kingdom would completely satisfy the soul thirsting for the knowledge of God. Jesus' new teaching was to make life easier and happier, inspiring visions of a more humane and loving human society and of hope for the life hereafter.

CHAPTER 8

AN ADULTERESS FORGIVEN

And the scribes and Pharisees brought unto him a woman taken in adultery; and when they had set her in the midst, They say unto him, Master, this woman was taken in adultery, in the very act. Now Moses in the law commanded us, that such should be stone; But what sayest thou? This they said, tempting him, that they might have to accuse him. But Jesus stooped down, and with his finger wrote on the ground, as though he heard them not. Jn 8:3-6.

Making marks on the ground is a common Near Eastern habit. Great thinkers, judges and wise men, while listening to debates and attempting to reach a decision, will bend down and scratch the floor with their forefinger, making geometric lines and crossing them in the form of a chess board but leaving no imprint. They would do this even if they were sitting on a rug or a rock. During council meetings and conferences, some men may finger a string of amber beads that they hold in their hands or other objects near them; or they may slowly shred a small piece of wood with their nails or with a knife. To a stranger, this might seem that men were concentrating on something else and not paying attention. In reality, they are deeply absorbed in careful thought

While Jesus was teaching in the outer courts of the temple, the scribes and Pharisees wanted to test him. So, they brought to him a woman who was caught in the act of adultery. They told him that, according to the law of Moses, women of this kind should be stoned. They were testing him to see how he would respond to this situation. They asked him, "What do you say about this?" While they were accusing the frightened woman of her adulterous act, quoting the law and waiting for an answer, Jesus bent down and began drawing on the ground with his finger. This entire situation was embarrassing. He was thinking about an answer and listening to the accusations of these men. He did not write anything on the ground, nor could these

113

accusers have read it if he had. Most Near Easterners at that time were illiterate. It would also be extremely difficult to write something on the hard, rough floor.

Jesus knew these men were crafty and he could read their judgmental thoughts and see through their evil intentions to trap him. If he said that the woman should be stoned to death, they would have taken her and stoned her. Then they would have had the legal excuse to blame him for her death. Jesus was not a temple authority vested with any power to condemn people. If he said she should go free, then he was not complying with the laws of Moses. And, again, they would be able to condemn him for breaking the law.

Jesus turned the situation around. He challenged them to cast the first stone if they were without sin. They knew by his voice inflection and demeanor exactly what he meant. They also knew that he was a prophet and could expose the men who sinned with her and, according to the law, suffer the same punishment. In addition to this, the fearful woman who stood in their midst could easily accuse them all of having committed adultery with her. Immediately, they fled. Now the woman was left standing alone with Jesus. He told her to go and not to do it again. Jesus came not to condemn but to forgive and restore people.

THE LIGHT OF THE WORLD

Then spake Jesus again unto them, saying, I am the light of the world: he that followeth me shall not walk in darkness but shall have the light of life. Jn. 8:12.

Light is the most precious element in the world. Some people would give everything they have for the light of their eyes. Light is also symbolic of God, who is the light and life of the world.

According to chapter one of Genesis, the first thing God said was "Let there be light." Metaphorically, this means "let there be enlightenment, intelligence and understanding." Light travels faster than anything. It is also symbolic of the Holy Spirit. And like light,

God's spirit—the divine presence—manifests everywhere in the universe. Wherever there is light, there is God. Light is the very source of human existence. Without light we would have no food, clothing and other necessities of life that are supported by the sun.

Jesus' teaching is a great luminescence, shining in a dark and periodically violent world. Anyone who practices his teaching does not walk in darkness (ignorance) but in light—that is, spiritual intelligence and understanding. His teaching dispels the shadow (fear) of death and brightens the hearts and minds of the human family.

MISGUIDED JUDGMENT

Ye judge after the flesh: I judge no man. Jn. 8:15.

The Pharisees and scribes judged people according to their understanding and interpretation of the Law and the Prophets. They relied on the traditions of men and the doctrine of the elders. They concluded, by their interpretation of Scripture, that a man's testimony of himself was worthless. He must be backed and recommended by other teachers of the law.

The expression "Ye judge after the flesh" refers to judgment based on materialism, worldliness and misunderstood religious teaching. The use of the term "flesh" is meant to be contrasted with "spirit." Flesh follows the letter of the law and not the spirit of the law. Flesh is weak but the spirit is life, light, grace and truth. Paul tells us: " For the material [minded] man rejects spiritual things; they are foolishness to him; neither can he know them because they are spiritually discerned. But the spiritual man discerns everything, and yet no man can discern him."[1] This was the case with Jesus; he judged matters spiritually, but no one could discern him.

"I judge no man" means "I do not criticize nor condemn any

---

[1] 1 Cor. 2:14-15, Aramaic Peshitta text, Lamsa translation.

one." Jesus was magnanimous in forgiving people and helping those who had lost their way. He never asked people to show their credentials to prove their integrity. He accepted all people as they were. His judgment was of the spirit and not by a rigid, inflexible understanding of religious law. According to the letter of the law, all transgressors are condemned. But the judgment of the spirit is tempered with compassion and the grace of God.

TRUE JUDGMENT

And yet if I judge, my judgment is true: for I am not alone, but I and the Father that sent me. It is also written in your law, that the testimony of two men is true. Jn. 8:16-17.

The Mosaic law required two witnesses in order to convict a man of a crime or of blasphemy against God. The judgment of two or three judges is more acceptable than that of a sole jurist. When Jesus said "I am not alone," he meant that "I do not pass judgment all alone, but God, who is my Father, also sits in judgment with me." Jesus did nothing by or of himself. He understood the true nature of God and consulted with his Father. Therefore, his judgment was according to God's compassionate and merciful judgment. Jesus was always in agreement and one with his father.[2]

The Scribes and Pharisees were not impressed by Jesus' discourse because he had no witnesses other than himself. In their eyes, his own testimony was not valid. Anyone could bear witness about himself and his works. However, everything Jesus did was according to the law, because Jesus' witness was his Father. Jesus was in harmony with God and was doing God's works. He was not alone and his deeds were sufficient proof that God was with him. No evil or ungodly individual could heal the sick and raise the dead

But the Pharisees and scribes did not know Jesus' God. Their idea of God was so different from the God of love that Jesus taught

---

[2]See Jn. 8:26.

and revealed. It is true that these teachers of the law revered the name of God and feared their deity, but they had no experience of that divine presence. These teachers of religion were blind to truth. Their eyes could not see the light of God that Jesus revealed through his good works. They had forgotten that God is a loving Father—the Beloved.

SHEOL AND SUICIDE

Then said the Jews, Will he kill himself? Because he saith, Whither I go, ye cannot come. Jn. 8:22.

An ancient belief held by many was that an individual who commits suicide is immediately cut off from this world and from the world hereafter. According to the belief, the suicidal soul goes to *sheol* or *hades*, a place of silence outside the jurisdiction of God, and remains there forever. The Jews believed that God had no power over *sheol*. This notion is still upheld in most Near Eastern countries; therefore, Near Easterners are less prone to commit suicide.

Jesus told the Jews that he was going to a place where they could not come. They thought that this place might be *sheol* because the only way to get there was by taking one's own life. In their estimation, Jesus was a heretic and deserved to go to *sheol,* especially if he would kill himself.

ETERNAL REGRET

I said therefore unto you, that ye shall die in your sins: for if ye believe not that I am he, ye shall die in your sins. Jn. 8:24.

"Ye shall die in your sins" means "You will die without knowing the truth and therefore will continue in your error." The term "sins" in this instance refers to "erroneous thinking and behavior." Many of the Pharisees and religious leaders would regret having rejected the

117

Messiah. Such strong remarks are made to people who are deliberately stubborn and difficult to change. "Unless you believe that I am he you will die in your sins." Jesus refers to himself as the anointed one of God, hence the term "Messiah."

Jesus had been with them for some time. He had preached truth, healed the sick, wrought miracles and wonders before their eyes, but they still rejected him as an ordained prophet and man of God. They continued to uphold the idea of a political messiah after the order of the Davidic kingdom. This was a great error in the Jewish teaching of the times and in their interpretation of the promised Messiah/Christ and his kingdom. The Messiah was to be a light to the Gentiles as well as to the Jews. God's light was to be shared with the entire world.

The ones who had rejected Jesus as the bearer of God's truth and light would die in their mistaken notions and errors. They would not know that God was a loving Father who always helps and guides people. They would die not knowing that forgiveness, loving kindness and meekness are the answers to humanity's sins and problems. After death, there would be no opportunity to rectify or change their mistakes.

JESUS IS TRUE

I have many things to say and to judge of you: but he that sent me is true; and I speak to the world those things which I have heard of him.
Jn. 8:26.

Generally, messengers are judged by the character of those who send them. If the sender is a man of good reputation, then his messenger is highly respected and his words do not come under any suspicion. A Near Eastern messenger represents his lord, and his lord instructs him to speak and act according to his wishes and on his behalf.

The Aramaic word *sharira* means "true" and "sincere." The argument that Jesus presents is proving that he is sincere like his

118

Father. This group of Jews believed that God was true, but they doubted that Jesus was his messenger. In his discourses, Jesus always attempted to impress his audience that he was sent by God and that he and God were of one accord. Semites often say, "What I am saying is true, just as God is true."

JESUS NEVER ALONE

Then said Jesus unto them, When ye have lifted up the Son of man, then shall ye know that I am he, and that I do nothing of myself: but as my Father hath taught me, I speak these things. And he that sent me is with me: the Father hath not left me alone: for I do always those things that please him. As he spake these words, many believed on him. Then said Jesus to those Jews which believed on him, If ye continue in my word then are ye my disciples indeed. Jn. 8:28-31.

Once Jesus was raised on the cross, then the people would realize that he was the promised Messiah/Christ, the man whom the prophet Isaiah had predicted—the suffering servant.[3] For everything that Isaiah had said in his prophecy would be fulfilled and the Messiah would rise from the grave and rule over a universal kingdom forever. The reason for this is that the Father who had sent him would not leave him alone, but would always be with him.

If the people would only believe in his words, then they would know the truth and become free of all false ideas, doubts, fears and worldly cares. Truth is spiritual food. It is the bread of life that causes one to transcend the physical and material world. These blind guides, teachers of the law, and even some of his own disciples, thought of freedom only from taxes, slavery and the Romans. But Jesus spoke of a greater freedom, one from the sin and error that create all human difficulties.

Being a descendant of Abraham would not free them from sin and foreign yoke. Abraham was a pious man. If these teachers of

---

[3]See Isa. 53.

religion who boast of their racial ancestry were true children of Abraham—that is, descendants of the spirit of Abraham and his faith—they would hear the voice of the Messiah and do the pious works of Abraham. Yes, they were heirs of Abraham by ancestry. But, they had forsaken the true teaching of their fathers, following their own religious imaginations and expecting the restoration of a national kingdom ruled by a political, warrior Messiah/King.

YOU SHALL KNOW THE TRUTH

And ye shall know the truth, and the truth shall make you free.
Jn. 8:32.

Shrara is the Aramaic word for "truth." It derives from *sharar*, "to be firm, sincere, truthful." People who are doubtful of their faith are easily shaken and may lose faith. Those who understand truth have a strong grasp on faith and cannot be shaken or weakened. Then faith becomes firmer and stronger because they understand that what they know is true.

During this time, sacred writings were only available to the high priests and doctors of the law. The general Jewish public did not know what their Scripture contained. All that they heard in the synagogue were the traditions of the elders who interpreted Scripture in the manner that suited them.

Sacred writings were soon to become common. The new movement was to expound authentic teaching and interpretation and reveal the inner truth that Scripture contained. Sacred scrolls that were locked in vaults were soon to be published and their words heard throughout the world. People would be free from misleading interpretations, false doctrines and bondage. They would soon be reading Scripture and understanding its inner meaning under the guidance of the Holy Spirit. Jesus' gospel of truth would set people free from false images of God. They would realize that God is the beloved Father of all nations, who brings peace, harmony and justice for all.

SERVANTS ARE NOT HEIRS

And the servant abideth not in the house for ever; but the Son abideth ever. If the Son therefore shall make you free, ye shall be free indeed. Jn. 8:35-36.

Stewards and servants are not hired permanently. Some of them change positions quite often. A servant always knows that he is a hired person and that his work may be temporary. He could be dismissed by his lord at any time. But a son is the heir, or one of the heirs, and stays at the home of his father forever.

The Pharisees and scribes were servants of God, but Jesus was the son and the heir to whom God had entrusted everything. Jesus spoke of freedom from ignorance, not political freedom. The Jews were subjected to foreign nations simply because they had departed from God's way and had worshiped strange gods.

The covenant between God and King David was conditional. David's descendants would sit on his throne provided they followed God's way and laws. But when they failed to remain loyal to the covenant that God had made with David, other nations would conquer them and take them into captivity. Both Israel and Judah, the southern and northern kingdoms, suffered the same fate and lost their freedom, becoming vassals and paying tribute, at different times to Assyria, to Egypt and to Syria.

When they knew the truth, became aware of their calling and of the divine promises, and repented from their evil doings, they would regain their freedom. But before the yoke of the oppressor would be removed, they must first turn back to God and move away from their erroneous ways.

THE DEVIL IS A LIAR

Ye are of your father the devil, and the lusts of your father ye will do. He was a murderer from the beginning, and abode not in the truth, because there is no truth in him. When he speaketh a lie, he speaketh of his own: for

121

he is a liar, and the father of it. Jn. 8:44.

The Peshitta text uses the Aramaic term *akelqarsa*. It means an "accuser, adversary, tempter, slanderer, one who tests or tries something out." It is he who we call "the devil." The root meaning is "to gnaw, ridicule." Figuratively, it was *akelqarsa*, the "adversary," who tempted Jesus—that is, tried him out, tested him, when he was in the wilderness. An adversary can be anything that is adverse to truth. Jesus was tempted as a human being; God cannot be tempted with evil, nor does God tempt anyone.[4] Jesus, in the desert, was engaged in an internal struggle, a battle within his own soul. The conflict is externalized as the adversary and three major temptations.[5]

The Pharisees and scribes who debated with Jesus claimed that they were the descendants of Abraham, the father of believers. But Jesus challenged their claim and told them that their father was *akelqarsa*, the "accuser." He called them children of the devil because they did not believe in him, and like the adversary, they accused him of blasphemy and wanted to trap him. Jesus told them if Abraham had been their spiritual father, they would have recognized and accepted his teaching, because he taught that which God had revealed to the holy prophets. Now the simple and true religion of Abraham and the prophets was almost forgotten. Man-made religious notions and doctrines and misleading teachings had replaced it.

The adversary is a liar and the father of lies. From the very beginning of creation, the devil—error—has caused men to miss the mark and turn from the way of God, which is truth, peace and harmony. Any negative and destructive thought that torments the human mind is the adversary. Any idea that deflects an individual from the true course of his/her life is truly an enemy. We know that God is not the author of evil or opposed to truth, for God is light and

---

[4] See James 1:13-14.

[5] See Errico and Lamsa, *Aramaic Light on the Gospel of Matthew*, Chapter 4, pp. 42-50.

truth.

There is no truth in error because error does not exist except in the minds of people who have revolted against truth and think that their error is truth. Nowhere in Scripture are we told that God created a devil and his kingdom of evil. Scripture testifies that everything that God created was good; goodness is an attribute of God. The devil is man's own creation, the revolter against truth, the opposing influence to the way of God. There is nothing in the nature of God that is capable of creating evil.

According to the fourth chapter of Genesis, Cain, the son of Adam and Eve, became the first murderer. He was the first child of God to revolt against his creator and, because of jealousy, murdered his only brother. And since Cain committed this crime, humankind has been possessed with a spirit that is contrary to the spirit of God.

THE SAMARITANS

Then answered the Jews, and said unto him, Say we not well that thou art a Samaritan, and hast a devil? Jn. 8:48.

The Samaritans were a mixed population composed of people that the King of Assyria had settled in the northern kingdom of Israel, replacing the ten tribes of Israel in 722 BCE. They were of the same stock as the people of Galilee, except that the Samaritans adhered more closely to the customs which their ancestors brought from Assyria. They adopted the Jewish faith in part but carried on their own traditions and worship as well.[6]

The people whom the Assyrian King brought from countries beyond the Euphrates river were of diverse religions. It is likely that the Assyrian authorities settled them in groups according to their faiths. During the time of Jesus, the Jews despised the Samaritans more than the Galileans. Although the Samaritans had accepted the

---

[6]See 2 Ki. 17:29.

five books of Moses, Genesis to Deuteronomy, the Jews thought of them as pagans. Samaritans resembled the Assyrians more than any other people in Palestine. They were tall, strong warriors like the Assyrians. Descendants of the Samaritans today, who are slowly vanishing, still bear resemblance to the Assyrians.

These people had accepted the Torah because this was the only sacred literature, oral or written, before the division of the state of Israel into two separate kingdoms, northern and southern. They probably rejected other books of the Hebrew Bible for political reasons. For example, the prophetic books contain writings that condemned the Assyrian Empire; and the books of Kings and Chronicles are largely against the northern kingdom of Israel and the kings of Samaria. The Samaritans thought it unwise to use books that were against their own people.

They had settled in Samaria, the capital of the northern kingdom, and they followed the customs and traditions of the land as established by Jeroboam and the kings of Israel. They worshiped at the sacred shrines on Mt. Gerizim and other high places that had been abandoned by the ten tribes. This custom of reviving old worship at forsaken sites still continues in many areas of the Near East. For instance, Moslems have converted Greek and Semitic Christian churches into mosques and carry on old traditions.

In this verse, Jesus was called a Samaritan in scorn because Nazareth was in the province of Samaria and a part of the northern kingdom. Moreover, the Samaritans were the traditional enemies of the Jews because their ancestors had come from Assyria and were occupying Israel's lands.

When Nehemiah and other elders of Judah were building the walls of Jerusalem and restoring the temple, the Galileans and the Samaritans came down to Jerusalem and offered assistance in the rebuilding. They said that since their forefathers were brought from Assyria into Galilee, they had been worshiping Yahweh, the God of the land. They also had been offering animal sacrifices to Yahweh.

The leadership at the time rejected their help on the grounds that the Galileans and Samaritans, although they worshiped the God of the

Jews, were descendants of the early Assyrian invaders.[7] They repudiated their claims to being a part of the Jewish faith. Their refusal widened the breach and increased the enmity between the people of the north and the south. Thus, the Galileans and the Jews despised each other bitterly. This hatred continued to the time of Jesus.

Usually, the Jews refused to eat or mix with Galileans. On the other hand, Galileans had no use for the ceremonial traditions and the teachings of the elders, which had become substitutes for true worship. This feeling was shared by Jesus and his disciples who were Galileans.[8]

The Pharisees and scribes, as well as the rest of the groups opposing Jesus' teaching, were enraged because he told them that Abraham was not their father and that the devil was their father. Thus, they called Jesus a "Samaritan" and said that he had a "devil." In other words, they meant that he was not a true Jew and he was "crazy." In Aramaic, the term "devil" also refers to someone who is psychotic and does not know what he is talking about.

Jesus denied that he was crazy; he did not teach or say anything contrary to God's truth, nor was he seeking his own glory. God had honored him by giving him power to heal the physically and mentally ill. This power was the proof that God was with him. His opponents were troublemakers; hence, they had no power to heal the sick and perform miracles. If they were doing God's works, they would also receive Jesus as a messenger of God and rejoice in his teaching.

ETERNAL LIFE

Verily, verily, I say unto you, If a man keep my saying, he shall never see death. Then said the Jews unto him. Now we know that thou hast a devil. Abraham is dead, and the prophets; and thou sayest, If a man keep my saying, he shall never taste of death. Jn. 8:51-52.

---

[7]See Ezra 4:1-3.
[8]Mt. 10:5; Lk. 10:33; Jn. 4:9.

According to the teaching of the elders, death was the end. Abraham, Jacob and the prophets had died and were in their graves. It was the people's belief in death that made it a finality.

On one occasion, Jesus had told them that God was the God of the living and not of the dead. "But concerning the resurrection of the dead, have you not read what was told you by God, saying I am the God of Abraham, the God of Isaac, the God of Jacob? And yet, God is not the God of the dead, but of the living."[9]

All Hebrew prophets and men of God were spiritually alive, but the people did not realize this truth. According to Jesus' understanding, people of good works were to live on through their good deeds forever. They would be transformed from one life to another.

Jesus, at another time, had told his disciples that some of them would never taste death. Their fame and teaching would be told from one generation to the next. They would become immortal. Today, the names of the prophets and apostles are read in more than eleven hundred languages.

Again, the Aramaic term "devil" refers to a "wild man, a crazy or insane person, a mentally disturbed individual." The Jews acquired this term when they were in exile in Chaldea (Babylon). The Aramaic text reads: " The Jews said to him, Now we are sure that you are insane. . ."

In the Near East, all forms of insanity and mental disturbances are attributed to devils, demons, and jinn. Medical terms, as we know them today, were unknown and in many areas of the Near East these terms are still not known. Psychological terms for mental and emotional difficulties and illnesses were alien to the minds of the people.

Jesus was called a crazy or insane person because those who heard him were shocked by his promise of not tasting death. It sounded ridiculous to them. How could they believe that this man from Nazareth was greater than Abraham and the prophets who were dead.

---

[9]Mt. 22:31-32, Aramaic Peshitta text, Lamsa translation.

126

THE AGELESS CHRIST

Then said the Jews unto him, Thou art not yet fifty years old, and hast thou seen Abraham? Jesus said unto them, Verily, verily, I say unto you, Before Abraham was, I am. Jn. 8:57-58.

When a Near Easterner reaches the age of fifty, he is considered an old man and will now sit in the Council of the Elders. His age is supposed to give him wisdom, and people seek his counsel because they regard him as an authority on what has happened in the past. He will tell them what he saw and heard when he was a young man. On the other hand, a young man, however learned he may be, is not consulted about social or religious matters. The elders are the only authorities on such questions.

"You are not yet fifty" is a Semitic saying that means "you are a young man." Any man between the ages of thirty and thirty-five is considered a young man. No birth records were kept and the age of people had to be guessed.

When Jesus said that he existed before Abraham ever existed, the Jews who debated with him became so angry that they wanted to kill him. They did not understand what he was saying and they took it at face value—that is, literally. They thought Jesus was telling them that he was older than Abraham, who had existed about two thousand years before their time.

What Jesus meant was that the Messiah or the Christ in him, which was the Word become flesh (human), was the promise that God had made to Abraham. The promise was that through Abraham's seed—that is, his descendants or teaching—all nations of the earth were to be blessed.

God's promise was also made to Eve many centuries before Abraham. Her seed, Christ, would crush the head of the serpent.[10] This meant that in due time, Christ—the truth—would destroy the forces of evil and death that bring the downfall of humankind.

---

[10]Gen. 3:15..

127

The Christ or truth always existed from the very beginning. Christ was preordained before the world was created. Christ is God's truth destined to correct the weaknesses in human nature, providing salvation for the entire world.

CHAPTER 9

A BLIND MAN HEALED

And his disciples asked him, saying, Master, who did sin, this man, or his parents, that he was born blind? Jesus answered, Neither hath this man sinned, nor his parents: but that the works of God should be made manifest in him. Jn. 9:2-3

Part 1—BLIND FROM BIRTH. Institutions for the blind are still unknown in most of the ancient biblical lands. Destitute blind men support themselves by working or begging. A few of them are taught to weave, grind wheat or do other manual labor, but most of them prefer begging rather than working. In the Near East, begging is a professional occupation.

Near Easterners, as with most people everywhere, would give to a blind or lame person rather than to a professional beggar who is physically fit. Some men, although not in need, successfully beg by pretending to be blind. This deception works against those who actually are blind.

Often these pretenders deceive men and women who are passing through the market places. People then become disinclined to give, not knowing if the person truly is disabled. Some beggars are totally blind, others only partially so, and still others pretend they are. It is difficult to believe an individual is blind when the person is seen gambling, quarreling, or if wrong change is given to him, he begins shouting curses and demanding proper change.

Jesus healed this man who was actually born blind. But the Pharisees did not believe in his healing because religious men are usually an easy mark for pretenders. On the way to the temple one often sees men sitting on corners, weeping and quoting scripture while asking for alms. We can easily understand why the Pharisees were reluctant to believe in this man's healing. This is the reason they went to his parents to see if the man was truly born blind. Although the parents confirmed their son's story, these Pharisees still could not believe in Jesus' healing power.

Part 2—WHO SINNED? In those days, blindness and deformities were blamed on the individuals who were handicapped or on their parents. People believed that good and evil attributes of the parents were inherent in their posterity. In those lands children were compelled to pay the debts of their parents. Hence, the meaning of the scripture that says: "The fathers have eaten sour grapes, and the children's teeth are set on edge."[1] Often, children were put to death for the sins of their parents.

The prophet Jeremiah had predicted that the day would come when the above saying would no longer hold true. The truth would be realized that every person would be responsible for his own iniquity. Thus, those parents who eat sour grapes would set their own teeth on edge and not those of their children.[2] A just and new law would supplant the old condemning law.

The prophet Ezekiel also tells us: "Son of man, why do you use this proverb in the land of Israel, saying, The parents have eaten sour grapes, and the children's teeth are set on edge? As I live, says the Lord God, this proverb shall never be used again in Israel. Because all souls are mine, the soul of the father, so also the soul of the son is mine; the soul that sins, it shall die."[3]

Near Easterners believed children can be stricken by placing curses on the parents.[4] They also thought that parents who break certain religious laws would bring illness on their children and that even babies could commit sin while in the womb.[5] Jesus believed in none of these notions. Jesus understood that neither the blind man nor his parents are to be blamed for the blindness. Sickness, blindness and other illness manifest because of many circumstances. Wars,

---

[1]Jer. 31:29, Aramaic Peshitta text, Lamsa translation.

[2]See Jer. 31:29-30.

[3]Ezk. 18:2-4, Aramaic Peshitta text, Lamsa translation.

[4]See Gen. 9:24-25.

[5]For the belief that babies can sin while in the womb and be born sick, see H.L. Strack and P. Billerback, Kommentar zum Neuen Testament aus Talmud and Midrach (5 vols., Beck, 1922-25), vol. 2, pgs. 528-29.

famines, malnutrition, drugs and many other factors create disease. Jesus saw this as an opportunity to reveal God's glory and power over sickness and the misunderstanding of illness.

Often there is a misunderstanding when reading the King James Version. The second part of the third verse and the first sentence of the fourth verse should go together to read as follows: "Neither did he sin nor his parents. But that the works of God might be seen in him, I must do the works of him who sent me while it is day." The man was not created blind so that Jesus might heal him. There were many ways that Jesus could reveal his miraculous power. The meeting of the blind man was incidental and providential, just as when Jesus met the son of the widow and raised him. Jesus healed the blind man so that God's works might be seen in him, and that he might carry out his mission of compassion as he had opportunity.

The story reveals that the real blind men were those religious authorities who were opposing Jesus. Although the blind man's parents verified the fact that their son was born blind, they had refused to see God's glory. They no longer had spiritual vision. These authorities were angry because people were flocking to Jesus and believing in him. They wanted the people to hear them and the teaching of the elders which they upheld..

Part 3—EXPECTORATE. Verses 6 and 7(a) read: "When he had thus spoken, he spat on the ground, and made clay of the spittle, and he anointed the eyes of the blind man with the clay, And said unto him, Go, wash in the pool of Siloam. . ." (K. J. V.) Spitting was often a way of repudiating disease and people's belief in sickness. Jesus could heal just by saying a word. He used clay so that the blind man would have to go and wash his eyes. The healing had already happened for the man.

ENLIGHTENMENT

I must work the works of him that sent me, while it is day: the night cometh, when no man can work. As long as I am in the world, I am the light

131

of the world. Jn. 9:4-5.

Darkness is symbolic of ignorance and superstition; light, of enlightenment. Jesus was light in the world because he spoke and revealed truth that brought enlightenment. As long as he was with his followers, they could see their way and do the work. But when he was gone, no one would be able to work because they would not have the light—that is, the depth of understanding about God that he had. So his disciples and followers were to work hard while he was with them, guiding and instructing them.[6]

In the Near East, when electricity and kerosene were unknown, men and women worked by the light of an oil lamp after six o'clock in the evening. When there was a shortage of oil they could not work. Man-made light is temporary and limited, but God's light is abundant and inexhaustible. The light of the Christ continues centuries after Jesus' death and resurrection.

WORSHIPING JESUS

He answered and said, Who is he, Lord, that I might believe on him? And Jesus said unto him, Thou hast both seen him, and it is he that talketh with thee. And he said, Lord, I believe. And he worshiped him. Jn. 9:36-38.

The Aramaic word *sagad*, "worship," also means "to bend, to kneel down." Usually when Semites greet each other, they bow their heads or bend down. When people greet a holy man, they kneel before him. "He worshiped him" does not imply that the man worshiped Jesus as one would worship God. That would be regarded as a sacrilegious act. In the eyes of the Jews it would be considered a breach of the first commandment and the man who showed respect to Jesus would have been stoned to death. The healed man knelt before the prophet from Galilee as a token of homage and gratitude.

This act also was a sign of self-surrender and loyalty. The man

---

[6]See Jn. 12:35.

132

who had been born blind worshiped Jesus in acknowledgment of his divine power and in appreciation of his compassion on him in opening his eyes. He had no knowledge of who Jesus was, nor was he interested in his teaching. But the man was convinced by the miracle that Jesus performed and respected him as a holy man and as one empowered by God.

SPIRITUAL BLINDNESS

And Jesus said, For judgment I am come into this world, that they which see not might see; and that they which see might be made blind. Jn. 9:39.

The man who had been born blind and then healed by Jesus could not read a word of the law and the prophets. Nevertheless, he believed in Jesus and venerated him. But the highly educated priests, Pharisees and scribes, who could read the law and interpret Scripture, refused to believe. Pride and hatred had blinded their eyes. They could not see truth.

It is common in the Near East to call one who makes mistakes blind. The reference here is to the Pharisees, scribes and priests. They were the learned men and guardians of religion and law. But as far as spiritual understanding was concerned, they were blind. They took everything literally and were blinded by traditions that had supplanted Scripture. These teachings had blurred their vision, and their thoughts could not go deeper than their own traditions.

The illiterate whom the learned had considered ignorant and blind could more readily see because they were not bound by traditions or false pride. Their eyes were to be opened by the new teaching that explained Scripture for the first time. The illiterate were blind through ignorance which was not their fault.

Many of the religious authorities were spiritually blind. Their sin (error) was great because they could see and read, but they were not willing to understand and accept the true, inner meaning of Scripture. Therefore, they were accountable for their own blindness.

133

CHAPTER 10

THE TRUE SHEPHERD

Verily, verily, I say unto you, He that entereth not by the door into the sheepfold, but climbeth up, some other way, the same is a thief and a robber. But he that entereth in by the door is the shepherd of the sheep. To him the porter openeth; and the sheep hear his voice: and he calleth his own sheep by name, and leadeth them out. And when he putteth forth his own sheep, he goeth before them, and the sheep follow him: for they know his voice. And a stranger will they not follow, but will flee from him: for they know not the voice of strangers. Jn. 10:1-5.

Part 1—THE SHEEPFOLD. Apparently, Jesus had spent his early life tending sheep, farming and doing other manual work that young people do in biblical lands before they reach adulthood. He knew a great deal about tending sheep.

Sheep are constantly guarded from thieves, robbers and predators. Sheep are very sensitive. They are afraid when strangers are around and feel disturbed by their presence, especially when they enter the sheepfold by climbing the wall or fence. Sheep know that the strangers are not their owners, because owners and shepherds always enter by the familiar and proper entrance.

In Scripture, the kings of Israel and Judah are called shepherds. God also is called the "Shepherd of Israel who never sleeps nor slumbers." God, like a skilled and good shepherd, constantly watches over his people.

Part 2—HIS OWN SHEEP. Every shepherd knows his own sheep and calls them by their names. A good shepherd also knows his neighbor's sheep. People name their sheep exactly the way those in the Western world name their domesticated animals. Sheep also bear the ear mark of their owners.

A shepherd who takes care of a large flock must know the marks of all the owners whose sheep are entrusted to his keeping. When a shepherd approaches the fold, his own sheep promptly recognize his

134

voice and bleat for him. He responds by calling the lead sheep by their names, and when he leads them to the pasture, the remainder of the sheep that belong to him follow. They know that their shepherd will feed them salt.

Jesus spoke this parable to show that the Pharisees and others like them did not belong to the fold of his teaching. They did not recognize his voice. He knew their mark and they were not his; therefore, they did not follow him.

THE DOOR OF THE SHEEP

Then said Jesus unto them again, Verily, verily, I say unto you, I am the door of the sheep. Jn. 10:7.

There are two kinds of sheep folds. One is a large square building covered with beams, branches of trees and a layer of straw and earth. This is used during the winter for the sheep. In the spring, summer and autumn, the sheep of the entire town are kept in a large square fold without a roof. There are walls around this fold to protect the sheep from wolves, bears and thieves. The walls also act as a barrier so that the sheep may not stray. This enclosure has a single entrance similar to the winter fold but without a door. After the sheep are brought in for the night, the shepherd sleeps at the entrance so that he can be awakened by the approach of a thief or a wild animal. No one is allowed to enter this fold except the owners of the sheep.

Jesus used the idea of the door as an illustration of himself as the door of the second sheep fold. He meant that he was the protector and guardian of the Jewish people in particular and of all people in general. No one could enter his fold without his knowledge. With his guardianship, people would live in security and peace. His teaching would protect and guard the people from all untrustworthy teachers, false notions, and dogmas.

SHEEP RESPOND TO THE SHEPHERD

All that ever came before me are thieves and robbers: but the sheep did not hear them. Jn 10:8.

The Aramaic text reads: "All who have come are thieves and bandits, if the sheep did not hear them."[1] The term "sheep" refers to "people." Hebrew prophets and songwriters (psalmists) called God the "Shepherd of Israel" and God's people "sheep."

In the olden days, just as today, there were good and bad shepherds. Good shepherds led the sheep to green pastures, bound their wounds and sought the lost sheep. Hired or bad shepherds led them astray, sold some of them and slaughtered others. The term "shepherds" was also a metaphor for kings, governors and other political and religious authorities who ruled over the people.

Jesus knew everything about sheep and shepherds, just as thousands of young Near Eastern men know today. He knew that the sheep recognize the voice of their shepherd when he calls them. He also knew that they became frightened when a stranger attempted to lead them. Sheep will not listen to the voice of a stranger.

Jesus, in this instance, made one of the strongest statements in his teaching. He plainly told the Jews who were opposing him that all religious, prophetic and political leaders of the past whom the sheep did not recognize as shepherds were thieves and bandits. If the sheep recognized their voices, then they were true shepherds of God.

The King James Version in this verse is not clear. It implies that all men of God, prophets and leaders of the past, were not true shepherds because the sheep did not hear them. The error exists in the Greet text because of the mistranslation of the Aramaic phrase *ella-la*. The phrase derives from *elola*. The Semitic character *waw,* "o," is a weak letter and changes to *aleph,*"a," and thus the phrase becomes *ella-la,* "if not."

This verse as it appears in the King James Version and in many

---

[1]Jn. 10:8, Aramaic Peshitta text, Lamsa translation.

other texts of the Bible has been an enigma to the readers of the gospels throughout the centuries. Jesus, on another occasion, had told the people that he had come to fulfill the Torah and the prophets. How could he condemn the prophets and men of God upon whom he based his teaching? According to the Aramaic text, Jesus commends the true prophets who came before him.

In ancient days, people listened to the prophets and followed them because they preached justice and righteousness and upheld the cause of the widows and orphans. Priests and scribes had turned to the worship of Baal. Those wicked religious leaders were opposed to reforms and they slew the prophets.

There were many true and false prophets in Israel and Judah, and the people of God heard only the voices of the true prophets. These holy men were loyal to God and taught truths that were inscribed in sacred scripture. The pious people knew and recognized the voices of these prophets and followed them. But they shunned the false prophets who had come to destroy them like thieves and bandits.

THE GOOD SHEPHERD

I am the good shepherd: the good shepherd giveth his life for the sheep But he that is an hireling, and not the shepherd, whose own the sheep are not, seeth the wolf coming, and leaveth the sheep, and fleeth: and the wolf catcheth them, and scattereth the sheep. Jn. 10:11-12.

In the Near Eastern world there are two kinds of shepherds— those who own the sheep and hired shepherds. Among Semites one of the highest occupations is that of a shepherd. For untold generations, a livelihood was made from the byproducts of raising sheep. One of the greatest desires of many women was to see their sons become shepherds. In cases where a man has no male children, a shepherd who is a stranger is hired for a set wage and food.

A shepherd who is the owner of the sheep not only loves them but also lays down his life for them. When robbers and predators attack the sheep, he will fight to the bitter end for the safety of his

137

flock. During attacks by bandits, these brave shepherds are often killed and the sheep are carried off. This would not be the case with hired shepherds. When they see an enemy approaching, they leave the sheep in the mountain or field and flee. Some hired shepherds would not try to rescue sheep from wolves or bears. They would rather see a score of sheep destroyed than suffer injury themselves. When David was a young man, he fed his father's sheep. He was a true shepherd because when the sheep were attacked by a lion and bear, he slew both animals; he did not run away.[2]

Jesus came not only to search for the lost people of the house of Israel, but also to bring the Gentiles and pagans into the fold of God. The Messiah/Christ was sent by God to shepherd all humanity and feed them with truth. Jesus knew the light of God must shine on all nations and races so that there may be peace, harmony and justice for everyone.

Some of the prophets in Israel were like hired shepherds. During conflicts and national calamities, they deserted the people and fled. The elders were the self-constituted shepherds of the people. However, their sole interest was in the revenues they were receiving. Their main concern was in the security of their office rather than in the welfare of the nation. Like David, Jesus was a true shepherd. He worked without wages or honors and was ready to give his life for all people. He knew that all races were children of his heavenly Father.

JESUS' GREAT POWER

And other sheep I have, which are not of this fold: them also I must bring, and they shall hear my voice, and there shall be one fold and one shepherd. Therefore doth my Father love me, because I lay down my life, that I might take it again. No man taketh it from me, but I lay it down of myself. I have power to lay it down, and I have power to take it again. This commandment have I received of my Father. Jn. 10:16-18.

---

[2]See 1 Sam. 17:34-36.

Jesus was willing to die for the sake of his gospel—that is, his teaching—because he knew that he would triumph over evil and rise again. No one had power over him, but he himself was willing to prove that death was not a finality or an end but the beginning of a larger life. No one before Jesus had ever dared to demonstrate this.[3] The great Hebrew prophets had feared death and when in danger escaped for their lives. They thought of death as a sinister force.

The term "other sheep" refers to the Gentiles and pagans who were not yet in Jesus' fold; they were soon to accept him as the savior of humankind through his teaching that they would put into action. Jesus, like the prophet Isaiah, saw the universality of the Jewish faith. Therefore, he advocated that the light of God, Holy Scripture, should be shared with the Gentile world. It was the only means of securing an everlasting peace and creating a new order for Jews, Gentiles and pagans. This was the way they could live together peacefully and harmoniously.

Isaiah had predicted that the Messiah/Christ would become a light to the Gentiles and rule over the universal state that would embrace all lands, to the uttermost parts of the world. The prophet had also envisioned the reign of everlasting peace and justice.[4]

JESUS KNOWS HIS OWN

And I give unto them eternal life; and they shall never perish, neither shall any man pluck them out of my hand. My Father, which gave them me, is greater than all; and no man is able to pluck them out of my Father's hand. Jn. 10:28-29.

"Pluck them out of my hand" means "snatch or seize them." A good shepherd would fight and die before he allowed his sheep to be seized by wild animals or stolen by thieves. "Sheep" refers to people—that is, those who believed in Jesus' teaching.

---

[3]See Acts 2:24.
[4]See Isa. 9:1-2.

Biblical authors frequently use the term "sheep" throughout Scripture. God is often pictured as a shepherd. Kings, prophets and men of God are also portrayed as God's shepherds, watching over the flock. Sheep are very timid and must be led by skilled shepherds. Thus, people must be led and guided by true prophets and men of God—that is, guided by truth, justice and love.

ONE ACCORD—JESUS' GOOD WORKS

I and my Father are one. Then the Jews took up stones again to stone him. Jesus answered them, Many good works have I shewed you from my Father: for which of those works do ye stone me? Jn 10:30-32.

From the very outset, Jesus told his followers to be aware and judge teachers and men not by what they say, teach and claim about themselves nor by what others say about them. They were to discern people by their works. He told the disciples that by their fruits (works) they would know them. Evil and crooked people cannot produce good works, nor can good people produce evil works.

Jesus' works were good and they validated him, but some people did not believe in him simply because they were not his sheep (people). He had told them that he and his father were one. This in Aramaic means "of one accord, agreement." He followed whatever the Father revealed to him and did the healing, restoring work of God. He came not to destroy but to restore. They were working together in one accord, like a father and son work together in the Near East. The father teaches his son and the son obeys his father, doing good works.

A HUMAN IS A CHILD OF GOD

The Jews answered him saying, For a good work we stone thee not; but for blasphemy: and because that thou, being a man, makest thyself God.

Jesus answered them, Is it not written in your law, I said, Ye are gods?
Jn. 10:33-34.

When Jesus made the statement that he and his Father were of
one accord, some Jews immediately construed it as blasphemy. In the
Jewish religion, no one dared to compare himself with God. To be
one with God, to be in one accord with God, or even saying one
would sit on the right hand of the Most High, was blasphemy. During
this deistic period of Jewish history, God was so holy that people
could not utter God's sacred name with their sinful lips.

People used euphemistic terms for God such as "heaven" or
made a sign when referring to God. Nevertheless, prior to the
Babylonian captivity, Yahweh, the God of Israel, was a Shepherd of
the people and was looked upon as a Father who loved and cared for
them.

Moses tells us that God created humankind in "his own image
and likeness."[5] This means that human beings are children of God,
born of God's spirit and essence. Jesus said: "It is the spirit that gives
life; the body is of no account." It is the Spirit that makes us children
of the living God. Paul says: "For you have not received the Spirit of
bondage, to be in fear again; but you have received the Spirit of
adoption whereby we cry, *Abba, awoon*, Father, our Father. And this
spirit bears witness to our spirit, that we are the children of God."[6]

Many Pharisees, scribes and elders had forgotten the teaching of
their forefathers. They had lost the true knowledge of sonship. The
Jews, since the Babylonian captivity, had been engaged in writing
commentaries. They were trying to find ways to go back to the
original teaching of the patriarchs and prophets. They did not know
that they were children of God.

In biblical days, Solomon was called God's son. Pious men were
also called sons of God; for instance, prior to the story of the flood,
the descendants of Seth, who were good people, were called "sons of

---

[5]See Gen. 1:26-27.
[6]Rom. 8:15-16, Aramaic Peshitta text, Lamsa translation.

God."[7] This ancient and true Jewish concept was supplanted by teaching and interpretations of the law that obscured this truth. These religious teachers had overlooked the scriptural truth that humanity, in its spiritual nature, is the image and likeness of God.

Jesus had said nothing that was not written on the pages of their holy book, the Torah. They had departed from the word of God and were relying on the traditions that were handed down. In the same way, many today do not follow the teaching of Jesus but the doctrines of men. Instead of helping people and pointing to the true way, their teaching only serves to obscure truth. The very truth that was once taught by the prophets has become blasphemy to dull ears.

Jesus quoted from the book of Psalms: "I have said, You are gods; all of you are children of the Most High."[8] On another occasion, Jesus told Mary of Magdala to go and tell his disciples and followers that he was ascending to his God and their God, to his Father and their Father.[9]

---

[7]See Gen. 6:2.
[8]Ps. 82:6, Aramaic Peshitta text, Lamsa translation.
[9]See Jn. 20:17.

CHAPTER 11

LAZARUS SERIOUSLY ILL

These things said he: and after that he said unto them, Our friend Lazarus sleepeth; but I go, that I may awake him out of sleep. Then said his disciples, Lord, if he sleep, he shall do well. Howbeit Jesus spake of his death; but they thought that he had spoken of taking of rest in sleep. Then said Jesus unto them plainly, Lazarus is dead. And I am glad for your sakes that I was not there, to the intent ye may believe; nevertheless let us go unto him. Jn. 11:11-15.

"He sleeps" is an Aramaic and Hebrew term that means "He is dead." When a king, prince or a holy man dies, people say, "He sleeps with his fathers."[1] Uneducated and simple folk who converse in the vernacular tongue often misunderstand. They take the expression literally. Jesus' disciples took Jesus literally when he said, "Our friend Lazarus sleepeth."

The problem is that the Aramaic word *shakhiw* means "asleep, lying down or dead." Jesus often used this term when speaking of people who had passed away. When he entered the house of Jairus, he told the people not to weep. He said, "The damsel is not dead, but sleepeth."[2] In this instance, Jesus used the more colloquial Aramaic word *damkha ye,* meaning "She is sleeping."

When Jesus heard about Lazarus being ill, he said, "This sickness is not unto death, but for the glory of God, that the Son of God might be glorified thereby."[3] He knew Lazarus was sick, but he also knew that God was able to raise him from the dead through him. The expression "This sickness is not unto death" means that the case was not hopeless.

Near Eastern healers and doctors often minimize the seriousness

---

[1]See 1 Ki. 2:10
[2]See Mk. 5:39.
[3]Jn. 11:4, K. J. V.

of an illness or wounds so that the patient, his relatives and friends may feel encouraged and cheered. Even if the sick person is at the point of death, they remark, "Tomorrow he will be all right and working."

These physicians and healers are never hurried when summoned to visit a sick person. They take their time. It often happens that they arrive two or three days late, partly because it is difficult to travel and partly because personal affairs may have detained them. Also, these men are not punctual in their engagements and visits; neither are they concerned about their reputations. In the Near East, doctors and healers were not paid for their work. They were given gifts as an offering when the sick person was healed. If the patient died, they would say: "Let him rest in peace. God gave and God took him away. Blessed be his name."

Jesus knew death had no power over those who have a deep and spiritual understanding of the infinite power of God. He once said, "There are some standing here, who will not taste of death, until they see the kingdom of God."[4] Again, "And fear not them which kill the body, but are not able to kill the soul."[5]

Although he knew Lazarus was dead, Jesus did not believe in death as a finality. He was aware of God's power that destroys the sting of death and unlocks the gates of *sheol*. Had he believed that death was an end, he would not have gone to Lazarus, for his visit would have been in vain. Lazarus' sisters would probably have been angry, as Semites generally are when a doctor is late and the patient dies. To Jesus, death was nothing more than a temporary rest or sleep. "I am the resurrection and the life; he that believeth in me, though he were dead, yet shall he live."[6]

Lazarus was buried in a cave because caves are abundant in Palestine, and more often than not, people use them for tombs. Usually the deceased are buried the same day they die, and their

---

[4]See Lk. 9:27.
[5]Mt. 10:28.
[6]Jn. 11:25, K. J. V.

bodies are never disturbed. Undertakers are unknown and the dead are not embalmed. Burying is the responsibility of the townsfolk. The dead are wrapped in a single, white garment. The head is covered with another piece. Then the deceased are laid as though merely sleeping.

By the time Jesus and his disciples arrived in Bethany, Lazarus had been in the tomb for four days. Now the Pharisees and Sadducees and those who doubted Jesus' healing power could not say: "Oh, he was not dead, he was just sick and would have recovered anyway." The truth was that Lazarus was dead and the Jews themselves had mourned over him and buried him. When Jesus came to the tomb, he asked that the stone be removed. Then, when he had prayed, he cried with a loud voice, "Lazarus come forth!"

This was one of the greatest miracles that Jesus performed. Lazarus was dead and was raised in the presence of both his friends and enemies. It was after the raising of Lazarus that the Pharisees and priests began to be aware of Jesus' work, its importance and its dangerous threat to their traditions and theologies.[7]

The Messiah/Christ had the keys to *sheol*. He was the author of life and therefore had power over death. Martha had faith in Jesus because she believed in his power. She had heard of the many miracles and wonders he had performed. She was sure Jesus could raise her brother from the dead.

A DISCIPLE'S LOVE

Then said Thomas, which is called Didymus, unto his fellow disciples, Let us also go, that we may die with him. Jn. 11:16.

Some of the Jewish religious authorities in Judea had tried to stone Jesus; therefore, his disciples were afraid to return to that region. But Jesus assured them that as long as they were walking in

---

[7]Near Eastern tradition teaches that later on Lazarus became the first Bishop of Cyprus.

the light—that is, doing God's work—they would be protected. His teaching, wonders and faith would protect them from all evils and dangers they might face. The raising of Lazarus would lighten the darkened hearts of many doubtful Jews, and they would begin to believe in Jesus and his mission.

Jesus' disciples were not sure of their master's resurrection although he had often assured them that he would be crucified and rise again. They could not understand it at all. The notion of the resurrection was at that time naive and not well crystalized.

The Pharisees believed in the resurrection, but the Sadducees denied it. Also there were other Jews who were satisfied with this life only and had no desire for a life in another age.

Some of Jesus' disciples loved him so much that they were willing to die with their master if he should be arrested and condemned. In the Near East, faithful servants who love their lord offer their lives in the place of the master. They are willing to die or go to prison with him. Thomas, who in Aramaic is called *"Thoma*, the twin,"* was willing to die with Jesus.

In Aramaic people often say, "I'll die for you," meaning "I'll die instead of you." They will also say, "I will make myself an offering for you."

JESUS THE RESURRECTION

Jesus said unto her, I am the resurrection, and the life: he that believeth in me, though he were dead, yet shall he live: And whosoever liveth and believeth in me shall never die. Jn. 11:25-26.

Jesus' gospel of God's sovereign presence (the kingdom of God) gave humanity a clear and definite hope of the resurrection and eternal life. In his teaching, Jesus proved that human beings are children of God, made in God's image and likeness, and that the spiritual nature of humanity is indestructible. He proved this teaching through his death on the cross and his resurrection from the grave. No other prophet or man of God has ever been able to rise from the

146

grave. Jesus' tomb is the only empty one.

Those who believe in Jesus as the Messiah/Christ are assured of life eternal. They will pass from this earthly life into life everlasting. No other religion, before the Jesus movement, has ever assured its adherents of such a true and sure hope of eternal life. Without the understanding of the resurrection and life hereafter, this life would be dark, hopeless and meaningless.

SITTING AT THE FEET

Then when Mary was come where Jesus was, and saw him, she fell down at his feet, saying unto him, Lord, if thou hadst been here, my brother had not died. Jn. 11:32.

When Near Easterners are entertained, they sit on a quilt or a mattress on the floor and have pillows and cushions placed behind them on which to recline. The honored guest is given the best sitting position in the center. Generally, people fold their legs under them while eating. After the meal, if tired, they stretch their legs outward.

Servants and ordinary men cannot sit with guests but sit in front of them near their feet, kneeling on one knee and talking to them. On some occasions cases are brought up before the guests for discussion and arbitration. Men and women kneel down at the feet of the honored guest and plead for mercy.

When a poor person comes to present his case, or to greet the honored one, he first takes off his shoes and then goes to where the guest is seated and bows before him. If the guest happens to be a holy man, he kisses his hand, his knee, or his feet. While pleading the case, he often says, "I throw myself at your feet," meaning "I am at your mercy." Then he bows down to the ground, lays hold of the feet, and continues to present his case. When Mary saw Jesus, she threw herself at his feet exactly the way a grief-stricken person would approach a holy man.

147

JESUS WEPT

Jesus wept. Jn. 11:35.

The Aramaic text reads: "Jesus was in tears." That is, he was moved by the sorrow of the grief-stricken sisters, their relatives and friends. "When Jesus saw her weeping and the Jews who had come with her weeping, he was moved in his spirit and was greatly disturbed."[8] The Aramaic word *etzi*, "moved," means "disturbed." It refers to a change in one's facial expression. Semites are emotional and are easily stirred at funerals. They cannot help weeping when others weep. Even priests give way to tears.

At first Jesus was calm, attempting to encourage the sisters. He told them that their brother was not dead and that he would rise again. But when he was confronted by a large crowd of mourners, he could not restrain his emotions. Tears began to stream from his eyes, and his countenance changed. It appeared to the mourners that Jesus was not only expressing sorrow but was also indicating the hopelessness of the situation.

Usually, a Semitic doctor weeps only when he sees that there is no hope for the recovery of his patient. However, this was not the case with Jesus. He was not weeping because Lazarus was dead and that everything was utterly hopeless. The deep sadness and loud wailing of the mourners moved the heart of Jesus.[9] He knew that they thought of death as a final calamity and that they had no hope in God's power. Jesus was soon to correct their mistaken notion about death, for he would bring Lazarus back to life.

BURIAL CUSTOM

And he that was dead came forth, bound hand and foot with

---

[8] Jn. 11:33, Aramaic Peshitta text, Lamsa translation.

[9] Interestingly, in the Near East if one does not wail and mourn at the death of a friend or neighbor, it would indicate that one is glad that the person has died.

graveclothes: and his face was bound about with a napkin. Jesus saith unto them, Loose him, and let him go. Jn. 11:44.

Burial in biblical lands is conducted in the following manner: A deceased individual is clothed with white cotton from the neck to the feet. The head is covered with a napkin or handkerchief. Cotton bands are wrapped around the body. This is the reason Lazarus had to be loosed and set free.

When the napkin was removed and Lazarus' wrappings loosened, he was able to stand up and come out of the tomb. In the Near East, no parts of the body are removed. The deceased is bathed and clothed. Some of the dead are placed in coffins and then buried in the ground. Others are placed in sepulchers, tombs or caves. Lazarus was placed in a cave that had become a burial tomb.

FEAR OF THE ROMANS

If we let him thus alone, all men will believe on him: and the Romans shall come and take away both our place and nation. Jn. 11:48.

The Aramaic text reads: ". . . and the Romans will come and take over both our country and our people." That is to say, they will put an end to home rule in Palestine and make Judea a Roman province like the provinces in Asia Minor and Syria. These territories were governed by Rome and the people were made citizens of the Roman Empire.

Judea was under Rome, but the Jews still maintained a restricted autonomy. They were granted certain political rights and complete religious liberty, which they were able to save from the wreckage of the Hasmonean dynasty. The Romans appointed the kings over Judea, but first they had to obtain the approval of the Jews.

These rights and privileges were seldom bestowed on other races by the Roman Caesars; therefore, the Jews were careful not to lose them. On the other hand, sedition and revolutions would give Rome an excuse for cancelling these freedoms. This was the reason many of the Pharisees were afraid of Jesus' teaching, which sounded revolutionary and subversive. They thought his teaching would cause dissatisfaction and create uprisings among the misruled and heavily taxed subjects of Palestine. But, what really concerned them was the security of their own social and political positions and not the welfare of the people.

CHAPTER 12

GENTILES SEEKING JESUS

And there were certain Greeks among them, that came up to worship at the feast. The same came therefore to Philip which was of Bethsaida of Galilee and desired him, saying, Sir, we would see Jesus. Philip cometh and telleth Andrew: and again Andrew and Philip tell Jesus. Jn. 12:20-22.

The Aramaic text of verse 20 reads: "Now there were some Gentiles [*ammeh*] among them who had come up to worship at the feast."[1] The Aramaic word for "Greeks" is *yonayeh*. This term is not present in the Peshitta text. However, the word for Greek does appear in the inscription on the cross, John 19:19-20.

Apparently, these Gentiles were a mixture of Idumeans, Arameans (Syrians), Armenians and other neighboring Semitic peoples. A few of them who had come to the feast may have been from Edessa and Mesopotamia. Some of the Gentiles in Edessa and Mesopotamia had accepted Jesus' gospel of the kingdom by the teaching of the seventy disciples. Their master had sent them to lands east of the River Euphrates to preach the good news to the lost sheep from the house of Israel, the ten tribes.

In the gospel of John, these Gentiles are called *ammeh*, meaning "kindred people." The Arameans of the Near East were closely related to the Israelites. Their language, culture and customs were the same.

When Jesus was informed of the presence of these Gentiles who wanted to see him, he was pleased. He told his disciples that the hour had come to bring people of all races to his all-inclusive message and that he would be glorified by God because his gospel would be preached to all nations. Nevertheless, his glorification would be accomplished through his death, resurrection and later through the outpouring of the Holy Spirit upon his disciples and followers. These

---

[1] Jn. 12:20, Aramaic Peshitta text, Lamsa translation.

151

Gentiles attending the feast were just the beginning and the first fruits of the labors of Jesus and his disciples for God's kingdom.[2]

THE SECRET OF LIFE

Verily, verily, I say unto you, Except a corn of wheat fall into the ground and die, it abideth alone: but if it die, it bringeth forth much fruit. He that loveth his life shall lose it; and he that hateth his life in this world shall keep it unto life eternal. If any man serve me, let him follow me; and where I am, there shall also my servant be; if any man serve me, him will my Father honour. Jn. 12:24-26.

Part 1—ETERNAL LIFE. Jesus realized the hour had come when he would be infinitely more powerful and influential through his death, resurrection and spiritual existence than he had been in his physical existence. Through the power of the spirit of life, he would multiply himself in the hearts and minds of his disciples, followers and many races and peoples throughout the world for ages to come. His teaching would permeate, germinate and grow all over the earth among all nations.

Jesus understood the secret of life and was willing to surrender his earthly existence. He illustrated the secret of multiplication in a plain and simple metaphor, a grain of wheat. This little seed, when it

---

[2]Dr. Lamsa also suggests that these Gentiles might have been Assyrians who were sent by Abgarus, king of Edessa, to invite Jesus to his kingdom. A document relative to the visit of these men and the exchange of correspondence between Jesus and King Abgarus was discovered by Eusebius about 400 CE. A copy is at the Vatican library.

In his reply to Abgarus, Jesus promised to send one of his disciples to Edessa after his resurrection, saying: "The hour has come that the Son of Man should be glorified." "Glorified" refers to Jesus' resurrection. In his letter to Abgarus he also says that he must die. These emissaries of the Assyrian king offered Jesus protection from the religious authorities who were opposing him.

Today these letters written in Aramaic have come under much scholarly scrutiny and debate. There are those who dismiss these letters as inauthentic, but there are also those scholars who admit to their credibility.

falls into the ground, germinates, sprouts and becomes a glorious stalk that produces more seeds. They, in their turn, will multiply themselves. Great and infinite is the power of a grain of wheat. Its ability to continue itself is unending, yet it does not appear as if it has such tremendous energies working in it. The seed knows how to die, trap solar energy and bring new life and substance into existence.

During the time that Jesus spoke these things, only a few people truly believed in the resurrection and life hereafter. Many believed in the power of one life only and that death was the end of all life for human beings. The masses never learned from the law of nature that death is not an end but a multiplication and glorification.

The seed that is planted in the ground does not die but changes, multiplies and will be replanted again and again. These simple facts were hidden from the minds of the people, whose thoughts were occupied with the observance of ordinances, ceremonies, and religious processions along with the temporal and material cares of this world.

Jesus' death was a necessity for the spread of his gospel. It would release the hidden power in the souls of men. It would ignite the hearts and souls of his followers who, after his death and resurrection, would not be afraid to face death themselves. Jesus would inspire and encourage his disciples in a new way of life and thinking. He revealed that life is worth living and that his gospel of the kingdom would be worth dying for. Therefore, his disciples and followers were told not to be concerned about this life that would come to an end sooner or later, but to be concerned about the spiritual and eternal life to which he had awakened them that begins here on earth.

Part 2—THE LORD AND HIS SERVANTS. When Semites entertain a nobleman, his friends and servants are also included. The honorable guest and his servants sit down at meals together, although more attention is paid to the master than to his servants. Special dishes are prepared for him. Fruit and other delicacies are offered only to him, but he passes them around to his servants.

A Near Easterner would be offended if his servants were not

153

treated with due homage appropriate to him. Some men would refuse the hospitality and comfort of a home if their servants were not provided for in like manner as he. At night some of the guests and their servants sleep on the floor in the same room, and the next morning their servants accompany them wherever they are invited.

Jesus assured his disciples of his abiding presence. He was not leaving them but was going to the spiritual world before them so that he might prepare a place for them. Wherever he would be, they also would be with him. They had left everything to follow him and he would not leave them like orphans. They were to share in his heavenly kingdom now and hereafter.

JESUS DESTINED TO DIE

Now is my soul troubled; and what shall I say? Father, save me from this hour: but for this cause came I unto this hour. Jn. 12:27.

Jesus was the first teacher of religion who saw victory after death. No other prophet or man of God had ever taught that death and the grave were conquerable. From the very beginning of his ministry, Jesus foresaw his rejection and death. The great prophet Isaiah, centuries before him, had predicted that this would happen to the Messiah. But, Isaiah's prophecies were not understood by the Pharisees and other learned Jews.[3]

No one believed that meekness would ever triumph over force and love over hatred. No one could see that force and the sword had failed and that all the nations who had resorted to them had perished by them. To put it more plainly, no one had ever before taken the words of the prophet Isaiah seriously. Most people believed that the Messiah was to live forever and never die. He was to conquer all the nations of the world and live gloriously ever after.

Jesus, as any other man would be, was disturbed. His body

---

[3]See Isa. 53.

154

resisted, but his spirit was willing to let his body die in order to demonstrate that death has no power over those who believe in God and who are created in the divine image.

During his trial, Jesus said to Pilate: "For this I was born, and for this very thing I came to the world, that I may bear witness concerning the truth."[4] Jesus had come to bear witness to the truth—that is, to die for the sake of the truth.

Death is one of the most difficult forces one has to face. We can understand why this is so. Death causes us to depart not only from this temporal life but also from family, relatives, friends and the physical joys of life. Jesus' disciples were poor and what they did have they left behind so that they might learn from him. Jesus was soon to leave a group of men who were very dear to his heart. He knew that after his death, they also would be hated and despised more than ever before and even put to death because of their teaching.

Jesus' soul was troubled. He had to drink from the bitter cup. If he should ask his Father to save him from the cross, he knew he would be turning from the reason he came into this world. The prophets had predicted his death and God was to reveal the depths of love and salvation through the cross. The nations were to be delivered not by the sword of the Messiah but by the power of the spirit and meekness. Jesus would not retreat from his stance. He knew and understood his destiny.

THE PRAYER OF JESUS

Father, glorify thy name. Then came there a voice from heaven, saying, I have both glorified it, and will glorify it again. Jn. 12:28.

Jesus had been glorified. His heavenly Father had endowed him with powers. God, as a father, had entrusted everything into his hands just as an Eastern father entrusts his possessions to his son. Jesus had raised the dead and opened the eyes of the blind. He had received

---

[4]Jn. 18:37, Aramaic Peshitta text, Lamsa translation.

honor and praise from so many people. He was acclaimed a king and deliverer of Israel. Multitudes followed him from town to town because of his popularity.

Now he was to be rejected, humiliated and meet with a torturous death, but the sudden disappointment and sadness that would befall his disciples and followers would soon turn to joy. He was to be further glorified by God, his Father, through his resurrection and ascension into the heavenly realms. Humanity was to share in this glory. Jesus would soon overcome death and open a new way to immortality for humankind.

JUDGMENT

Now is the judgment of this world: now shall the prince of this world be cast out. And I, if I be lifted up from the earth, will draw all men unto me. This he said, signifying what death he should die. Jn 12:31-33.

Part 1—THE WORLD IS JUDGED. The day of judgment for the world was at hand. A new gospel had been preached and the seeds of a universal kingdom ruled by the Messiah/Christ had already been planted. God's sovereign presence among all nations would judge the rulers of the world. Princes and kings will ultimately lay down their crowns at the feet of the prince of peace.

The reign of God was upon all nations. Jesus' final demonstration on the cross was destined to change the whole world. It was meant to remove racial boundaries, humble the proud and exalt the meek. A new world system was to begin, bringing a new creation into existence; the old was passing away with the success of the teaching of Christ.

Part 2—PRINCE OF THIS WORLD. The "prince of this world" refers to the Jewish high priest, the Herodian and Romans who ruled over the people. These ambitious and controlling leaders and authorities were dominated by greed, hatred, pride and worldly power. But now their days were numbered.

The holy temple was soon to be destroyed. Jesus' gospel of the kingdom was to triumph over the Roman Empire. The kingdom of genuine justice and piety envisioned by the Hebrew prophets was to be established on the earth.

Jesus was facing the darkest hour of his life. He was soon to be delivered into the hands of wicked princes and leaders of this world. An innocent one was to be tried, convicted and crucified by the sinful.

Part 3—JESUS AWARE OF THE CROSS. The Aramaic phrase "lifted up" is another way of saying "crucified." Victims were lifted up to their crosses and then crucified. Evidently, the crosses were erected beforehand even as the victims were watching the procedure.

"This he said, signifying what death he should die." This verse (33) was probably a marginal note that was added to the text much later. It was to show that Jesus knew beforehand what manner of death he was to die. Death on the cross was the severest punishment that could be inflicted.

When Jesus was lifted up, hundreds of men and women who had heard of him but had never seen him would now see him dying like a criminal. Many of them believed he was a righteous man dying the death of a sinner. In the eyes of others he was dying as a malefactor should.

But from that moment on, Jesus began to draw men and women to him. The cross would stand forever in the hearts of those who would believe in him. Had Jesus died in Nazareth, the world would have been robbed of his wonderful message. The gospel he proclaimed was the good news of the power of meekness and freedom from evil that was made possible through his death on the cross. Without the cross he could not have demonstrated that death was not the end of life and that it was surmountable.

THE SUFFERING MESSIAH

The people answered him, We have heard out of the law that Christ abideth for ever; and how sayest thou, The Son of man must be lifted up? who is this son of man? Jn. 12:34.

According to Jewish traditional interpretation of Scripture, the Messiah was to restore the glorious Davidic kingdom and establish a monarchy that was to surpass in wealth and power the glory of Assyria, Babylon and Persia. Most of the prophets of Israel predicted the rise of such a strong political leader as a means of establishing God's kingdom on earth. In the later prophecies, however, the whole messianic picture was changed.

The prophecies suddenly shifted from the notion of an earthly, militant ruler to a suffering servant, and from a long expected and welcomed Messiah to a rejected one. (Compare Isaiah chapter 11 with chapter 53.) The reason for this change was that the prophets began to see that as a small nation, the Jews could never overthrow stronger nations and attain political supremacy. But they foresaw that Israel was destined to exercise a spiritual influence over the entire world.

In accordance with these prophecies, Jesus invariably proclaimed that the messianic kingdom, God's kingdom, was at hand. His announcement of the messianic reign induced people to seize him and attempt to make him a king by force. His early ministry was largely confined to this first aspect of prophecy and to the political restoration of Israel. Then he changed and shifted his policy. He predicted that his departure to the holy city would not be to receive a crown that would make him a king but to be betrayed and crucified.

The long, overdue political kingdom turned out to be a spiritual kingdom and the death of Jesus was the only means to establish this spiritual reign on earth. By his death, Jesus would save not only Israel but all nations. The political salvation of Israel depended on the spiritual salvation of the world. The later prophets were aware of this. They saw great kingdoms rising and falling. The Davidic kingdom had also disappeared. A spiritual kingdom was the answer for the salvation of the world. And this could not be realized without the crucifixion and death of the Prince of Peace.

WALK IN THE LIGHT

Then Jesus said unto them. Yet a little while is the light with you. Walk while ye have the light, lest darkness come upon you: for he that walketh in darkness knoweth not wither he goeth. While ye have light, believe in the light, that ye may be the children of light. These things spake Jesus and departed, and did hide himself from them. Jn. 12:35-36.

Where electricity is unknown, work and travel are done during the day, and people rest when it is dark. In emergencies some people work and travel at night and take the risk of accidents and other mishaps that take place in the dark.

Jesus spoke of his departure. He had been as a light to his disciples. He had explained Scripture to them and revealed things that were hidden from the foundation of the world. Now the light was to disappear for a while. Darkness would soon settle everywhere. Temptation would overtake his followers. However, the sun was to rise again and its golden rays would penetrate the farthest corners of the world.

Jesus wanted his disciples to use every opportunity to understand these things while he was with them. The days of his trial and crucifixion were approaching. Some of his followers had already left him in disappointment. Others were soon to desert him. These men could not understand the prophecies about the Messiah. How could the Messiah suffer? In this critical period Jesus concentrated all his thought on his disciples. He had to show them from holy Scripture that the Messiah had to die so that he could rise again in glory and triumph.

THEY HAVE BECOME BLIND

He hath blinded their eyes, and hardened their heart; that they should not see with their eyes, nor understand with their heart, and be converted, and I should heal them. Jn. 12:40.

159

The Aramaic text reads: "Their eyes have become blind and their hearts darkened, so that they cannot see with their eyes and understand with their hearts: Let them return and I will heal them."[5] The Aramaic word *awaro* is the third person plural passive voice of the word *awar* and means "they have become blind." The Greek translator confused this term with *awar,* the third person singular active tense, meaning "he made them blind." This mistake was doubtless due to the translator's unfamiliarity with Aramaic or perhaps the text had become mutilated and the manuscript was not clear.

When Near Easterners lose their interest in religion they are called blind. Wealth and luxury close their eyes to spiritual needs. Selfishness and greed dominate their hearts. They oppress the poor and weak. All who are afflicted by such blindness lose their spiritual sight. They cannot think of God, love and justice. God did not bring this misfortune on them, as the King James version of this verse tells us. It was through their own heedlessness and indifference to God's truth. They were morally guilty and needed divine forgiveness so that they might be restored as the Aramaic text reads: "Let them return and I will heal them."

JESUS SPOKE FOR GOD

For I have not spoken of myself, but the Father which sent me, he gave me a commandment, what I should say, and what I should speak. And I know that his commandment is life everlasting: whatsoever I speak therefore, even as the Father said unto me, so I speak. Jn. 12:49-50.

Jesus gave all glory and honor to God, his Father. He said nothing of his own accord but only that which God had revealed to the prophets and that which God had commanded him to say. Jesus, as a man, was sent by God, and he acted as a representative for God on earth. He who sends is greater than the one who is sent. This is the

---

[5]Jn. 12:40, Aramaic Peshitta text, Lamsa translation.

reason Jesus said: "My Father is greater than I. I of myself can do nothing. The Father does it."[6]

Jesus wanted people to know that he was not introducing an alien religion and asking people to worship him. He always gave honor and glory to God. Jesus was an ambassador. He told the Jewish people and his disciples that God had ordained him and given him power to be a light in the world. He had power to heal and forgive sins, and whoever saw him saw the action of God who sent him. Jesus was the image and likeness of God. Being spirit, God cannot be seen. But the human Jesus in whom God dwelt could be seen. According to John's gospel, the Christ in Jesus existed with God from the very beginning. The man Jesus, however, was born in time with an earthly beginning and ending—that is, subject to birth and death.

---

[6]See Jn. 8:38.

CHAPTER 13

JESUS SHOWS THE WAY

So after he had washed their feet, and had taken his garments, and was set down again, he said unto them, Know ye what I have done to you? Ye call me Master and Lord: and ye say well; for so I am. If I then, your Lord and Master, have washed your feet: ye also ought to wash one another's feet. Jn 13:12-14.

The gospel writers revealed the heart of Jesus, which was behind all his teaching. They revealed his love for humanity, his humility and his willingness to surrender his life for those who had gone astray and lost their way. Jesus desired that his disciples and followers conduct their lives differently from that of the masses and the political and religious leaders of the world. Concerning their behavior as leaders, they were to be equal in rank and the greatest one among them was to be servant of all.

Any apostle rejecting this simple ceremony that Jesus performed would not be able to participate in the ministry of the Messiah/Christ. The refusal on the part of that disciple would indicate that he wished to be a lord over the others. Although Jesus was their master and teacher, he became an example for them. He showed them the way of meekness and humility. Up until this time no teacher had ever washed the feet of his servants or disciples. No great nobleman had served the humble and poor. Jesus' way was so entirely different from anything they had ever known.

Jesus' gospel of the kingdom was not to be taught like other teachings but was to be demonstrated. Love and care for one another was to be practiced by this new leadership among the twelve. At that time, however, his disciples did not comprehend the full significance of the example. After his death and resurrection, the apostles began to see and reason more clearly about what Jesus had taught them. The Holy Spirit was to nurture and increase everything that he had planted in their hearts while he was with them.

BETRAYAL OF FRIENDSHIP

I speak not of you all: I know whom I have chosen; but that the scripture may be fulfilled, He that eateth bread with me hath lifted up his heel against me. Jn. 13:18.

When you eat bread and salt with a neighbor and then later betray that person, you have committed one of the worst breaches of Near Eastern etiquette. Most Semites refuse to eat bread in the homes of those with whom they are not on good terms or of their enemies upon whom they seek vengeance. If they once eat bread and salt, they have to forget all their differences and in time of trouble lay down their lives for each other.

The Aramaic idiom "he hath lifted up his heel against me" means "He has revolted against me and is ready to fight me." Near Easterners fight with their feet to kick each other and use their fists to strike one another. Once the enemy has fallen down, he is trodden under the heel of his opponent until he becomes helpless and unconscious.

Judas was rebelling against his master. He had broken bread with him for several years, but now he was ready to betray him and see him mocked, scourged and punished. It was not only a breach of discipleship but also a breach of a long established and cherished Near Eastern tradition of great worth, the covenant of bread and salt.

The thought of Jesus' betrayal dismayed all of his disciples. And when Jesus saw that they were all sorrowful and troubled, he told them that he did not mean all of them; only the one who would eat bread with him would revolt against him. "Yea, mine own familiar friend, in whom I trusted, who did eat of my bread had lifted up his heel against me."[1]

Judas was the treasurer. Apparently he was one of the most trusted of Jesus' disciples; yet he would betray him for money and for the doubts he had in his new teaching. It was Judas whom Jesus

---

[1] Ps. 41:9, Aramaic Peshitta text, Lamsa translation.

pointed out by giving him the sop.

In biblical lands, only friends give their sops to one another. Jesus still counted Judas as a friend, and even when Judas betrayed him he addressed him as a friend. Jesus did this because there was still time for Judas to change his mind and turn to God for forgiveness.

SIMON WINKING AT JOHN

Simon Peter therefore beckoned to him: that he should ask who it should be of whom he spake. Jn. 13:24.

Generally, Semitic guests and disciples are shy and quiet in the presence of a nobleman or a holy man. On such occasions they keep silent. The master of the house and his honorable guest or guests carry the conversation. Other guests merely listen or exchange thoughts and ask or suggest questions by winking their eyes or making facial expressions and gestures. Every move of an eye means something. Thus questions and answers are easily communicated. The Aramaic text reads that Peter winked at John.

During the last supper Simon Peter was not seated near Jesus. He could not wait until the supper was over. He wanted to know at once who was to betray their master. But Jesus did not want all the disciples to know who this was to be. It would have caused trouble and perhaps a rift in the ranks. Therefore, Peter winked at John, who was sitting near Jesus, to ask him who was the traitor.

Jesus indicated the guilty party by dipping the bread in the dish, creating the sop and then giving it to the traitor. John immediately knew who the guilty one was and later passed on the information to Peter. This might have been the reason that Peter took a sword with him into the garden. The other disciples were unaware of what was going to happen, nor did they suspect Judas.

"And when he had dipped the sop, he gave it to Judas Iscariot, the son of Simon. And after the sop Satan entered into him. Then said Jesus unto him: 'That thou doest, do quickly.' Now no man at the

164

table knew for what intent he spake this unto him. For some of them thought because Judas had the bag, that Jesus had said unto him, Buy those things that we have need of against the feast; or, that he should give something to the poor."[2] "Satan entered into him" is an Aramaic expression meaning "to follow through with an evil intent." In other words, the scheme that he had devised was now to be carried out.

And when he had dipped the sop, he gave it to Judas Iscariot, the son of Simon." At Syrian feasts, especially in the region where Jesus lived, such sops are handed to those who stand and serve the guests with wine and water. But in a more significant manner those morsels are exchanged by friends. Choice bits of food are handed to friends by one another, as signs of close intimacy. It is never expected that any person would hand such a sop to one for whom he cherishes no friendship.

I can never contemplate this act in the Master's story without thinking of "the love of Christ which passeth knowledge." To the one who carried in his mind and heart a murderous plot against the loving Master, Jesus handed the sop of friendship, the morsel which is never offered to an enemy. The rendering of the act in words is this: "Judas, my disciple, I have infinite pity for you. You have proved false, you have forsaken me in your heart; but I will not treat you as an enemy, for I have come, not to destroy, but to fulfill. Here is my sop of friendship, and "that thou doest, do quickly."

Apparently Jesus' demeanor was so cordial and sympathetic that, as the evangelist tells us, "Now no man at the table knew for what intent he spake this unto him. For some of them thought, because Judas had the bag, that Jesus had said unto him, Buy those things that we have need of against the feast, or that he should give something to the poor."

Thus in this simple act of the Master, so rarely noticed by preachers, we have perhaps the finest practical example of "Love your enemies" in the entire Gospel. Is it therefore to be wondered at that in speaking of Judas, the writer of St. John's Gospel says, "And after the sop Satan entered into him"? For, how can one

---

[2]Jn. 13:27-29, K. J. V.

165

who is a traitor at heart reach for the gift of true friendship without being transformed in the very spirit of treason?[3]

THE DISCIPLES COMFORTED

Little children, yet a little while I am with you. Ye shall seek me: and as I said unto the Jews, Whither I go, ye cannot come; so now I say to you. Jn. 13:33.

Jesus called his disciples "little children," not because they were too young or immature, but because they were inexperienced in religion and knew so little of the problems and difficulties that were ahead of them. It also conveys a Semitic teacher's love for his students and followers. Jesus was expressing his deep love for and closeness to his disciples.

An ecclesiastical authority in the Near East, when addressing a letter to the members of his church, will write, "My beloved sons." One often hears people engaged in conversation, calling each other "My Father" or "My son." An elder will usually address a younger person as "my son."

Again, unlearned men, no matter how old they may be, are also called "my sons" or "little children." When God called Jeremiah to preach to the people, Jeremiah said, "I am a child." This means, "I am unlearned." God would not call a child to go and stand before kings and princes. In Arabic, such persons are called *jahil*, "inexperienced."

Nearly all of Jesus' disciples were simple, common folk with little or no training and without material and political influence or support. He felt compassion for them as a father who grieves when he leaves his little children behind him.

The disciples, like the Jews, would seek him but would not find him. For where Jesus was to go no one would be able to follow. Nonetheless, his disciples would see him later, after he had risen and

---

[3]Abraham M Rihbany, *The Syrian Christ,* Chapter VI, "Feast and Sacrament," pp. 68-70.

166

gained a victory over death. His disciples would rise in consciousness and realize their master-teacher and his glorious message were greater than the grave and death. They would come to him and see him again.

A NEW COMMANDMENT

A new commandment I give unto you, That ye love one another: as I have loved you, that ye also love one another. By this shall all men know that ye are my disciples, if ye have love one to another. Jn. 13:34-35.

The old commandment that was given by Moses reads: "Thou shall not avenge, nor bear any grudge against the children of thy people, but thou shalt love thy neighbor as thyself; I am the Lord."[4] Jesus commanded his disciples to love one another, just as he had loved them. They were told to love all of those who believed in him, and even to love their enemies regardless of race or religion.

To love one another was the manner in which humanity would know that these men were disciples of Christ. When people loved just their own relatives, friends and neighbors, it was nothing, for everyone loves those who love them in return.

On the other hand, love was to serve as a binding force and thus strengthen the ranks of the apostles and their followers. Love would remove jealousy, greed, rivalry and worldly aspirations so that this movement would become an example for Jews, Gentiles and pagans. These people would see love in action. Also, ruling powers of the world would see spiritual principles governing the hearts and souls of men and women, bringing peace and harmony wherever they were. The disciples were to become a true loving family. They would be examples to future generations and to the world. Love is the only way for people to bond to each other.

Jesus was soon to be crucified. He was to accept the challenge and drink of the cup from which no one else would wish or dare to

---

[4]Lev. 19:18, K. J. V.

drink. He was to travel a path that no one else knew. Jesus was to show that death and the grave had no power over truth. These terms of speech were difficult for his disciples to understand. No one had spoken in such a manner before. No one in the history of the world had ever said that he would be put to death, buried, and rise again.

Religious teachers in those days sought their own interests and were jealous of one another. They did not really love each other. Prior to his journey to Jerusalem, Jesus had noticed that rivalry and jealousy had already begun working among his disciples They were arguing over leadership and who would occupy the high seat in the Davidic kingdom. They were interested in themselves rather than in the work they were to do. Loving one another was a new commandment for a teacher to give his disciples.

CHAPTER 14

THE HEAVENLY HOME

Let not your heart be troubled: ye believe in God, believe also in me. In my Father's house are many mansions: if it were not so, I would have told you. I go to prepare a place for you. Jn 14:1-2.

The Aramaic text reads: "Let not your heart be troubled; believe in God, and believe in me also. In my Father's house are many rooms; if it were not so, I would have told you. I go to prepare a place for you." In Aramaic, "Let not your heart be troubled" means "Don't worry." The disciples felt fear and were confused and worried. Jesus knew that they must have strong faith in God and that they were also to trust and have faith in him.

The term "mansion" is not in the Aramaic text. *Awaneh*, "rooms" or "abodes," is the proper term and is used figuratively, meaning "place." Here it is also used as a metaphor. Heaven has no partitions, rooms, keys and bars. Heaven is a state of harmony and peace.

From time immemorial shortage of housing has existed in biblical lands. Houses are always crowded because many family members continue to live together, and they even share their dwellings with strangers. Until the advent of Western culture in the Near East, houses were usually one story structures, and during the summer season people slept on the roof. In many places in the Near East this still holds true.

In the winter, travelers and strangers who find no lodging usually sleep in stables and caves. Until recent days in Palestine and Syria, housing conditions were always bad. The lack of space in over-crowded homes caused unsanitary conditions often resulting in leprosy.

While in Jerusalem, Jesus and his disciples often slept in Gethsemane, a public park, because the city was too crowded during festivals. (Princes and noblemen send their servants ahead to prepare a place for them.)

169

One of the highest desires of a Semitic family is to have a home of their own. One can find food and clothing, but it is very difficult to find a dwelling place. There is nothing more alluring than when a lord promises his servants their own house.

In God's kingdom there are many rooms. Jesus called God's kingdom his Father's house. In other words, there will be room for people of all nationalities, regardless of race. God's kingdom is open to everyone.

Jesus was soon to leave his disciples. While they were with him, they were cared for and their needs met. They were afraid that after he left them they would be destitute and without a home. Jesus assured them of an eternal habitation. Even though their earthly expectations of a home and luxuries had come to an end, their hopes would be granted in the realization of eternal life. In his Father's house there were many rooms and comforts. Fears, worries and suffering were soon to vanish and the disciples were to be inheritors of the heavenly kingdom and its eternal glory and peace. Their master had prepared a place for his followers so that they might be with him.

TO PREPARE A PLACE

And if I go and prepare a place for you, I will come again, and receive you unto myself; that where I am. There ye may be also. Jn. 14:3.

Migrations are always preceded by an advance party composed of one or two experienced men. They are sent in search of a place as a temporary or permanent settlement. Among sheep-raising people, men are sent in search of green pastures and water for the flocks. No one would venture to leave his town or his pasture without the assurance of something better.

These men are empowered by the tribe to negotiate and make written or oral treaties with the people among whom they are to dwell. Houses, fields, seeds and other necessities are provided in advance for the newcomers. The natives, among whom they are to dwell, are well informed about the immigrants and are ready to receive them with open arms. Jesus' death was to open a new way to immortality and prepare an everlasting home for his followers.

In those days, death was considered an ending. Souls of the departed ones went to an unknown land. Only a few believed in the resurrection. Jesus' death was a departure from this life into eternal life. His followers were not to go down to *Sheol* but were to follow him into his everlasting kingdom. He was to go ahead and prepare a place for them. The assurance of this kingdom came to them after the triumphant resurrection and ascension of Jesus. His disciples followed in his steps and were thus immortalized. The kingdom has been established and there are places in it for all the faithful who want to live forever.

JESUS IS THE WAY

Jesus saith unto him: I am the way, the truth, and the life: no man cometh unto the Father but by me. If ye had known me, ye should have known my Father also: and from henceforth ye know him, and have seen him. Jn. 14:6-7.

This verse has been misunderstood by many interpreters and students of the Bible. They interpret this verse as if Jesus were presenting himself and his teaching in a sectarian, exclusive manner. "I am the way, the truth and the life" means "what I teach is the path of truth and eternal life." Jesus personified his teaching. He was the living example of truth in action and the image of the living God.

Urha in Aramaic means "path, way, religion." To really understand God as a Father, one would have to come to the son. It is the son who reveals the Father. In the Near East, there exists a special relationship between a father and a son. A father will reveal everything to his son. There is no secret that he will keep his son from knowing. Thus, if one wishes to know more about the father and his secrets, one must go to the son. Jesus revealed the true, loving nature of God because he knew him as a father, the Beloved, and not as a "God." The term "father" in Aramaic also means "beloved."

171

No one has ever seen God except Jesus as the Christ, who came from God. For the Christ—that is, the spirit, truth and life—existed with God from the very beginning. It is through the Christ that one can see God. The works of Jesus were the works of God; his healing power was the power of God. The realization is that God manifested and worked through Jesus. Those who saw him saw the Father at work. Thus, one comes to the son to see the Father at work.

The Jewish concept of God was vastly different at that time. People were told that God was so holy that no one could draw near his presence and that he could only be approached through sacrifices and intermediaries. And yet the forefathers of the Jews, Abraham, Isaac and Jacob, had neither priests, prophets nor intermediaries.

Now even Jesus' disciples, who had been with him throughout his ministry, did not believe that he was the image and likeness of God. Their old concepts of God still dominated their minds and hearts. Jesus said: "All this time I have been with you, and yet you do not know me, Philip? He who sees me has seen the Father: and how do you say, Show us the Father?"[1]

ASSURANCE OF GREATER WORKS

Verily, verily, I say unto you, He that believeth on me, the works that I do shall he do also; and greater works than these shall he do; because I go unto my Father. Jn. 14:12.

In Palestine and Syria, an artist always assures his apprentice that some day he will surpass him in his skill and workmanship. An apprentice learns his master's trade and its secrets and, at the same time, he discovers new methods and tools that were unknown to his master. The master is aware of future discoveries and progress in his trade and he has absolute confidence in the success of his faithful apprentices. This is also true of a good teacher. A student, though lacking confidence and experience, hopes that some day he will be as

---

[1]Jn. 14:9, Aramaic Peshitta text, Lamsa translation.

skilled as his master or even better.

Jesus' disciples were students learning the secrets of the new gospel of the kingdom. They were learning to preach, teach and heal. They were astonished at the cures and miracles their master had performed. These men were eager to do these things themselves, wondering if they would ever have the secret of this power and wisdom. Jesus' apostles had some faith but little confidence and experience. At times they had failed to heal the sick who were brought to them.

Jesus encouraged them and assured them of utmost success, saying that they and those who would follow them would do even greater things. In his preaching and debates, Jesus had silenced the religious teachers of Galilee and Judea. In healing, he had surpassed the prophets, doctors and healers of all times. His disciples would stand before governors and kings and would even silence the high priests. They would restore the insane, cleanse the lepers, raise the dead and teach more people than Jesus had. Jesus had sown the seeds in Galilee and Judea, and his disciples carried on in the larger and more powerful centers, synagogues and temples in Jerusalem, Syria, Mesopotamia and Rome.

His disciples would be able to do these things because he was going to his Father. He would grant them greater powers because the work of the Gospel would be greater.

Jesus' disciples would teach people of many races and religions. The Holy Spirit would fully operate through them and help those who believe in the name of Jesus. God would grant the disciples more gifts and favors in the presence of men so that the needs for the expansion of the gospel could be met. Anything that they would ask in his name—that is, through his way, his method—would be granted. Throughout the ages greater works have been done by men of God through the teaching of Jesus.

JESUS' METHOD

And whatsoever ye shall ask in my name, that will I do, that the Father may be glorified in the Son. If ye shall ask anything in my name, I will do it. Jn. 14:13-14.

B'shemi, "in my name," means "according to my method, my way of doing things." Jesus' way was different from that of any other religious teacher of his time. He taught people to pray to God and ask his blessings as one would ask a loving Father and not as an earthly Near Eastern potentate whom people feared and worshiped as a god.

In many lands, members of various religions mention the names of their patron saints when petitioning God. The Jews invoked the names of their patriarchs, Abraham, Isaac and Jacob, who had been close to God.

Jesus' way was meekness, forgiveness, inclusiveness and loving kindness. Turning the other cheek and going another mile were new ideas, a new approach to God and religion. Jesus had power from God to grant favors; all power in heaven and on earth were his.

Even today, great inventions and discoveries are credited to and are known by the names of their creators and authors. Jesus was the author of the simplest, yet most practical, method of praying and seeking God's blessings ever discovered.

The disciples and followers of Jesus were assured of greater miracles and wonders than those Jesus himself had performed. Anything they would ask of God, believing in Jesus' teaching, using his method and knowing that God had sent him, would be granted. Jesus' method was direct and sure. A father would do anything for his children.[2]

---

[2]See Mt. 7:7-8, Jn. 15:7-8. Also Rocco A. Errico, *Setting a Trap for God: The Ancient Aramaic Prayer of Jesus,* "Praying in Jesus' Name." pp. 15-17.

LOVE MUST BE PROVEN

If ye love me, keep my commandments. And I will pray the Father, and he shall give you another Comforter, that he may abide with you forever; Even the Spirit of truth; whom the world cannot receive, because it seeth him not, neither knoweth him: but ye know him; for he dwelleth with you, and shall be in you. Jn 14:15-17.

Part 1—KEEPING JESUS' COMMANDMENTS. Loyalty to Jesus and his teaching cannot be demonstrated just by confessing his name and saying, "I believe in him." Actualizing his teaching is the proof of loyalty to him. Only by obeying Jesus' words and demonstrating their works would others know that the disciples were true followers of the Christ.

Jesus gave his disciples and followers a set of great commands, not just to be read but to be demonstrated in their daily lives. One who obeys his words and lives by them engraves them on the hearts of men and women of generations to come. This individual then becomes a light to those who walk in darkness.

The Pharisees, scribes and pious Jews believed in all of the laws and ordinances of Moses, but many did not practice them. Believing without action is like an empty cloud or a dry well. Jesus' disciples were to be more than just believers; they were to keep and practice his teachings.

The comforter, the Holy Spirit, was to be their teacher of the new law and commandments. The Spirit was to guide the followers of Jesus and teach them the new way, the way whereby they could demonstrate that they were children of God. Their loyalty to him was the same as loyalty to God who sent him and to the Holy Spirit.

Part 2—THE COMFORTER. The Aramaic word *paraqleta* has several meanings. It means "comforter, one who saves or encourages." "Savior" in Aramaic is *paroqa*. *Paraqleta* is probably the participle of the verb *praq*, "to save." The title of Savior belongs to the Messiah/Christ.

According to the literal translation, the Comforter would seem to be another person, but this idea cannot be harmonized with Semitic

175

thought, especially with the unity of God. What Jesus meant was a reference to his own spirit or influence that would abide with his disciples forever. "If I do not go, the Spirit will not come" does not mean that Jesus had to go and force the Spirit to come. It means "If I do not die, I will have no influence over you and my spirit will not abide with you."

If Jesus had not gone to the cross, he would have returned to Galilee, grown old and died, leaving nothing behind. His movement would have died with him. It was his death on the cross that fired the hearts of his disciples with zeal. It was the spirit of Jesus that made the disciples travel over land and sea and even meet horrible deaths for his sake. Jesus left them, but his spirit abided with them in power and enabled them to see things spiritually.

While he was with them physically, they reasoned in a literal and material way. When Elijah was about to depart, Elisha, his student and servant, prayed for a double portion of his master's spirit to be given to him.[3] This was needed if Elisha was to continue his master's mission. It was the same with Jesus' disciples, who needed the Spirit of Jesus—that is, the Christ—to guide them as we also are guided.

ORPHANS

I will not leave you comfortless: I will come to you. Jn. 14:18.

The Aramaic text reads: "I will not leave you orphans or bereaved." Orphanages and other institutions for the poor are unknown in most areas of the Near East. The destitute are left to roam the streets and seek livelihood by begging and servitude. When a man dies, his family becomes disorganized. His widow returns to her father's home or seeks work. The children are left to the mercy of his relatives or they will have to fend for themselves in the streets.

Jesus was as a father to his disciples. They had trusted his

---

[3]See 2 Ki. 2:9.

counsel and judgment. He shared with them what he received from people. They feared that his death would not only scatter their material hopes and happiness but that he would leave them orphans and destitute.

Jesus promised to provide for them by entrusting them to the care of his Father. The spirit was to help and guide them. After his death, his disciples were to be more popular and independent. They would stand before governors and kings. The spirit of their lord would tell them what to say. Men and women would sell their possessions and entrust their money to the apostles. They would lack nothing, just as when he was with them.

DISCIPLES NOT BEREAVED

Yet a little while, and the world seeth me no more; but ye see me: because I live, ye shall live also. At that day ye shall know that I am in my Father, and ye in me, and I in you. He that hath my commandments and keepeth them, he it is that loveth me; and he that loveth me shall be loved of my Father, and I will love him, and will manifest myself to him.
Jn 14:19-21.

Jesus spoke of his death, which was to take place soon. Those who did not believe in him would no longer see him. But his disciples would see him again after his triumphant resurrection from death and the grave. Their names would be inscribed in his eternal gospel. The disciples' voices would be heard in strange and unknown tongues, even in the languages of races and people who were not yet born.

All of Jesus' loyal followers who were keeping his commandments would see him in spirit and in truth. Wherever they would go, preaching his gospel of the kingdom, Jesus' spirit would be with them, backing them with power. His spirit would guide them, speak for them before judges, governors and kings. Jesus would never leave them bereaved.

The Aramaic text of verse 20 reads: "And in that day, you will know that I am with my Father, and you are with me and I am with you." The letter "beth" in Aramaic is a preposition and it has many meanings. In this case it does not refer to the preposition "in." It refers to "with."

Jesus told them that he would be with them even until the end of the world. He also told them he would not leave them as orphans. The expression "to be with them" means he would support them in all that they would teach and do to spread the gospel of the kingdom just as the Father had endowed him with authority and power.

LOYALTY TO JESUS

Judas said unto him, not Iscariot, Lord, how is it that thou wilt manifest thyself unto us, and not unto the world. Jesus answered and said unto him, If a man love me, he will keep my words; and my Father will love him, and we will come unto him, and make our abode with him. He that loveth me not keepeth not my sayings: and the word which ye hear is not mine, but the Father's which sent me. Jn 14:22-24.

One of Jesus' disciples, Judah (not the traitor) wondered how Jesus could manifest himself to them and not to the rest of the world. Judah thought in terms of a physical or corporeal manifestation. But, Jesus was referring to a spiritual appearance. That is, he would be seen, felt and even heard from time to time by his disciples and followers, and even by others who did not believe in him yet would be called to preach his gospel. The apostle Paul is a perfect example of one who at first did not believe but then heard from the ascended Christ on the road to Damascus.

Now only those who loved him and kept his commandments and believed in him would see him. The eyes of the world would be closed to his gospel and therefore they could not see him. All these things that Jesus spoke to his disciples were extremely difficult and challenging for them. They could not grasp or understand these spiritual matters at that time. His kind of teaching and commandments were so alien to their simple minds.

PARAQLETA—THE TEACHER

But the Comforter, which is the Holy Ghost, whom the Father will send in my name, he shall teach you all things, and bring all things to your remembrance, whatsoever I have said unto you. Jn. 14:26.

The term paraqleta is an Aramaic word. It is a compound noun: *Praq* means "to save," *porqana*, "salvation," *paroqa*, "savior," and *leta* means "the accursed ones, those who have gone astray from the way of God." (*Leta,* in Aramaic is spelled with the letter *thet*, which is not found in Western alphabets.) Such people in Jesus' day were called the accursed ones because they did not know the law. *Paraqleta*, "Holy Spirit," was to strengthen, comfort and gather the disciples together.[4]

Since the gospel of Jesus Christ reached the Western world through the Greek language, the term *paraqleta* is supposed to be Greek. But we know that the gospel was preached in Aramaic to Aramaic speaking people. *Praq* is an Aramaic verb.

The Greeks borrowed many Aramaic words and changed their form into Greek expressions, just as the English and Germans borrowed hundreds of Latin words, and Latins borrowed from the Greek tongue. But Armenians and Arabs also borrowed this Aramaic word. Arabs used the Aramaic term *porqana* for "salvation;" they call it *porqan*, while the Armenians call it *perqueton*.

The Holy Spirit was to encourage, teach and guide the apostles and their followers, who were soon to be left. They would be comforted by the Spirit for their great loss. The work of the Holy Spirit would recall for the disciples Jesus' teaching and bring understanding to his words. The spirit would also enlighten those who were living in darkness and bring them to the truth of Jesus' gospel of God's kingdom.

---

[4]See p. 175 of the commentary, Part 2, "The Comforter."

THE PEACE OF CHRIST

Peace I leave with you, my peace I give unto you: not as the world giveth, give I unto you, Let not your heart be troubled, neither let it be afraid. Jn. 14:27.

The peace of Jesus is just, sure and everlasting. It is the peace of God that passes all understanding. It is not the kind of conditional and unjust peace that kings and princes of this world offer to one another after one has defeated the other. Such peace does not endure because when the defeated become strong again, they avenge themselves. The peace that the world gives is selfish and only temporary. The Christ peace is free of political and economic interests of this life. This is what makes it just and everlasting. The world has two yardsticks for measuring peace. One is for the victor and the strong and the other is for the weak and vanquished.

Jesus was not only leaving his peace with his disciples to protect them; it was peace of mind and soul, the peace that would make them surrender to God. All the disciples were, sooner or later, to suffer for the sake of the gospel because they had surrendered their bodies and souls to God. Peace in Aramaic is *shlama,* in Hebrew, *shalom*, and in Arabic, *salam,* and it also means "surrender"—that is, "I place everything under the care of God."

God's peace is difficult to understand because when it is in action—that is, actualized—the strong want to make peace with the weak and the great become servants. When people surrender to God's peace they pray for their enemies and bless those who hate them. Such a simple way of life and peace is practical, but challenging, for the proud rulers of this world to accept.

THE FATHER IS GREATER

Ye have heard how I said unto you, I go away, and come again unto you. If ye loved me, ye would rejoice, because I said I go unto the Father: for my Father is greater than I. And now I have told you before it come to pass; that, when it is come to pass, ye might believe. Jn. 14:28-29.

"I go away" means "I will die and come again to you" or "I will rise up again and come back to you." Jesus wanted his disciples to be cheerful because he was going to his Father, who was greater than he. His Father would grant them more power than they now had. And after he had gone, they would perform greater miracles and wonders in his name. The Holy Spirit would open their eyes and inspire them to understand the inner meaning of their lord's teaching.

All Semites honor their fathers regardless of their own position and influence. Jesus here refers to himself as the messenger of God. The Aramaic word *rab*, "great," also means "important, famous." For example *nasha rabba* means "a famous or important man."

Jesus was a humble man. He always referred to himself as "Son of man," meaning "a human being." He did not want people to honor him more than God, his Father. When they asked him certain questions, his reply was, "no one knows, not even the Son but the Father alone." In all circumstances he referred everything to God. This is the thought brought out by Paul, according to the Aramaic text: "Who was in the likeness of God and did not consider this resemblance as something to be grasped, but he emptied himself and took the appearance of a servant and he became in the likeness of men."[5]

Any claim that Jesus might have made to be greater than God or even for him to be God would certainly have caused misunderstanding even among his own followers. He always declared that he was in accord with God, who is greater than he. This is in harmony with Near Eastern thought. A Semitic son of the East reverences his father and considers him more important than himself.

---

[5]Philippians 2:6-7.

POLITICAL AND RELIGIOUS POWERS

Hereafter I will not talk much with you: for the prince of this world cometh, and hath nothing in me. Jn. 14:30.

The "prince of this world," the Roman Emperor, had nothing against Jesus. He had committed no crime and broken no state law. But the princes of this world, the political and religious authorities, were accustomed to persecuting and even putting to death any person who opposed them, regardless of any guilt or crime, just as King Herod did to John the Baptist. Herod had nothing legal against John but had him beheaded to please his wife, Herodia.

The imperial power of Rome had appointed the religious and political powers in Jerusalem, and now those powers were preparing to arrest Jesus, judge him and put him to death. But these authorities also had nothing legal against Jesus. He had not broken a single law of the imperial or Palestinian governments nor any laws of his religion. He was ready to die on the cross so that the world might know that he loved God and humanity. Jesus was an innocent man. He was ready to suffer at the hands of the sinful. As Pilate had said concerning Jesus, he had done nothing worthy of death.

Jesus gave his followers teachings that were contrary to the religious traditions that were taught by the Jewish authorities and government officials. Now Jesus had to pay the price for such teachings.

CHAPTER 15

THE TRUE VINE

I am the true vine, and my Father is the husbandman. Every branch in me that beareth not fruit he taketh away: and every branch that beareth fruit, he purgeth it, that it may bring forth more fruit. Now ye are clean through the word which I have spoken unto you. Jn. 15:1-3.

Part 1—JESUS THE TRUE VINE. In many parts of the Near East vines grow wild. They resemble the cultivated vines, but their grapes are smaller and somewhat bitter. A good vineyard is noted for the quality grapes it produces. A vine is symbolic of a family or a church. The vine has its branches just as a family and church have their members. When good vineyards are neglected or abandoned, the fruit becomes poor in quality and the vine resembles one that is wild and uncultivated.

The prophets declared Israel as God's vineyard. These men of God were husbandmen, but Israel had for many centuries been without prophets and seers. They had lost touch with their spiritual power and were like salt that had lost its savor.

Jesus was to prune this vineyard. He had to remove the dry branches and those that did not bear fruit. He now was the true vine. Those who believed in him were the branches that were to abide with him so that they might bear fruit.

Part 2—ABIDING IN JESUS. As we have said, there were two kinds of vines: the vine that is pruned and produces quality grapes and the wild vine that produces sour grapes. The grape vine must be pruned to stay healthy and produce good grapes. Just as unfruitful branches are cut off, so would the unfaithful be cut off from the life force of the vine.

The same way the branches remain an integral part of the vine so that it may bear fruit, so Jesus' followers must remain loyal to him, i.e., his teaching. They must abide in one another so that they might produce fruits of the spirit

183

The vine and its branches exist and work together and depend on one another for growth and nourishment. But branches that do not draw from the root are cut off and are used for fuel. Jesus' disciples and followers were to remain in him—that is, draw from his spirit and teaching. If they do not abide in the Christ teaching, they actually cut themselves off by not remaining in the truth of his gospel of God's kingdom.

The only condition that Jesus required was that they obey his commandments. By so doing, they would remain in him. Otherwise, his followers would be cut off from the vine that gives nourishment and strength to bear the fruits of the kingdom. Their loyalty to Jesus was to be demonstrated by keeping his word and loving one another.

The spirit strengthens those who bear good fruit. These branches are pruned so that they may produce abundant fruit. Jesus' disciples were pruned through the word that he taught them. Now they were clean and ready to produce abundant fruits of the Spirit.

LOVE ONE ANOTHER

As the Father hath loved me so have I loved you: continue ye in my love. If ye keep my commandments, ye shall abide in my love; even as I have kept my Father's commandments and abide in his love. These things have I spoken unto you, that my joy might remain in you and that your joy might be full. This is my commandment, that ye love one another as I have loved you. Jn. 15:9-12.

One of the last things Jesus wanted to impress on the minds and hearts of his disciples, whom he was soon to leave in this world, was that they love one another. Without love there would be no unity and accord among them; their ranks would quickly weaken and their cause be lost.

Love is the only binding force that can bring people of many races and ideas close to one another. Love is the cement that holds people together and builds God's kingdom. Jesus kept his disciples in his love by caring and nurturing them in the message of the kingdom. He showed his love for them constantly and was ready to die for the truth so that they could carry on his work. He wanted them to follow through on his word that they love one another. By so doing they would have joy and contentment working together.

NOT SERVANTS BUT FRIENDS

Henceforth I call you not servants; for the servant knoweth not what his lord doeth: but I have called you friends; for all things that I have heard of my Father I have made known unto you. Jn. 15:15.

In Syria, Arabia and some other parts of the Near East, the status of a servant is that of a slave. Disciples are also considered servants of their teacher because they obey his commands. Warriors serve and die for their leader. The position of a lord and the respect shown him are much higher than in the West.

Servants and disciples are timid and even afraid in the presence of their master. They serve him very humbly at home or when they travel. Some lords are fond of displaying this authority and power over their servants. They often rebuke and chasten them for no reason, and when they speak of them, they refer to them as servants. For example they say, "My servant is not here." Kindly lords, when addressing their servants, call them "my son" or, at times, "my father." Jesus used the term "friends," and once he called them "my sons."

As rivalry and intrigue are common, most masters hesitate to make their secrets known to their servants. Occasionally when a servant is faithful, his lord makes him overseer and confides all his secrets to him just as Potiphar did with Joseph.[1] Then, there are those teachers who become jealous of their pupils, and artisans of their apprentices. They hide their wisdom and secrets from them, fearing that some day they may become their competitors. A teacher would dislike seeing his disciples knowing more than he, just as a lord

---

[1]See Gen. 39:4.

would not wish to see his servant acquiring a higher position than himself.

Jesus told his disciples everything they could grasp and even some things they could not understand until after his death and resurrection. He taught them to take his place when he was gone. They were not to be his competitors but his heirs. This is the reason he called them friends and not servants.

THE WORLD HATED JESUS

If the world hate you, ye know that it hated me before it hated you. If ye were of this world, the world would love his own; but because ye are not of the world, but I have chosen you out of the world, therefore the world hateth you. Remember the word that I said unto you, The servant is not greater than his lord. If they have persecuted me, they will also persecute you: if they have kept my saying, they will keep yours also. Jn. 15:18-20.

Jesus reminded his disciples that the world would hate them because the world loves evil and hates truth. The adherents to the system of the world do not change easily. They hated Jesus and will hate his disciples.

Jesus' disciples had renounced their citizenship of this world and had become citizens of God's kingdom. The principles that governed them were different from those which govern the world. Therefore, they were no longer of this world and could not remain loyal to the worldly ways. In a short while material interests would vanish from their minds and thoughts. They would begin to think of the new world order to come, the realm of the spirit. The disciples would be absorbed in spreading the gospel of God's kingdom and hope for a better and surer future. These would be their everlasting rewards.

The world would hate them simply because their good life and pious behavior would contradict the lives and wants of the world's system of doing things. Evil attracts evil, and good attracts good and contradicts evil. Jesus reminded them that a servant is not greater than his lord. They would be persecuted and imprisoned because of their new way of life. It was the way of God, which the world does not know because it is beyond its understanding.

SIN EXPOSED

If I had not come and spoken unto them, they had not had sin: but now they have no cloke for their sin. He that hateth me hateth my Father also. If I had not done among them the works which none other man did, they had not had sin: but now have they both seen and hated both me and my Father. But this cometh to pass, that the word might be fulfilled that is written in their law, They hated me without a cause. Jn 15:22-25.

Sin is dormant until the law is revealed and sinful things are pointed out. As long as a man has not been told that certain things are unlawful and wrong to do, he does not break any law by doing them. But when the law says, "Thou shalt do this and not do that," then the transgression becomes operative. That is, that which was dormant and unknown becomes active and known, and that which is evil is classified as an evil so it may be differentiated from good.

Jesus had pinpointed the sins of the religious authorities and the wrongs of some of the people; therefore, their sin was exposed and their guilt would be greater. Now, they would have no excuse. The gospel of God's kingdom had been preached and its power demonstrated, but they had rejected it. Their sin would be greater because they had seen miracles and wonders and had heard the words of truth and light. Yet they had refused to receive the teaching. They had hated him without a cause and had chosen to remain with their blindness and sin.

THE PROMISE OF THE COMFORTER

But when the comforter is come, whom I will send unto you from the Father, even the Spirit of truth, which proceedeth from the Father, he shall testify of me: And ye also shall bear witness, because ye have been with me from the beginning. Jn. 15:26-27.

187

After the resurrection, the Comforter would confirm all the works of Jesus. It was to be through the power of the Holy Spirit that his followers would perform greater miracles and wonders in their master's name. His own disciples would testify of the great works they had seen when they were with him. Now because of the greater things they would witness coming through them from the Spirit, they would become willing to die for his gospel of God's kingdom.

CHAPTER 16

ADMONISHING HIS DISCIPLES

These things have I spoken unto you, that ye should not be offended. They shall put you out of the synagogues; yea, the time cometh, that whosoever killeth you will think that he doeth God service. And these things will they do unto you, because they have not known the Father, nor me. But these things have I told you that when the time shall come, ye may remember that I told you of them. And these things I said not unto you at the beginning, because I was with you. But now I go my way to him that sent me: and none of you asketh me, Wither goest thou? Jn. 16:1-5.

Jesus' disciples had never heard their master speak in such a dark manner before. When he told them about his death, a great many of his followers left him. But now he was soon to leave his faithful disciples bereaved. He knew what would happen to them. So he wanted them to know in advance how the religious authorities and misguided men would treat them and what to expect after his departure. However, he told them all that they were about to face so that their faith might be strengthened in him. For when these things happened they would say to each other, "He forewarned us."

No matter how sorrowful these things were and how dark the future might be, he let them know that it was better for them to know everything ahead of time so that later no one would say, "he had deceived us." The leaders of this world make alluring promises to the people, but they hardly ever follow through with them; therefore, people lose faith in them.

Jesus was up front and unequivocal with his disciples. He told them the truth. Their task would not be easy, for it would be fraught with dangers and persecution. In the final outcome, many of them would carry their own crosses and drink from the same bitter cup as he.

189

TRUTH

Nevertheless I tell you the truth: It is expedient for you that I go away: for if I go not away, the Comforter will not come unto you; but if I depart I will send him unto you. Jn 16:7.

The Aramaic word for "truth" is *shrara*. It derives from *sharar*, meaning "to sustain and affirm." While conversing with one another, Near Easterners often exaggerate their compliments to each other. At times what they say is in the form of a joke. During heated debates, they try to contradict or convince each other. Thus the word "truth" is frequently used so that their statements to one another may carry conviction. However, the expression "I tell you the truth" means "what I am telling you is true and not a joke or an exaggeration but something that I can sustain." When such a remark is made there is no further argument. The matter is closed.

Jesus' disciples had frequently heard their master teach in parables and figures of speech. When he spoke of his death, they did not take it seriously because Semites often speak of their death with no intention of dying soon. They say to each other, "I'll die for you," but this a mere pleasantry and no one takes it seriously.

Jesus knew it was difficult for his disciples to think of a suffering Messiah/Christ because they had been taught that the Messiah would be a great conqueror. Therefore, he wanted to impress on their minds that he had to die so that he could accomplish his mission. Jesus used the expression "I tell you the truth," or its equivalent "Truly, truly," whenever he wanted to emphasize the seriousness of his utterances.

Jesus also wanted his disciples to know that if he stayed with them, they would continue to rely on him for preaching, healing and teaching. Once he had gone, they would rely on the Holy Spirit so that the things he had done they would do also. The spirit of truth would guide them, strengthen their souls and give them power to speak, teach and heal. The Holy Spirit would also, through the disciples, reprove the world for not believing in the way of humility and meekness which was Jesus' gospel.

190

Jesus had to leave this world. It was imperative in order for his disciples and followers to come to the realization that death is not an end but the beginning of a new life. And, how they lived their lives on earth would give them power of victory over the grave and the sting of death.

HOLY SPIRIT REBUKING WORLD

And when he is come, he will reprove the world of sin, and of righteousness, and of judgment: Jn. 16:8.

The Aramaic word *ruha,* "spirit," also means "expansion." In this verse of scripture, the writer uses it in the sense of effectiveness. Jesus spoke of a hidden power that was to come and confirm his work.

There were many things that Jesus did not wish to explain or discuss, but he assured his disciples that certain matters would be revealed in the near future. His followers had not reached the point where they could see things spiritually; they still understood things literally. They had to come into a greater awareness before the Spirit could commune with them. The Spirit was there, but it was unknown to them.

"If I do not go, the Spirit will not come" means that if he did not die, they would not see spiritually. The Spirit could not reveal matters to them. The disciples were relying on Jesus totally. After his death, they were to be comforted by his spirit and the influence he was leaving behind in their minds and hearts.

The Spirit would reprimand the political and religious authorities of sin because they had rejected him—that is, his teaching. They deliberately continued to live in moral bondage. He would reprove them of righteousness because they crucified him unjustly and of judgment because the princes of this world were already condemned for their unjust ways.

The new kingdom was established and the new king inaugurated on the cross. The power of men had come to an end. Political and

191

religious leaders were to face final judgment, and the new era of justice and truth under the guidance of the Spirit was to begin.

THE SPIRIT OF TRUTH

I have yet many things to say unto you, but ye cannot bear them now. Howbeit when he, the Spirit of truth is come, he will guide you into all truth; for he shall not speak of himself: but whatsoever he shall hear, that shall he speak: and he will shew you things to come. Jn. 16:12-13.

It was very challenging and difficult for Jesus to explain everything to his uneducated disciples before his death and resurrection. The Jews were taught that the Messiah would live forever; therefore, it was hard for the disciples to reconcile what he had told them with what they had been taught for years.

But after his death and resurrection, things would be different. The fear of death would be dispelled. Death's secrets would be revealed, the grave unveiled and evil powers exposed. They would see him alive again. The spirit of truth would teach them and confirm their faith in their risen master. Then they would understand more fully what he had said to them while he was with them.

When he told them, "A little while and you shall not see me," they did not understand what he meant. How could they believe that the one who had raised the dead, opened the eyes of the blind and unstopped the ears of the deaf, would be put to death? They were simple-minded and they did not understand the hidden and inner meaning of Scripture.

IMPENDING SORROWS

Verily, verily, I say unto you, That ye shall weep and lament, but the world shall rejoice: and ye shall be sorrowful, but your sorrow shall be turned into joy. A woman when she is in travail hath sorrow, because her hour is come, but as soon as she is delivered of the child, she remembereth

192

no more the anguish for joy that a man child is born into the world. And ye now therefore have sorrow: but I will see you again, and your heart shall rejoice, and your joy no man taketh from you. Jn. 16:20-22.

Part 1—A SORROWFUL TIME. Jesus plainly told his disciples that they were soon to weep over him, but the rest of the world would rejoice over his suffering and death. The princes of the world had hated him and rejected his teachings.

But Jesus assures his disciples that their sorrow will in a little while turn into joy. In due time, his disciples will forget their sorrow and see him alive once more. Jesus was to triumph over death, and the victory of his gospel of the kingdom would make them forget their temporary defeat.

Part 2—A MALE CHILD. In olden times and in some areas of the Near East today, the birth of girls was not welcomed. Expectant mothers are always anxious and nervous because they want to give birth to a male child. The news of a male birth often strengthens the relationship between a wife and her husband. On the other hand, failure to give birth to a baby boy can result in separation and divorce. Sometimes women who have no male children are hated by their husbands.

When a woman gives birth to a female child, the news is kept from the mother, especially if she is in serious condition. If it is a boy the mother is informed immediately. The good news cheers and helps her. She rejoices exceedingly because she gains favor in her husband's eyes. No longer will she be reproached by her neighbors for not having a male child.[1]

Male children are very important in Near Eastern families because men are always engaged in wars and revolutions, and women could not inherit property. If a man should die leaving a wife and five girls, his estate goes to his nearest male relative and his family is left destitute. In some Near Eastern countries, the birth of a girl is greeted with sorrow and tears by the grief-stricken mother and her friends.

---

[1]See Gen. 35:17.

193

Sometimes a black piece of cloth is placed on the door as a sign of mourning. The birth of a boy is regarded as a good omen and is welcomed with joy, merry-making and lavish banquets. Food is distributed to the poor and offerings made at shrines. The whole community joins in welcoming the newborn boy.

The sudden trial and crucifixion of Jesus were to create fear, distress and great loss for his followers, but they were soon to be cheered by the good news of the resurrection, just as women are cheered by the birth of a male child.

IN THAT DAY

And in that day, ye shall ask me nothing. Verily, verily, I say unto you, Whatsoever ye shall ask the Father in my name, he will give it you. Hitherto have ye asked nothing in my name: ask, and ye shall receive, that your joy may be full. Jn. 16:23-24.

Until this time, the disciples had relied on Jesus for their clothes, food and other necessities. People who came to be healed brought gifts of food or money. The disciples' needs were met abundantly. They did not have ask for anything.

The term "in that day" refers to the day of separation. Jesus, after his triumph over death and *sheol*, was to ascend to his Father. His disciples no longer would be able to depend on him as the healer and teacher who provided them with their material needs. Now they were to ask God in Jesus' name—that is, according to his method. The disciples were to pray to God in the way Jesus had taught them. They also would heal the sick and perform miracles and wonders.

God as a Father supplies the needs of his children day by day. They were not to worry about what they would eat or with what they would clothe their bodies. Their Father in heaven would supply these needs just as God supplies the needs of other creatures and clothes the flowers and birds with glory and majesty.

The disciples were to depend on God. Their lord had shown them the way. In addition to this, Jesus' spirit was to be with them

194

always. He would guide them in his truth and grant them courage to withstand the trials and difficulties that were ahead of them.

DESERTION

Behold, the hour cometh, yea, is now come, that ye shall be scattered, every man to his own, and shall leave me alone: and Yet I am not alone, because the Father is with me. Jn. 16:32.

When a leader surrenders himself willingly, his followers flee. His safety largely depends on their actions and behavior. Any resistance on their part would endanger his life. On the other hand, when a leader is seized by force, his followers fight to the last and lay down their lives for him.

Jesus had constantly predicted his arrest, humiliation and death in Jerusalem. He had willingly come to Jerusalem to die without resistance. His departure from his messianic mission as a king was puzzling for his disciples. Some of them were armed and ready to lay down their lives for him. However, some others deserted him on his way to Jerusalem. Still others were discouraged by Judas' revolt and the cold reception given Jesus by the authorities of Jerusalem. They reluctantly and fearfully followed him to Gethsemane.

They were almost convinced that their lord would surrender and the only thing for them to do was flee and await the outcome. They thought that he would probably be arrested, rebuked, chastised and released, as was often done to religious teachers who were condemned as heretics. None of them believed he would be sent to the cross. There had been rumors of his arrest but no serious charges to justify capital punishment. This is the reason they allowed the guards to seize him. Had they known he would be crucified, they would have fought to the finish. The high priests and soldiers understood the character of these warlike Galileans, and so they were well armed for the occasion.

Jesus' faith in his Father was stronger than that of his followers'. He would not be alone because God would always be with him. As

195

long as Jesus was with his disciples, they had peace of mind and felt secure. When he was arrested, they scattered. Nevertheless, he knew his Father would not forsake him but would stand by him through his trials, beatings and crucifixion. God would vindicate his unjust death.

CHAPTER 17

PRAYER FOR DISCIPLES

These words spake Jesus and lifted up his eyes to heaven, and said, Father, the hour is come: glorify thy Son, that thy Son also may glorify thee: As thou hast given him power over all flesh, that he should give eternal life to as many as thou hast given him. Jn 17:1-2.

Jesus' entire prayer (verses 1-26) was for his disciples, for those who would believe in him through his disciples, and for all those who would come after them. It was a prayer for men and women who would leave their families, fields, houses, synagogues and even risk their lives for the sake of his teaching. His disciples and followers would need strength and courage in the dark hour of tribulation.

This prayer was not for the worldly rulers who had rejected him and his teaching and who were about to condemn and put him to death. It was too late for these people to change. They made their decision and were determined to do away with Jesus and his gospel.

The only thing Jesus could do for his disciples and followers was to entrust them to God, his Father, who had sent him. For only God had power over the princes of this world.

LIFE ETERNAL

And this is life eternal, that they might know thee the only true God, and Jesus Christ, whom thou hast sent. Jn. 17:3.

According to this part of the prayer, the only way to secure everlasting life is to believe that God is the only true God and that there is none other. Also one must believe in Jesus the Christ, whom God had sent to bring people to the way of God. Moses declared that there is only one God: "Hear O Israel, the Lord our God is one Lord"[1]

To believe in Jesus Christ is to believe in his gospel of the kingdom, justice, love, harmony and peace. This was his way or religion. All other ways and philosophies that people sought as a means of salvation were misleading or destructive. Jesus had been leading people to the way and truth that God had revealed and given to the Hebrew prophets.

DEDICATION

And for their sakes I sanctify myself, that they also might be sanctified through the truth. Jn. 17:19.

The Aramaic and Hebrew word *kadish* means "to set aside for a purpose." Things that were called holy and sacred were things that were set aside as a portion which belonged to God and could not be touched. For example, the ark of the covenant was so holy—that is, set aside—that no one could touch it. (See 2 Samuel 6:6-7, the story of Uzzah and the ark of God.) A holy man is one who has surrendered the material things of this world and dedicated himself to God.

Jesus had dedicated his life to the truth that he was teaching to the Jewish people. The task was so great that he had to devote all of his time, strength and mind to the work that was ahead of him. He had tutored his disciples to follow his way of life, to put God's truth first in their lives, and if necessary to die for it.

Jesus had accomplished a tremendous mission through the power of God. His disciples needed the same power so that they could undertake the mission for which he had prepared them. As a master-teacher, he knew that if the world hated him, the world would also hate his disciples. If the leaders of this world were soon to crucify him, they would crucify his followers also.

Every great and difficult task in this world can be accomplished

---

[1] Deut. 6:4, Mk. 12:29.

if the person who undertakes the work is willing to sanctify himself and even to give this life for it if called upon to do so. True sanctification means one must put God first and love God with all one's mind, heart and strength. When we love God, we love the whole world. When we love just our interests in this life, our life is cut off from its eternal, universal source.

UNITY IS ESSENTIAL

That they all may be one; as thou, Father, art in me, and I in thee, that they also may be one in us; that the world may believe that thou hast sent me. Jn.17:21.

The Aramaic preposition *bee* means "with me" or "by me." It is a term used for one who stands by another. Jesus did not mean that he was *in* his disciples and they were *in* him, but that he would stand by them as his Father stood by him.

He urged them to be of one accord just as he and his Father were of one accord. He prayed for them that they might become perfected in their relationship with one another and live in unity so that the world might see what his mission was all about.

The success of Jesus' gospel of God's kingdom depended on the harmony and unity of his disciples and their followers. He was leaving them in the world and everything was in their keeping. They were to be unified so that they could withstand and triumph over opposing evil forces. Discord would disrupt the progress of the gospel and delay its work, as it actually has done.

GLORY

And the glory which thou gavest me I have given them: that they may be one, even as we are one: Jn. 17:22.

Jesus' name was glorified by all classes of people because of the

199

miracles and wonders that he performed. He raised the dead, opened the eyes of the blind and healed the sick. People honored and praised him.

Jesus had assured his disciples that they would do greater things than they had seen him do if they would strictly adhere to his method and approach to God. Jesus had disclosed everything to his disciples. He knew they would be glorified—that is, praised and honored—just as he was glorified by the people for the good works he had done. The disciples would do the same works as their master. People would sing songs of praise to their names.

In the Near East, most religious teachers, magicians and philosophers claim that they are the ones who understand the deeper things of life. They are so proud of themselves that they seldom share their glory with their students or even promise them that they will be able to do greater things.

Jesus is credited with saying, "No student is greater than his master." However, we are inclined to believe that a scribe put these words on the lips of Jesus in the text. Many students have surpassed their teachers. For example, we have surpassed Benjamin Franklin, Alexander Graham Bell, Thomas Edison and many other inventors and teachers. Americans who walked on the moon wrought the greatest wonder in world history. Even to this day many Near Easterners are guided by past writings of ancient teachers of religion, not realizing that each day gives birth to new ideas that were not known yesterday. Scientists of centuries ago would not even be qualified to enroll in classes today.

Jesus knew that his disciples would do greater things than he had done. Through their teaching, a new and better world order would be instituted. He knew distances would be conquered and his gospel of the kingdom would be written in hundreds of languages and preached to many nations. During Jesus' life his teaching was spreading throughout Galilee, Samaria and Judea, but his apostles made it known world wide.

JESUS PROMISES A PLACE

Father, I will that they also, whom thou hast given me, be with me where I am; that they may behold my glory, which thou hast given me: for thou lovedst me before the foundation of the world. Jn. 17:24.

This reference is to life hereafter. The prayer implies that God would grant a place in the heavenly kingdom for those who had accepted Jesus, believed in him and left everything. These disciples and followers had been called and guided by God to follow Jesus. Therefore, "to be where he is" means to be in heaven, a spiritual dimension, so that his disciples might see his glory and know how God loved him before the world was created.

In the Near East, a good lord who loves his faithful servants always sees that they are treated as he is; they sleep where he sleeps and eat what he eats. This prayer was meant to comfort his disciples and followers.

GOD'S NATURE REVEALED

And I have declared unto them thy name, and will declare it: that the love wherewith thou hast loved me may be in them, and I in them. Jn. 17:26.

The Aramaic text reads: "And I have made thy name known to them, and I am still making it known, so that the love with which thou hast loved me may be among them, and I be with them."[2]

The Jewish people reverenced their God, just as people around them feared their deities. All of the pagan gods and goddesses, as well as the God of the Jews, had mysterious names and their natures were unknown to the people. All were in awe when they stood in the presence of the gods in the temples.

Jesus, in his teaching, gave his disciples and followers a new concept of the true nature of God. He revealed to them a God who is

---

[2]Jn. 17:26, Aramaic Peshitta text, Lamsa translation.

loving and who cares for the people: a God who forgives their iniquities, heals their sicknesses and binds up their wounds. For centuries, this true concept of God was lost. The loving shepherd of Israel had to be appeased by means of sacrifices, drink and cereal offerings that the priests themselves consumed. This new concept given by Jesus was contrary to that of the priests and scribes who were the interpreters of holy Scripture.

Jesus was continuously revealing the true God of Abraham and the prophets to his disciples. He did this to show them that just as God had loved him, so should this same love be among his disciples. Jesus' followers were to love one another.

Through his love for his disciples, Jesus would constantly be with them. Love is supreme and never dies. Love is the cohesive force that binds people together because God is love.

CHAPTER 18

JESUS ARRESTED

When Jesus had spoken these words, he went forth with his disciples over the brook Cedron, where was a garden, into the which he entered, and his disciples. And Judas also, which betrayed him, knew the place: for Jesus ofttimes resorted thither with his disciples. Judas then, having received a band of men and officers from the chief priests and Pharisees, cometh thither with lanterns and torches and weapons. Jesus therefore, knowing all things that should come upon him went forth, and said unto them, Whom seek ye? They answered him, Jesus of Nazareth. Jesus saith unto them I am he. And Judas also, which betrayed him, stood with them. Jn. 18:1-5.

The rank and file of the Jewish people had never seen Jesus. The high priests, learned men and members of the Council may have had a glimpse of him when he addressed some of the people on the temple grounds, but they paid little attention to the prophet from Galilee. They had seen and sought remedies for their ills from other teachers, preachers and leaders who, from time to time, addressed the people.

Jesus' work had been limited to the common people, tax gatherers and sinners—people whom the religious authorities called the unlearned and scum of the earth. That is why the Council paid Judas thirty pieces of silver, a good sum of money, so that he could point out his master.

CONFRONTING THE ENEMY

As soon then as he had said unto them, I am he, they went backward, and fell to the ground. Jn. 18:6.

When enemies confront each other suddenly, they immediately fall back to hold positions. Some fall on the ground for protection. Others seek shelter behind large rocks and trees until they are ready

203

to fight.

Judas had heard Jesus tell his disciples to buy swords. He undoubtedly took the saying literally and warned the priests and temple guards that his master and his Galilean disciples would offer resistance. Simon Peter carried a sword with him, probably for cutting wood and meat and as a means of protection from wild animals.

The guards saw Peter ready with his sword. They feared that the other disciples would suddenly attack, so they fell back a short distance to arm and protect themselves. This is the reason they fell to the ground, but when they heard Jesus rebuking Peter and commanding him to put up his sword, they immediately made the arrest.

THE HIGH PRIEST

And led him away to Annas first: for he was father in law to Caiaphas, which was the high priest that same year. Jn. 18:13.

The Aaronic high priesthood was hereditary. Even though the high priest's jurisdiction was over religious matters, he also exerted a great influence in political and social affairs. This type of priesthood still exists among Assyrian Christians, where patriarchs and bishops who do not marry are succeeded by their nephews.[1]

In the period of the Judges, Eli the high priest was also ruler over Israel. He was succeeded by Samuel; the office was never held thereafter by a prophet.

During the reign of David when the kingdom was strongly established, priests had sole jurisdiction over religious affairs. In the reign of Solomon, the priesthood was highly organized and the office of high priest was important. This was largely due to the Temple and its rich revenues. Rivalry between kings and priests broke out from

---

[1]The past patriarch of the Church of the East was Mar Eshai Shimun XXI, Catholicos Patriarch of the East. He was the twenty-first succeeding patriarch of his family, a line of succession for over 600 years.

time to time. Jealousy and usurpation of power were shown by both sides. At times kings removed priests and appointed new ones. Sometimes priests accused rulers and initiated rebellions, as when Jehoiada overthrew Athaliah and proclaimed Josiah as King.[2]

The Aaronic priesthood continued unbroken until the Babylonian captivity when the temple was destroyed and Judah was taken to Babylon in 486 BCE. It was reestablished by Ezra and Nehemiah. During the Greek conquest of Syria, the priesthood was again disorganized. Simon, the founder of the Hasmonean dynasty, became the ruler and high priest. His successors were also invested with the same authority. The welding of these two offices was necessary for the solidarity of the nation so that they could withstand pagan invaders.

When the Romans conquered Palestine, they succeeded in weakening the Jewish ranks by appointing rival high priests who had restricted temporal jurisdiction. These men were selected from candidates not because of moral character but because they favored the Roman government and did not oppose high taxation. Although the Mosaic law required only one high priest for life, there were times when there were two rival high priests. (Compare what happened in the Roman Church during what is known as the Babylonian captivity when there were two rival popes.)

The office of high priest was often sold to the highest bidder and not given to a man of merit. This practice used to be followed in Near Eastern countries that were ruled by Europeans. Religious authorities not in accord with the prevailing government were deposed and others appointed in their place.

In the time of Jesus, the high priest had some temporal authority, but it was limited to Judea. Had Jesus belonged to the province of Judea, he would have been stoned, but he was a Galilean arrested in Jerusalem. The priests had no authority over Galilee, which was under Herod. But the Roman procurator had authority over all territories ruled by native kings or princes. This was the reason the

---

[2]See 2 Ki. 11:13-21.

high priest had to go to Pilate for permission. Pilate was willing to let Jesus be tried by the Jews, but when he found that he was from Galilee, he immediately sent him to Herod.

JESUS TO DIE INSTEAD OF THE PEOPLE

Now Caiaphas was he, which gave counsel to the Jews, that it was expedient that one man should die for the people. Jn. 18:14.

The Aramaic text reads: "It is better for one man to die instead of the people."[3] The priests were afraid that Jesus' acts and words might cause sedition. His messianic claims had already enlisted on his side the peasant population of Galilee and the neighboring country. They had tried to make him a king, and there was fear of an uprising.

The Romans had already crushed several revolutionary attempts in Galilee, causing the massacre not only of the participants in the revolt but also of their sympathizers. Such political disturbances usually ended with the death of the leaders and the massacre of their supporters. The high priests and leaders of the Jews were anxious to avoid mishaps. Hence they decided that it was better to put Jesus to death and lose one man rather than exposing thousands to danger and death at the hands of the Romans. They did not want to chance having their country taken away from them.

Jesus was put to death so that the country and the Jewish people might avoid a revolution and disaster. But his death had a different meaning and intention. It was to save Jew and Gentile from the power of sin and evil. The cross would reveal that violence is not the answer to humanity's ills. It was to give humanity a new hope and a new way of living. His death was meant to bring peace to the entire human family.

---

[3]Jn. 18:14, Aramaic Peshitta text, Lamsa translation.

JESUS' TEACHING SUSPECTED

The high priest then asked Jesus of his disciples, and of his doctrine.
Jn. 18:19.

Since Jesus was a Galilean, the high priests and others in authority, who belonged to the state of Judea, felt that his teachings were suspect. Although Galileans were members of the Jewish faith, the Jews in the south regarded them as Gentiles. Galilee was inhabited largely by Gentiles, such as Assyrians and Syrians. The Jewish religious authorities were suspicious of the Galilean notions and traditions and afraid that foreign teaching might corrupt their faith. Many Jews were influenced by Roman civilization, and the tendency among them was toward modernization. The priests were aware of the danger and suspicious of alien influences.

The high priest wanted to know more about Jesus and his gospel from eyewitnesses and others who were familiar with his teaching. These teachings were doubtless misrepresented by his enemies, who confused their purpose and placed them in a misleading context. For instance, when he spoke of the destruction of the temple and his rebuilding in three days, he was referring to his body; however, the Jews thought that he meant the temple in Jerusalem.[4] Then the notion that he was the son of God was interpreted in a pagan manner. Pagan gods had wives, concubines and children.

The high priest was convinced that Jesus was influenced by the pagan religions of Syria, which had many adherents in Galilee. Doubtless, this notion was due to the fact that Jesus had preached more frequently in Galilee than in Judea. It is evident that the high priests were ignorant of the actual teaching of Jesus. Naturally, they treated the whole matter at first as having only local significance and not of sufficient importance to command their attention. But now the situation had changed.

---

[4]See Jn. 2:19-20 and comments in Chapter 2, "Destroy This Temple," "A Spiritual not a Structural Temple," pp. 38-41.

STRUCK ON THE CHEEK

And when he had thus spoken, one of the officers which stood by struck Jesus with the palm of his hand saying, Answerest thou the high priest so? Jn. 18:22.

The Aramaic text reads: ". . . struck Jesus on his cheek." This is in accord with Near Easter custom. When people fight they strike one another on the cheek. When a man is punished for a minor offense, he is struck on the cheek. In the same way, pupils are punished by their teachers and soldiers by their officers. In the case of grievous offenses, the victim is punished by scourging on the back. This guard was standing by Jesus when he replied to the high priest.

DEFILED IN PASSOVER WEEK

Then led they Jesus from Caiaphas unto the hall of judgment: and it was early; and they themselves went not into the judgment hall, lest they should be defiled; but that they might eat the passover. Jn. 18:28.

It is an established custom among Near Eastern Christians not to touch any unclean thing or to converse with a heretic soon after they have taken Holy Communion. Some strict Assyrian Christians would not talk with a Moslem or a Jew during Holy Week. Moslems likewise have their restrictions. In case one is touched even by accident, he has to make a new ablution and prayer then begins all over again.

The Passover was celebrated on Thursday, but to the Jews the entire week was holy, just as Holy Week is so regarded by Christians. The Jews would not enter the Praetorium for fear of being touched by Pilate's Gentile servants. On such occasions, the Jews generally remained exclusively at home. But this was an emergency, and they had to take Jesus to Pilate to have him crucified before Saturday. Yet, at the same time, they had to take precautions and not be defiled by touching any Gentiles, even accidentally.

CAPITAL PUNISHMENT

Then said Pilate unto them, Take ye him, and judge him according to your law. The Jews therefore said unto him, It is not lawful for us to put any man to death: Jn. 18:31.

Crucifixion as a capital punishment was a Roman and not a Jewish custom. The Jews stoned their victim and then hung the dead body on a tree to expose the crime.[5] Although the Jewish authorities were under Rome, they had some authority to inflict capital punishment on men convicted of blasphemy or heresy, as seen in the case of Stephen.[6]

This is the reason Pilate reminded them of their right to judge a prisoner according to their own law. At first the charge against Jesus was religious, but this was outside the sphere of the Roman governor, who had jurisdiction only over political matters. Then, the charge was shifted from blasphemy against their God to treason against Caesar.

Crucifixion was inflicted by the Romans chiefly on their Gentile subjects. Jesus was a Galilean; therefore, he expected to die on the cross instead of by stoning.

THE PRAETORIUM

Then Pilate entered into the judgment hall again, and called Jesus, and said unto him, Art thou the King of the Jews? Jn. 18:33.

The Aramaic text reads: "Then Pilate entered the Praetorium." Praetorium is the Latin name for the residence of Roman generals. This name was also given to the tent where the general lived during campaigns. The newly conquered countries and turbulent regions were ruled by Roman generals who were appointed procurators by the emperor. Their chief functions were to collect revenues, suppress

---

[5]See Lev. 24:14-16; Deut. 21:22-23.
[6]Acts 7:59.

209

rebellions and administer justice. Lesser duties were assigned to native kings and princes, who ruled under the authority of the governor general, appointed directly by the emperor.

Cases of high treason, which required the death penalty, were always referred to the procurator, who decided them himself or referred them to the governor general, who resided in Antioch, the capital of Syria. Roman citizens had the privilege of appealing even to the emperor, who was the supreme ruler, as was done by the apostle Paul, who was a Roman citizen. He was entitled to be tried before Caesar. [7]

Pilate was procurator over Judea, whose capital was Jerusalem. Galilee and other regions were under other Roman governors, who were responsible to the governor general. Pilate's palace is now an Armenian monastery. The building and courtyards resemble old Turkish and Roman palaces. The edifice has a large courtyard in the center and is surrounded by buildings with open porches. Some of these structures were doubtless occupied by the governor's staff and other buildings were for receptions and meetings.

THOU SAYEST

Jesus answered him, Sayest thou this thing of thyself or did others tell it thee of me? Jn. 18:33-34.

The Aramaic phrase *at amarat,* "you say that," means "You say that I am a king or have others told you falsely concerning me?" What Jesus was saying was this: "But I have not said it. If I were a king my servants would have fought for me and I would not have been delivered into the hands of these religious authorities. These men are demanding my life. They are waiting outside with knives and staves. How can I be a king to these people? To this end I was born and for this cause came I into the world, that I should bear witness to the truth. I am to suffer for the sake of the truth." The Aramaic word

---

[7]See Acts 25:11.

for "yes" is *aen* and for "no" is *la*. Jesus used neither of these words and placed the responsibility for decision on the governor.

The answer was so emphatic in its denial of a political kingdom that Pilate immediately realized the charge made against Jesus was false. The man who was standing before him did not possess the characteristics and demeanor of an earthly king or of one who aspired to such a position. His own people and the high priests had delivered him and their charges about taxation and rebellion were trumped up.

Pilate, therefore, sought to release him. He saw that the whole affair was a religious controversy between Jesus and the Pharisees and priests and had nothing to do with political claims. This is the reason Pilate asked the Jews to judge him in their own way. The government had no interest in religious matters.

THE SPIRITUAL KINGDOM

Jesus answered, My kingdom is not of this world: if my kingdom were of this world, then would my servants fight, that I should not be delivered to the Jews: But now is my kingdom not from hence. Jn. 18:36.

Readers of the Bible often misunderstand the term "kingdom." Some students of Scripture believe that the kingdom of heaven will be like the kingdom on earth, with soldiers and officials occupying high government seats.

In Aramaic, "kingdom" means "counsel." Therefore, the Kingdom of God means "God's counsel." The kingdom that the prophets and Jesus had envisioned is a realm governed only by God's counsel. When God's kingdom comes into full manifestation, our lives will be ruled by God and all evil forces will cease.

Jesus was accused of having proclaimed himself the political leader of Israel and heir of the Davidic kingdom, the Messiah/Christ. When Pilate asked him if he were a king, Jesus was able to satisfy the Roman governor with one sentence. Jesus said to him, "Do you say this yourself or have others told it to you concerning me?"

211

WHAT IS THIS TRUTH?

Pilate therefore said unto him, Art thou a king then? Jesus answered, Thou sayest that I am a king. To this end was I born and for this cause came I into the world, that I should bear witness unto the truth. Everyone that is of the truth heareth my voice. Pilate saith unto him, What is truth? And when he had said this, he went out again unto the Jews, and saith unto them, I find in him no fault at all. Jn. 18:37-38.

Jesus, prior to his entry into the holy city, knew that he would suffer death on the cross. He knew that he would be rejected by those in power in Jerusalem and be betrayed by one of his own disciples, arrested, judged and condemned to die.

But Jesus also knew that the cross and the crown were his destiny of victory. The Hebrew prophets had foreseen his rejection and death. The cross was the only means whereby he could change the sword into meekness and hatred into love and thus save humankind. His death on the cross was to reveal to humanity a new way of living, a way of meekness and love.

Naturally, Jesus' humanness wanted to escape the horrible death, but his spirit was aware that crucifixion was his destiny. Scripture must be fulfilled and death must be given a new meaning. A few days later, when Jesus stood before Pilate in the judgment hall, he said to the governor that he had come into the world to bear witness concerning the truth—that is, suffer for the sake of the truth.

While he was on the cross Jesus cried out: "O God, O God, for this purpose you have kept [spared] me."[8] Peter in his first epistle says: "Who [Jesus Christ] verily was foreordained for this very purpose before the foundation of the world, and was manifest in these last times for your sakes."[9] Jesus had said: "Now my soul is dis-

---

[8]See Mt. 27:46; Mk. 15:34, Lamsa translation. See also Errico and Lamsa, *Aramaic Light on the Gospel of Matthew*, "Jesus' Triumphant Cry," pp. 346-352, and *Aramaic Light on the Gospels of Mark and Luke*, "Jesus' Death Foretold," Parts 1-3, pp. 90-96.

[9]1 Pet. 1:20, Aramaic Peshitta text, Lamsa translation.

turbed, and what shall I say? O my Father, deliver me from this hour; but for this cause I came to this very hour."[10]

Part 2—TRUTH. In his answer to Pilate's question, "Art thou a king then," Jesus pointed out that he was not an earthly king but had come to suffer on the cross for the sake of the gospel of the kingdom of God in which he was the king. Pilate then understood that Jesus had no political aspirations and that the accusations against him were based on religious prejudices.

"What is this truth?" as the Aramaic text renders the words means "What is your religious belief and what do you represent?" The governor was aware of the hostile rivalries between the Jewish sects of the Pharisees, Sadducees and Essenes. He did not wait for an answer. There was no need to examine Jesus' views. These were matters for the Jews to settle among themselves and not for the Roman procurator. Therefore, when he went out of the palace, he told the Jews: "I have examined him and find no fault in him." Jesus was no political leader but a spiritual king to rule in the hearts of nations and races everywhere.

---

[10]Jn. 12:27, Aramaic Peshitta text, Lamsa translation.

CHAPTER 19

JESUS SCOURGED

Then Pilate therefore took Jesus, and scourged him. Jn. 19:1.

The Aramaic text tells us that Pilate "had him scourged." This is more in accord with the custom. High government officials never punish people themselves. They give orders to soldiers or servants to inflict punishment. Some officials refuse even to be present when the victim is whipped. This was a soldier's task and not one that a governor should perform. It would be a disgrace for one of high position even to smite a criminal in public. Some would become unclean by touching a condemned individual.

PILATE HAD NO POWER

Jesus answered, Thou couldest have no power at all against me, except it were given thee from above: therefore he that delivered me unto thee hath the greater sin. Jn 19:11.

"He that delivered me unto thee hath the greater sin" refers to the high priest, for it was he who turned Jesus over to Pilate. Therefore, his sin was greater than Pilate's and that of the men who were to crucify Jesus. The high priest had access to Scripture, but the governor was not acquainted with Jewish theology. In the eyes of the high priest, Jesus was guilty and must, therefore, be put to death. But Pilate thought otherwise. The high priest and the members of the Council who had instigated his arrest, judgment and death were the guilty ones. The rest of the Jews in Jerusalem and provinces, except for the unruly crowds, were innocent.

Jesus could have escaped earlier but he chose not to flee. His death on the cross was predicted by the Hebrew prophets. Jesus had to die to reveal the power of God over death and to open humanity's eyes to the workings of sin and evil forces.

Pilate was a military governor. He had to comply with imperial policy and the wishes of the people over whom he was ruling or answer to the emperor. According to Jesus, God had given the authority to Pilate. The cross was inevitable. The apostle Simon Peter says it was preordained from the foundation of the world that the Messiah/Christ must suffer these things.

GABBATHA

When Pilate therefore heard that saying, he brought Jesus forth, and sat down in the judgment seat in a place that is called the Pavement, but in the Hebrew, Gabbatha. Jn. 19:13.

The Semitic word *gab-batha* is an Aramaic compound noun: *gab* means "side; *betha* or *batha* means "house." *Gabbatha* means "on the side of the house."

Nearly every Near Eastern house has a place at its entrance where people sit down. It is about three feet high and three feet wide and constructed of large stones. This is where Eli, the high priest, was seated when he heard the bad news that the ark of the covenant was captured by the enemy. The news was so startling that he fell off the seat backward and broke his neck.[1]

On important occasions gatherings of people are addressed from this place by speakers who sit on the *gab-batha* as a platform. At the homes of the rich and of government officials, it is also used as a resting place by servants and soldiers.

This was the last appearance of Pilate in defense of Jesus. The Jews usually entered the palace and the judgment hall, but at this time, the crowd had increased and become excited. There was danger of tumult and violence. The governor had already been accused of being lenient toward the man whom the high priests had condemned. It would have been unsafe for Pilate and his household to allow the

---

[1] 1 Sam. 4:18.

frenzied mob to enter the palace. Therefore, he came out and used the *gab-batha* as a platform to address the large crowd that had gathered. He wanted to make his final appeal to them.

THE HOUR OF THE CRUCIFIXION

And it was the preparation of the passover, and about the sixth hour: and he saith unto the Jews, Behold your King! Jn. 19:14.

Part 1—THE HOUR. The authors of the three synoptic gospels (Matthew, Mark and Luke) agree on the hour of the crucifixion, but the author of the fourth gospel does not. John's gospel reads that Jesus was still with Pilate at the sixth hour. "It was Friday of the Passover, and it was about the sixth hour, and he [Pilate] said to the Jews, Behold your king!"[2] The sixth hour would be twelve o'clock. The authors of the other gospels say it was the sixth hour when Jesus was crucified on the cross and darkness fell upon the land. It remained dark until the ninth hour when Jesus cried out and then died.[3]

We must remember that all of Jesus' disciples except John had fled. John was the only one present when Jesus was crucified. The other disciples received their information from others who had been in Jerusalem on that fatal Friday. In those days there were no watches or clocks. Time was measured by the slant of the shadows of the cliffs and trees and the crowing of the cock.

Then, too, Semites were not concerned with exact time. During such a great tragedy, no one would be mindful of time or even care to know the exact hour or minute of the crucifixion. We must realize that all the apostles one way or another agree that it was on Friday, after the Passover. Some of the disciples may have counted the time from the hour when Jesus was delivered to Pilate; others from when he was crucified. Regardless, there is no theological point in this.

---

[2]Aramaic Peshitta text, Lamsa translation.
[3]See Mt. 27:45-46; Mk. 15:33; Lk. 23:44.

216

Part 2—FRIDAY NOT PREPARATION DAY. *Erota* means "weekend day"—that is, Friday. The Jews called it the sixth day. According to Jewish custom, at 6:01 p.m. the Sabbath dawns. The Hebrew week, like the Chaldeans', begins with the first day, Sunday, and ends with the sixth day, Friday. Sabbath, or the seventh day, is the holy day.

According to Mosaic law, bodies of crucified victims must not remain on the crosses on the Sabbath but must be lowered from the cross and buried.

Jesus and his apostles ate the Passover on Thursday and not on Friday as some scholars erroneously teach. This error is caused by the fact that at times Friday is also called the preparation day—that is, preparation for the Sabbath. This is because the Jews cannot cook food or do any other work on the Sabbath.

Jesus died on the cross on Friday. He arose early Sunday morning while it was still dark.[4]

THE HEBREW LANGUAGE

And Pilate wrote a title, and put it on the cross. And the writing was JESUS OF NAZARETH THE KING OF THE JEWS. This title then read many of the Jews: for the place where Jesus was crucified was nigh to the city; and it was written in Hebrew, and Greek, and Latin. Jn. 19:19-20.

Hebrew here means Aramaic, the language of the people at that time. Hebrew is the name of the race and not the language. The Jews spoke Aramaic after their return from Babylon. Hebrew primarily derives from Aramaic. The two languages are so alike one can hardly make distinctions.

Abraham was an Assyrian. Jacob's children were born in Assyria and later sojourned in Egypt and Palestine. The people of Palestine called them Hebrews, which means "those who crossed over the river Euphrates." What we call Hebrew ceased to be the

---

[4]See Jn. 20:1.

217

spoken language from 450 BCE to the ninth century CE. Aramaic was the literary and colloquial language of the Jewish people. Hebrew remained a classical language and was only read by Jewish teachers and during services in the synagogue. It was then interpreted into Aramaic. Even today Aramaic prayers are used in the Jewish prayer book.

> . . . Josephus considers Aramaic so thoroughly identical with Hebrew that he quotes Aramaic words as Hebrew ("Ant" iii, 10, section 6), and describes the language in which Titus' proposals to the Jerusalemites were made (which certainly were in Aramaic) as Hebrew ("B.J." vi 2, section 1). It was in Aramaic that Josephus had written his book on the "Jewish War" as he himself informs us in the introduction, before he wrote it in Greek. . . .
>
> . . . In Hebrew philology, Aramaic was especially useful in the explanation of Hebrew words in the Bible; and it served as the foundation for a comparative philology for the Semite languages inaugurated by Judah in the Koreish and Saadia. . . .
>
> . . . For more than a thousand years Aramaic remained the vernacular of Israel, until the conquests of the Arabs produced another linguistic change, as a sequel of which a third Semitic language became the popular tongue for a large portion of the Jewish race, and the vehicle of their thought. The spread of Arabian supremacy over the whole country formerly dominated by the Aramaic tongue produced with extraordinary rapidity and completeness an Arabizing of both the Christian and Jewish populations of western Asia, who had hitherto spoken Aramaic (Syriac) . . . [5]

The literary form of Eastern Aramaic was pronounced differently in the western countries under Roman rule and its Byzantine successor, and became a western dialect, influenced by Greek grammar and style. In the Parthian Empire, the language retained its archaic style, syntax, and pronunciation. Greeks had called Aramaic by a word they coined, "Syriac," and this artificial term was used in the West, but not in the East, where it

---

[5]From *THE JEWISH ENCYLOPEDIA,* Vol. 2, published by Funk and Wagnails Co., New York and London by special permission.

has always been known by its own name, *lishana aramaya,* [The Aramaic tongue]. Modern Eastern Aramaic has sixteen dialects, spoken by Christians and Jews, and a widely spoken western dialect. Modern Western Aramaic, akin to the dialect of Galilee, is spoken in three small villages north of Damascus, but in a very mixed form with words borrowed from Arabic and Turkish. . . . The advantage of Eastern Aramaic dialect, is that it shares a common morphology and idiom with Judaean and Galilean Aramaic of that period.[6]

The inscriptions were written on a stone tablet and placed above the cross. Greek was used because Alexandrian Jews who had come for the Passover could not read Aramaic. In 300 BCE, the Bible was translated into Greek because the Jews in Egypt could not understand Aramaic. Latin was used because it was the official language of the Roman Empire. Some of the soldiers and other Romans could not read either Aramaic or Greek. Aramaic was the language of the common people.

THE SEAMLESS ROBE

Then the soldiers, when they had crucified Jesus, took his garments, and made four parts, to every soldier a part; and also his coat: now the coat was without seam, woven from the top throughout. They said therefore among themselves, Let us not rend it, but cast lots for it, whose it shall be: that the scripture might be fulfilled which said, They parted my raiment among them, and for my vesture they did cast lots. These things therefore the soldiers did. Jn. 19:23-24.

When a dispute arises over certain articles between various parties, the decision is made by throwing lots. This is chiefly done when a special article of value and beauty is desired by everyone

---

[6]*The New Covenant Aramaic Peshitta text with Hebrew translation,* edited by The Aramaic Scriptures Research Society in Israel, "Editors' Note" pp. iii, iv, The Bible Society, Jerusalem 1986.

present and it cannot be divided into parts without damaging it.

If several articles are to be disposed of they are placed in separate piles. Stones of different colors and sizes are then chosen and each person selects his own stone. These stones are then dropped over the articles by a disinterested person and each man has to take the article or articles over which his stone falls. In case there is a single article to be disposed of, like the seamless robe of Jesus, four stones are selected and one of them is thrown upon the article. The person to whom the stone belongs becomes the owner of the article.

This robe was probably woven by Mary or presented to Jesus by one of his devoted friends. Near Eastern women often weave special garments for their loved ones as a token of affection. Such garments are used only on special occasions like weddings or the Passover festival.

HIS BEREAVED MOTHER

When Jesus therefore saw his mother, and the disciple standing by, whom he loved, he saith unto his mother. Woman, behold thy son! Then saith he to the disciples, Behold thy mother! And from that hour that disciple took her unto his own home. Jn. 19:26-27.

When Jesus saw his bereaved and mournful mother standing in the crowd of Galilean men and women near the cross, he thought of her future and in particular of her long journey back to Nazareth. Mary's head was bowed down in grief, occasionally looking up at him. She had come to the feast with him, his disciples and his brothers.[7] But now his disciples, with the exception of John, had fled. Some of them had gone home to Galilee. Others were hiding in Jerusalem and in nearby towns. His brothers from the outset did not want anything to do with him. They did not believe in him and were embarrassed because of his preaching and actions. They did not want to be identified with his movement. Therefore, after the Passover all

---

[7]These brothers were probably sons of Joseph from another wife or wives.

220

of them had left for Galilee.

All of Jesus' relatives, friends and disciples had heard the rumors that the high priests, Pharisees, scribes and elders had decided to do away with him. His kinsmen were afraid they would be arrested and put to death also, so they had to leave the city as soon as possible.

When Jesus looked again at the dense crowd, he saw his beloved disciple, John, who had been so close to him. Regardless of the danger, this disciple had dared to remain to the end. Thus Jesus entrusted his mother to him so that he could take her home and care for her. Jesus knew that his brothers would not support her.

JESUS THIRSTY ON THE CROSS

After this, Jesus knowing that all things were now accomplished that the scripture might be fulfilled, saith, I thirst. Now there was set a vessel full of vinegar: and they filled a spunge with vinegar, and put it upon hyssop, and put it to his mouth. When Jesus therefore had received the vinegar, he said, It is finished: and he bowed his head, and gave up the ghost.
Jn. 19:28-30.

Part 1—VINEGAR INSTEAD OF WATER. In these lands, government officials and jailers have no sympathy for prisoners who have been convicted of treason against the government or blasphemy against God. The prisoners are kept hungry and thirsty and are beaten from time to time.

Jesus had not had any water since his arrest on Thursday night. He had been doomed to be crucified; why should the soldier give him water that was so scarce in Jerusalem and, at times, very difficult to procure. Even rich people and government officials sometimes went to sleep thirsty.

Jesus was thirsty. He had been punished severely and had lost much blood. He needed water to quench his thirst, so he asked for some. Instead of giving him water the soldiers gave him vinegar, and when he tasted it he refused to drink it. Then he cried in a low tone, "It is fulfilled!"

Scriptures were now fulfilled. Everything the holy prophets had written concerning him had come true. Jesus had drunk of the bitter cup. He had challenged the forces of political and religious evils and he was soon to triumph over death and the grave.

Part 2—PROPHECIES FULFILLED. The Aramaic text reads, "It is fulfilled." All prophecies concerning Jesus had taken place. As Isaiah had predicted, Jesus was found weak—that is, a weak leader without any army and supplies, who was rejected as the Messiah/Christ. And according to the prophetic Psalm, his garments were divided among the jailers. When Jesus was thirsty, they gave him gall to drink. When he had tasted the gall he refused to drink it. This is because gall was given to the victims to lessen their suffering. Jesus did not want a sedative.

The words "It is finished" are not translated properly. Jesus' work was not finished. He had just inaugurated his kingdom on the cruel and blood-stained cross. The symbol of the cross was soon to be worn on the crowns of Emperors, Kings and Princes of the kingdoms of the world.

There was nothing that was written that was not fulfilled. He had come to fulfill the prophecies to reveal to the world a new way of salvation, the way of meekness and loving-kindness that some day would supplant force, violence and weapons of war.

FRIDAY

The Jews therefore, because it was the preparation, that the bodies should not remain upon the cross on the sabbath day, (for that sabbath day was a high day) besought Pilate that their legs might be broken and that they might be taken away. Jn. 19:31.

The Sabbath was approaching and Passover had been celebrated on Thursday. The preparation for Passover was done on the day before and not after it. The Aramaic text does not read "preparation day" but "because it was Friday."

Near Easterners count the day from sunrise to sunset. The Jews

222

did not want to see the men alive on the crosses on the Sabbath, because they could not then act as guards. They asked the governor to have their legs broken so as to be sure that they were dead, because the Sabbath day was approaching and they wanted to leave the place.

However, this was merely an excuse. Jesus and the two criminals were crucified by Romans and their death had nothing to do with the Jewish Sabbath. Even if they had remained alive on their crosses on the Sabbath, the holy day would not have been broken because the Romans were not Jews. There was something more than the Sabbath behind the demand that their legs be broken. The religious authorities wanted to be sure that Jesus was dead before they left the scene of the crucifixion. They were afraid that after they were gone, the soldiers might get tired of watching and abandon the bodies before the victims were completely dead.

Jesus might then be taken away alive or his body be lowered, supposing him to be dead, and his disciples could possibly take him and heal his wounds. This has happened in many countries. Men shot by a firing squad and given up for dead have often recovered or escaped the bullets. Others who were given up for dead have been taken away by relatives and have recovered.

These authorities wanted to see that Jesus' legs were broken to prevent this mistake. They did not want to take any chances. But Jesus had died long before. Thus, in order to convince these men, a soldier pierced him with a spear. This was to relieve the soldiers of any blame or charge of bribery and leniency toward Jesus.

A NEW HEWN TOMB

Now in the place where he was crucified there was a garden; and in the garden a new sepulchre, wherein was never man yet laid. Jn 19:41.

Semites bury their dead shortly after death. If an individual should die in the morning, he or she is buried at noon; if the death should occur in the afternoon, then the person is buried in the evening. A corpse is seldom kept until the next day except when death occurs at night. The body is buried quickly because Semites consider a corpse unclean. Also, there are no undertakers and no means of preserving the body. The climate causes early decay, and it is contrary to religious belief and custom to leave a corpse in the house, where many families live under the same roof. In emergencies the dead are taken to the church.

Jesus died late Friday afternoon. It was against the Jewish law to bury him on the Sabbath day, which begins on Friday evening. The body was, therefore, temporarily laid in a nearby tomb, hewn in a rock, to be removed on Sunday and buried permanently. Caves and hewn tombs are very abundant in Palestine. These are the only places to which a corpse could be removed. This applies particularly to the dead bodies of slain robbers and criminals who are not given a decent burial and could not be brought into the city.

CHAPTER 20

BURIED WITH GARMENTS

And the napkin, that was about his head, not lying with the linen clothes, but wrapped together in a place by itself. Jn. 20:7.

The deceased are bathed, then clothed in a white burial shroud woven all in one piece. Both bathing and the white garment are symbolic of immortality and resurrection. The dead are thus prepared for the resurrection day when they will be met by angels clothed in white.

Bathing and white burial apparel are also symbolic of purity and preparedness for the future life. The deceased must be clothed when they arise on the last day. Semites never bury their dead wearing ordinary clothes or garments worn during life. The burial shroud must be a new white garment of cotton or linen.

Bandits, criminals and persons publicly put to death, are not usually given these religious burial rites that Near Easterners consider sacred. They are buried in the garment that the soldiers reject as worthless and leave on them. Provincial soldiers are entrusted with these tasks. They are seldom paid for their services and they provide their own clothes. They obtain what they can from the people, especially from prisoners who are under their charge.

When a person is put to death, most of his valuable outer garments and other belongings are the property of the soldiers and prison guards. At times, the guards do not wait. So that others cannot take them, the prisoner is stripped and relieved of the best of his outer garments before he is bound in chains.

When Jesus was crucified, his garments were divided among the soldiers. Undergarments, which consist of a light cloak and several shirts, were not taken. In the case of a man who is being crucified publicly, it is improper to strip him of all his garments. A portion of

Jesus' garments were left on him when he was crucified. There were many women and children standing near the cross. The chief priests and elders who were present would have resented the crucifixion of a person without garments.

The burial of Jesus was rather hasty because of fear and lack of time. The Sabbath was approaching and the dead must be buried before the end of the day. Jesus' body was lowered from the cross and wrapped in a white burial garment. His undergarments were not removed and his body was neither washed nor embalmed. Thus when Jesus arose from the tomb, the burial garment having been laid aside, he appeared to the disciples as they had last seen him.

THE RESURRECTION

Jesus saith unto her, Mary. She turned herself and saith unto him, Rabboni: which is to say, Master. Jesus saith unto her, Touch me not: for I am not yet ascended to my Father: but go to my brethren and say unto them, I ascend unto my Father, and your Father; and to my God, and your God. Jn. 20:16-17.

Part 1—MARY. Mary was looking for Jesus in a cemetery on the hill of Golgotha, "the skull." The hill resembled a human skull. Mary, like others of Jesus' followers and disciples, never expected to see her lord alive again. She had come to prepare the body for a final burial. The burial of Jesus had been so hasty because Friday was spent and the Sabbath day was approaching, so his body was temporarily placed in the tomb.

When Jesus called her name, "Mary," she turned to him and said *Rabboli*, a term of endearment for someone who is precious, meaning "Oh, my great teacher, my master!" Then she rushed to him to embrace him. In these ancient lands when a man is thought to be dead and appears alive, women rush to kiss him.

Jesus did not want Mary to touch him or embrace him. People who were passing by the garden would have misunderstood her good intentions. Then again, Jesus appeared to her in a bodily form,

226

clothed in his under garments[1] and looking like a gardener. These men who hold the position of a gardener usually remove their outer garments and work the garden in their long under (lower) garments.

Part 2—TOUCH ME NOT. The Aramaic text reads: "Do not come near me." The Aramaic word *kraw* means "to approach, come near, to touch," but in this instance the better rendering is "come near." Near Eastern women never touch men in public. During conversation they are not supposed to be close to the men. A violation of this custom is often misunderstood and looked upon with suspicion.

There are exceptions: For instance, when a man returns from a long journey, when a person given up for dead is found to be alive, or when the lost return. Women then hasten to embrace and kiss such individuals, whether they are relatives or neighbors.

Jesus rose from the dead early in the morning. When Mary saw him, there were other people passing by or at work. She drew near to embrace and kiss him as one who was given up for dead but is alive. Such an act would certainly have aroused suspicions of those who were around the area. They would have given the situation a wrong and immoral interpretation They knew nothing of the circumstances about Jesus' death and resurrection.

Part 3—I AM NOT YET ASCENDED. "Ascend" in Aramaic also means "transcend." Christ, which is the Spirit of God, dwelt in the prophet from Galilee. Jesus was human, but the Christ in him was the very Spirit of God. After the resurrection, Jesus' physical body had transformed into a spiritual body. He said, "it is the spirit that gives life; the body is of no account. . ."[2]

There is no doubt that Jesus must have had a secret that no one else in the world knew. He knew the secret of transcending the physical and material plane of life. The risen Christ had the power to materialize and dematerialize, integrate and disintegrate his human form. He had told his disciples that he would be crucified and buried

---

[1]See p. 226, last paragraph about under garments.
[2]Jn. 6:63.

227

but would rise again. Being the Messiah, he had power over his body, which existed in the limits of space and time. Physical things are constantly changing, but Spirit is unchangeable.

The process of this transformation may have taken forty days. The Egyptian embalming process took forty days to complete.[3] Jesus, during these forty days, suddenly appeared and disappeared among his disciples. After the forty days were over he never appeared again.

We must realize that his disciples were transformed in their minds and had transcended the material world so that they could see the risen Christ. Their faith was strong in Jesus. All matters that he had told them had been fulfilled. Prior to the crucifixion, they had not understood him. Their minds were still subject to the teaching of the elders and the notions of the material world. In the beginning the disciples thought that the Messiah would be a militant, political leader sent by God to restore the Davidic kingdom. Even to the last moment, before Jesus ascended into the heavens, his disciples expected him to restore the political kingdom of Israel.[4]

Part 4—MY GOD AND YOUR GOD. Jesus always addressed Yahweh, the God of Israel, as "my God and my Father." As a man, Jesus was a child of God just as other people were. He never made himself equal with God although the Spirit of God was on him more than any other prophet. When Mary saw him, he told her to go to his disciples. "But go to my brethren and say to them, I am ascending to my Father and your Father, and my God and your God."

It is through the teaching of Jesus as the Messiah/Christ and Lord that we know that God is our Father. Prior to the Jewish exile, the Fatherhood of God was known to the Israelites. During the exile, this spiritual truth was lost just as other teachings were lost. God was known as the God of Abraham, Isaac and Jacob. Jesus, through his gospel of the kingdom, revealed the true nature of God as a loving Father of all nations and races. God was the beloved.

---

[3]See Gen. 50:2-3.
[4]See Acts. 1:6.

SHLAMA AMKHON – PEACE BE WITH YOU

Then the same day at evening, being the first day of the week, when the doors were shut where the disciples were assembled for fear of the Jews, came Jesus and stood in the midst, and said unto them Peace be unto you. Jn. 20:19.

Jesus greeted his disciples with the common Semitic Aramaic greeting: *shlama amkhon*, "Peace be with you." The ancient meaning was "I surrender to you," but in modern days it simply means "hello." After they saw him, he greeted them again with the same words and commissioned them to go out and preach his gospel of God's kingdom to all nations that there might be peace and harmony among all people of the earth.

HE BREATHED ON THEM

And when he had said this, he breathed on them, and said unto them. Receive ye the Holy Ghost. Jn. 20:22.

This is an Aramaic idiom commonly used even to this day. The Aramaic verb *npakh* means "to blow into." Near Eastern people say that the prophets were blown into by the Holy Spirit so they could speak for God. It is like a wind instrument that must have air blown into it so that it can make musical sounds. The prophets and Jesus' disciples were God's instruments. The disciples were to sing and sound the notes of the new kingdom.

"He breathed on them" means "he encouraged them." They had to know and feel this encouragement so that they could carry on his mission. After the crucifixion, the disciples were discouraged. Their messianic hopes and aspirations were shattered. Their lord had met the death of a criminal. They thought their careers had come to an end. Thus, they returned to Galilee and their fishing trade.

Jesus then appeared and conversed with them, reminding them that the Son of Man had to die and rise again so the Scriptures might

229

be fulfilled. They had to realize that his death was a victory. He impressed on them that he was alive and would be with them always. These encouraging words and promises helped the disciples to be courageous. Once again they took up the challenge and followed him spiritually.

SINS FORGIVEN

Whose soever sins ye remit, they are remitted unto them; and whose soever sins ye retain, they are retained. Jn. 20:23.

After Jesus' spiritual presence had encouraged them and they had received the Holy Spirit, the disciples were empowered to heal the sick and forgive sins. According to the Jewish concept of God's way in the Old Testament, God can forgive sins only through intermediaries such as the high priests. But in the New Testament, the new order, the disciples and their successors were granted the power to forgive sins and even to raise the dead.

The term "sin" means "transgression against the law" or "deviation from truth or justice." Any human act that causes harm to others, whether a woman, man or child, is sin. Nevertheless, some sins are offenses that can be easily forgiven and forgotten; others are mortal sins, such as murder,[5] blasphemy and adultery. These can be forgiven providing that those who had committed them are willing to repent and make restitution. Offenses are mere faults, misdemeanors that are often committed unknowingly and are therefore forgivable.

According to Jesus' teachings, one does not have to offer animal sacrifices and other offerings to seek forgiveness of sins. This power was already granted Jesus' disciples and their followers by means of the Word, just as Jesus himself did when he said, "Your sins are forgiven, go and sin no more." A sincere penitent will be forgiven

---

[5]Although murder can be forgiven, if the government upholds capital punishment, the murderer cannot be saved from death ordered by law. This act in the Bible is called "a sin unto death."

230

and restored.

JESUS APPEARS TO THOMAS

The other disciples therefore said unto him, We have seen the Lord. But he said unto them, Except I shall see in his hands the print of the nails, and put my finger into the print of the nails, and thrust my hand into his side, I will not believe. And after eight days again his disciples were within, and Thomas with them: then came Jesus the doors being shut, and stood in the midst, and said, Peace be unto you. Then said he to Thomas, Reach hither thy finger, and behold my hands: and reach hither thy hand and thrust it into my side: and be not faithless, but believing. And Thomas answered and said unto him, My Lord and my God. Jn. 20:25-28.

Part 1—DOUBTFUL THOMAS. Semites become excited over sad, cheerful or unexpected news and are bewildered. They usually say, "I cannot believe you!" When lost persons are found they say, "I cannot believe it. It must be a false vision." Such statements are not always due to actual doubt but to an excess of joy creating the feeling that it is too good to be true. Also, false rumors are common and good news is often exaggerated.

Thomas was cautious in believing the news of his risen lord. He had fled from Jesus in the garden of Gethsemane. Then, when he heard the sad news of the crucifixion, it meant to him that everything was over. His master had been slain by the religious authorities and was dead and buried like other prophets. Suddenly he heard the news of the resurrection, and finally Jesus himself appeared before him.

These events followed in such rapid succession that he was overwhelmed and did not know what to make of all this news. When he finally did see Jesus, at first he thought it was a false vision; then doubts crept into his mind, and he thought probably his lord was not slain and the news concerning his death had been nothing but a rumor as so often happens. Men are frequently reported killed but return home safe.

Jesus most likely knew that Thomas thought he had not been

231

crucified but had, as on other occasions, escaped from his enemies. Jesus told Thomas to come forward and touch his feet and hands and see the wounds for himself so that he might believe he had been crucified and was risen again.

Part 2—MY LORD AND MY GOD! This was the third time Jesus greeted his disciples with the salutation of peace. They needed peace of mind and soul. They had been greatly agitated by the loss of their master and were holding the fear and worry that they might be implicated and convicted the same as he was. Now Jesus' gentle words of greeting removed the anxiety. He calmed them and inspired and encouraged them to continue the work of his gospel.

It was very difficult for Thomas to believe that his lord had conquered death and risen from the grave. The others were doubtful also. They did not believe until he showed them his hands, feet and side and told them to touch him.

Prior to his crucifixion and resurrection, Jesus was never addressed as God, but as Messiah, the son of the living God. Even the angel of the Lord, when announcing Jesus' birth to Mary, said, "He will be called the son of the Highest." The angel did not say, "He is the son of the Highest," but "he will be called . . ."[6] This is because God, being Spirit, cannot have a physical son, but rather a spiritual son.

It is difficult to determine whether or not Thomas' exclamation, "My Lord and my God!," was a confession that Jesus was God or that he was astonished to see his risen lord standing before him. Near Easterners, when they receive shocking or surprising news, exclaim, "Oh, my God! Oh, my lord!" Such remarks are common not only in Aramaic and Arabic but in English and other languages as well.

Regardless, Jesus' disciples traveled with him and he never told them he was God. Had he made such a statement, his disciples would never have followed him. Jesus was specific and positive about his status. He called himself "Son of Man," "human being." He always

---

[6]See Errico and Lamsa, *Aramaic Light on the Gospels of Mark and Luke,* "Son of the Highest," Part 1—HE WILL BE CALLED, pp. 119-120.

said that he could do nothing of himself, that it was his Father who did the works. Jesus prayed to God and glorified God's name. His disciples accepted him as the blessed Messiah/Christ, the one who had been sent by God to bring, hope, love and salvation to the world. When Jesus appeared to Mary in the garden, after his resurrection, he told her, "I am ascending to my Father and your Father, and my God and your God."[7]

---

[7]Thomas's statement also might have been a gloss—that is, a marginal note—and later copied into the scripture. However, one cannot be completely sure.

CHAPTER 21

PETER'S LOYALTY

So when they had dined, Jesus saith to Simon Peter, Simon, son of Jonas, lovest thou me more than these? He saith unto him, Yea, my Lord; thou knowest that I love thee. He saith unto him, Feed my lambs. He saith unto him the second time, Simon, Son of Jonas, lovest thou me? He saith unto him, Yea, Lord; thou knowest that I love thee. He saith unto him, Feed my sheep. He saith unto him the third time, Simon, son of Jonas, lovest thou me? Peter was grieved because he said unto him the third time, lovest thou me? And he said unto him, Lord, thou knowest all things; thou knowest that I love thee. Jesus saith unto him, Feed my sheep. Jn. 21:15-17.

Part 1—PETER'S LOYALTY TESTED. The Aramaic word *halein* means "these" and here it refers to things and not to Jesus' disciples who were also present with Simon Peter. If Jesus had meant his disciples, then the word *talmeedeh* would have been inserted in the sentence. And, it would have read *talmeedeh halein*, "these disciples."

It is not likely Jesus would have asked Peter such a question, for he knew Peter loved him more than he loved the other disciples. In the Near East, every disciple loves his master more than his fellow students. Peter had already shown his love by following Jesus to the courtyard of Caiaphas while the other disciples had fled the scene during his master's arrest in the garden. Peter loved his master more than the other disciples loved their teacher with the exception of John, who stood by Jesus while he was dying on the cross.

After the crucifixion most of the disciples went to Galilee where they resumed their business of fishing. To leave their commissions and return to the old occupations may appear like a hasty act, but the fact is that their teacher had left them no money. They had eaten their last meal at the Passover with him. Where could they get their next meal? They had made their living from Jesus' popularity and shared the hospitality extended to him.

Now that their lord was taken away, they either had to beg or return to their former occupations. They could not beg in Jerusalem without being exposed to danger. They had to return to Galilee. It was either return or starve in Jerusalem.

Jesus found them fishing and told them to cast their nets into a particular area of the lake. They did so and made a large catch. It was while they were sorting the fish that Jesus said, "Simon, son of Jonah, do you love me more than these?" Jesus meant, "Do you love me more than these material things?" He was testing Peter to see if he would give up the business of a fisherman and continue with his mission of teaching the gospel of the kingdom.

Peter's messianic hope had been shattered by the cross. Jesus had to win him again through his resurrection. It was the risen Christ that spoke with Simon Peter. When Peter answered, "Yea, Lord," Jesus commanded him to feed his sheep and his lambs. This was in accordance with his teaching. Men were asked to leave everything and follow him. This was the second call to Peter, but it was the greatest and most important of all. Peter was to become the chief shepherd of the flock that Jesus was leaving behind.

Part 2—PETER'S COMMISSION. The Aramaic text reads, "Feed my male lambs." The sixteenth verse reads, "Feed my sheep," and the seventeenth, "Feed my ewes." This is in accordance with Near Eastern custom, where three different flocks consist respectively of sheep and goats for milking, male lambs and rams, and ewes (female lambs). These flocks are kept separately during the summer months in the milking season. Sheep are raised not for meat, as in other countries, but for milk, cheese and byproducts on which the people live.

The three flocks are in the charge of several shepherds, but they are all under a head shepherd, whose advice is sought in matters of grazing, water and the protection of the sheep. He is the one who searches for new pastures and orders the sheep to a new location.

Jesus gave Peter charge of three flocks. These were symbolic of the Jewish people, Galileans and pagans. His disciples were soon to shepherd all races. Peter was to be their leader and counselor in

235

Jerusalem.

When Jesus asked Peter if he loved him more than his former occupation, he was referring to devotion and faithfulness. The Aramaic word for love is *hooba*. The root of this Semitic term is *haw*, meaning "to set on fire." It refers to ardent devotion in a spiritual sense. All epistles in Aramaic begin with the phrase "My beloved."

It was the risen Christ that spoke these words to Peter. It appears that Simon had forgotten that he had traveled with Jesus for three years and that he called his master "The Messiah/Christ, Son of the living God." Now Peter was totally taken up with his old occupation. When the risen Christ pointed to the catch of fish and asked, "Do you love me more than these things?" he was implying, "You have deserted your mission and resumed your old business." Only true and ardent devotion to his master would make Peter abandon his former trade and follow Jesus' commission.

Now Simon Peter had seen and spoken to the risen Christ, and he himself was raised in consciousness and his faith strengthened. Instead of seeing things from a material point of view, he looked on them from a spiritual perspective. He now began to see that the preaching of the living gospel is far more important than fishing and other material things.

OTHERS WILL TIE YOUR GIRDLE

Verily, verily, I say unto thee, When thou wast young, thou girdedst thyself and walkedst whither thou wouldest; but when thou shalt be old, thou shalt stretch forth thy hands, and another shall gird thee, and carry thee whither thou wouldest not. Jn. 21:18.

"Another shall gird thee" means "you will lose your liberty and you will be in prison; your hands will be tied and you will be led by another." In the Near East, prisoners were usually chained and their hands tied. Today only the more dangerous prisoners are chained. When a prisoner is taken to court for trial, the jailer puts the sash on him. This custom prevailed in many parts of the Near East until

236

World War II and is still practiced in some remote, backward areas, where the government authorities are trying hard to stop crime.

Jesus predicted that the day would come when Simon Peter, the shepherd of his flock, would be arrested and, with his hands tied behind him, be thrown into prison. Peter was to follow Jesus even to death.

Now Simon Peter's faith was strong. He would preach the good news of God's kingdom. He would even die for the cause of his beloved master's teaching. There would be no more weakness or denials facing Peter. He was now ready to serve fully. Further on in the chapter, Jesus hinted that John would outlive Peter and would see the kingdom of God established. Peter did die before John; his death was foretold symbolically by Jesus.

JOHN LIVED A LONGER LIFE

Jesus saith unto him, If I will that he tarry till I come, what is that to thee? Follow thou me. Jn. 21:22.

Jesus loved John so much that he wished John would live to see the success of his mission. "Till I come" means "till the establishment of the kingdom."[1]

Jesus was repudiated as the Messiah/Christ, judged, convicted and crucified as a malefactor. Humanly speaking, he died a defeated man, but he was soon to come to power and glory. In Aramaic, when a defeated man recovers from his losses and regains his strength and power, people say, "He has come back" or "He has risen."

When a politician loses his power, Easterners say, "He is dead." When he returns to power, they say, "He has risen" or "He has returned," meaning "He has succeeded."

Jesus did not mean that John would be living when he returned. Such a remark is generally mere wishful thinking. In the Near East, people say, "I pray you will live a thousand years." Jesus said that no

---

[1]See Mt. 16:27.

one would know the hour and the day of his coming, but that it would be as unpredictable as a thief who comes in the night.

John saw Jesus' movement and the power of the gospel of the kingdom spreading in many lands. He saw Jesus' teaching in written form. He died about 90 CE., but Peter had died before him.

Peter took Jesus' words literally and wondered why he was not included. What Jesus meant by "What is that to you?" is, "I am talking to John," and that is all. Prior to Jesus' death there was some rivalry among the disciples over leadership. They wondered who would succeed him. Jesus even upbraided some of them because of this competition and rivalry. His gospel was not to foster overlords and a hierarchy.

BIBLIOGRAPHY

ARAMAIC AND SEMITIC STUDIES

Black, Matthew, *An Aramaic Approach to the Gospels and Acts*, Peabody, Mass., Hendrickson, Third Edition, 1967 & 1998.

Burkert, Walter, *The Orientalizing Revolution*: *Near Eastern Influence on Greek Culture in the Early Archaic Age*, Harvard University Press, 1992.

Charlesworth, James H., *Jesus Within Judaism*: *New Light from Exciting Archaeological Discoveries*, New York, Doubleday, 1988.
_____, *Jesus' Jewishness*: *Exploring the Place of Jesus in Early Judaism, New York*, Crossroad Herder, 1996.

Chilton, Bruce, *Pure Kingdom: Jesus' Vision of God*. Grand Rapids, Michigan, Eerdmans, 1996.

Chilton, Bruce & Neusner, Jacob, *Judaism in the New Testament*, London, Routledge, 1995.

Eisenberg, Azriel, *The Synagogue through the Ages*, New York, Block Publishing Company, 1974.

Errico, Rocco A., *Setting A Trap For God*: *The Aramaic Prayer of Jesus*, Unity Village, Unity Books, 1997.
_____, *Let There Be Light*: *The Seven Keys*, Smyrna, GA, Noohra Foundation, 1994.
_____, *And There Was Light*, Smyrna, GA, Noohra Foundation, 1998.
_____, *The Mysteries of Creation*: *The Genesis Story*, Smyrna, GA, Noohra Foundation, 1993.
_____, *The Message of Matthew*: *An Annotated Parallel Aramaic-English Gospel of Matthew*, Smyrna, GA, Noohra Foundation, 1991.
_____, *Aramaic Light on the Gospel of Matthew*, A Commentary on the teachings of Jesus from the Aramaic and unchanged Near Eastern Customs, Smyrna, GA, Noohra Foundation, 2000.

_____, *Aramaic Light on the Gospels of Mark and Luke,* A commentary on the teachings of Jesus from the Aramaic and unchanged Near Eastern customs, Smyrna, GA, Noohra Foundation, 2001.

Falla, Terry C., *A Key to the Peshitta Gospels*, New York, Brill, 1991.

Fitzmyer, Joseph, *A Wandering Aramean: A Collection of Aramaic Essays*, Chico, CA, Scholar Press, 1979.
_____, *Essays on the Semitic Background of the New Testament*, Chico, CA, Scholar Press, 1974.

Gibson, Margaret D., *The Commentaries of Ishodad of Merv: The Gospels of Luke and John* (Aramaic) Cambridge, University Press, 1911.

Hitti, Philip K., *The Near East in History*, Princeton: D. Van Nostrand Co., 1960.

Lamsa, George M., *The Oldest Christian People*, New York, Macmillan, 1926.
_____, *My Neighbor Jesus: In the Light of His Own Language, People, and Time*, Philadelphia, A. J. Holman, 1932.
_____, *New Testament Origin*, New York, Ziff Davis, 1947.
_____, *The Kingdom on Earth*, Unity Village, Unity Books, 1966.
_____, *The Holy Bible: From the Ancient Eastern Texts*, San Francisco, Harper Collins, (originally A. J. Holman) 1957.

McCullogh, W. Stewart, *A Short History of Syriac Christianity to the Rise of Islam*, Chico, CA, Scholars Press, 1982.

Moffett, Samuel H., *A History of Christianity in Asia*, Vol. 1, Harper, San Francisco, 1992.

Rihbany, Abraham M., *The Syrian Christ*, Boston, Houghton Mifflin, 1916.

Segal, J. B., *Edessa: The Blessed City*, Gorgias Press, 2001.

Stewart, John, *Nestorian Missionary Enterprise: The Story of a Church on Fire*, Kerala, India, Mar Narsai Press, 1961.

Torrey, Charles Butler, *The Four Gospels*: *A New Translation*, New York, Harper and Publisher, 1947.

Vermes, Geza, *Jesus the Jew*, Philadelphia, Fortress Press, 1981.
_____, *Jesus and the World of Judaism*, Philadelphia, Fortress Press, 1983.
_____, *The Religion of Jesus the Jew*, Philadelphia, Fortress Press, 1993.

Wigram, W. A., *The Assyrians and Their Neighbors*, London, G. Bell and Sons, 1929.

Wilson, E. Jan, *The Old Syriac Gospels: Luke and John, Vol. 2*, Notre Dame University de Louaize, Lebanon and Gorgias Press, 2002.

Zeitlin, Irving M. *Jesus and the Judaism of His Time*, London, Polity Press/Basil Blackwell, 1988.

STUDIES ON THE HISTORICAL JESUS

Chilton, Bruce & Evans, Craig A., *Studying the Historical Jesus*: *Evaluations of the State of Current Research,* New York, Brill, 1998.
_____, *Authenticating the Words of Jesus*, New York, Brill, 1999.
_____, *Authenticating the Activities of Jesus*, New York, Brill, 1999.
_____, *Jesus in Context*, New York, Brill, 1997.

Evans, Craig A., *Jesus & His Contemporaries*, New York, Brill, 1995.

Meier, John P., *A Marginal Jew*: *Rethinking the Historical Jesus*, New York, Doubleday, Vol 1–1991, Vol. 2–1994, Vol. 3–2002

GENERAL

Brown, Raymond E., *The Death of the Messiah*, Volumes 1 & 2, New York, Doubleday, 1994.

_____, *The Gospel According to John,* A New Translation with Introduction and Commentary, Vol. 1and 2, The Anchor Bible, Doubleday, 1985.

Burkitt, F. Crawford, *The Earliest Sources for the Life of Jesus*, New York, E. P. Dutton, 1922.

Charlesworth, James H., *Jesus and the Dead Sea Scrolls*. New York, Doubleday, 1992.
_____, *John and the Dead Sea Scrolls*, New York, Crossroads Press, 1990.

Countryman, L. William, *The Mystical Way in the Fourth Gospel: Crossing Over into God*, Philadelphia, Fortress Press, 1987.

Dalman, Gustaf, *Jesus–Jeshua*, New York, Macmillan Co., 1929.

Dungan, David Laird, *A History of the Synoptic Problem*: *The Canon, the Text, the Composition, and the Interpretation of the Gospels*, New York, Doubleday, 1999.

Ellis, Peter F., *The Genius of John : A Composition-Critical Commentary on the Fourth Gospel*, Collegeville, MN, Liturgical Press, 1984.

Farmer, William R., *The Synoptic Problem: A Critical Analysis*, North Carolina, Western North Carolina Press 1976.

Robinson, John A. T., *The Priority of John,* London, SCM Press Ltd., 1985.

Stanton, Graham, *Gospel Truth? New Light on Jesus & the Gospels*, PA, Trinity Press International, 1995.

Renan, Ernest, *The Life of Jesus*, New York, World Publishing, 1941.

von Wahlde, Urban C., *The Earliest Version of John's Gospel: Recovering the Gospel of Signs*, Wilmington, Delaware, Glazier, 1989.

STUDIES ON THE CROSS AND SACRED VIOLENCE

Alison, James, *Raising Abel: The Recovery of the Eschatological Imagination*, New York, Crossroad Publishing, 1996.

Baile, Gil, *Violence Unveiled: Humanity at the Crossroads*, New York, Crossroad Publishing, 1997.

Girard, Rene, *The Girard Reader*, edited by James G. Williams, New York, Crossroad Publishing 1996.

Hamerton-Kelly, Robert G., *Sacred Violence: Paul's Hermeneutic of the Cross*, Minneapolis, Fortress Press, 1992.

Levenson, Jon D., *The Death and Resurrection of the Beloved Son: The Transformation of Child Sacrifice in Judaism and Christianity*, New Haven and London, Yale University Press, 1993.

McEntire, Mark, *The Blood of Abel: The Violent Plot in the Hebrew Bible*, Mercer University Press, 1999.

Mendel, Arthur P., *Vision and Violence,* Ann Arbor, The University of Michigan Press, 1992.

Wallace, Mark I., Smith, Theophus H., editors, *Curing Violence,* Sonoma, CA, Polebridge Press, 1994.

Williams, James G., *The Bible, Violence and the Sacred: Liberation from the Myth of Sanctioned Violence*, San Francisco, Harper, 1991.

ABOUT THE AUTHOR
George M. Lamsa

George M. Lamsa, Th.D., a renowned native Assyrian scholar of the Holy Bible, translator, lecturer, ethnologist and author, was born August 5, 1892 in a civilization with customs, manners and language almost identical to those in the time of Jesus. His native tongue was full of similar idioms and parables, untouched by the outside world in 1900 years.

Until World War 1, his people living in that part of the ancient biblical lands that today is known as Kurdistan, in the basin of the rivers Tigris and Euphrates, retained the simple nomadic life as in the days of the Hebrew patriarchs. Only at the beginning of the 20th century did the isolated segment of the once great Assyrian Empire learn of the discovery of America and the Reformation in Germany.

Likewise, until that same time, this ancient culture of early Christians was unknown to the Western world, and the Aramaic language was thought to be dead. But in this so-called "Cradle of Civilization," primitive biblical customs and Semitic culture, cut off from the world, were preserved.

Lamsa's primary upbringing as a boy was to tend the lambs. But, as the first-born in his family, while yet an infant he was dedicated to God by his devout mother. Years after her death, when Lamsa was 12 years of age, her vow was renewed by native tribesmen, an ox killed and its blood rubbed on his forehead. Lamsa claimed this vow to God had always been part of him. "God's hand," he affirmed, "has been steadfastly on my shoulder, guiding me in the divine work."

Lamsa's formal education and studies began under the priests and deacons of the ancient Church of the East. Later he graduated with the highest honors ever bestowed from the Archbishop of Canterbury's Colleges in Iran and in Turkey, with the degree of Bachelor of Arts. Lamsa never married, but dedicated his life to "God's calling." He spoke eight languages and his lowest grade in any subject was 99.

At the beginning of World War 1, when Turkey began its

invasions, Lamsa was forced to flee the Imperial University at Constantinople where he was studying. He went to South America where he endured great hardships during those years. He knew but three words in Spanish at that time—water, work and bread. As best as he could he existed—in the British Merchant Marine for a time, then working on railroads, in mines and later in printing shops, a trade he had learned while attending college in Iran.

After arriving in the United States in his early 20s, Lamsa worked by day as a printer, and by night he went to school. He later studied at the Episcopal Theological Seminary in Alexandria, Virginia, and at Dropsie College in Philadelphia.

It was through his struggles, during these years, with the English idioms that Lamsa gradually launched into his "life's work" of translating the Holy Bible from Aramaic into English. Yet many years were to pass before the world received his translations.

First as a lecturer in churches and seminaries, in halls and auditoriums, before statesmen, theologians, groups of artists, actors and others, Lamsa received recognition as a poet-philosopher and as an authority on all phases of Near Eastern civilization.

It was his own inner compulsion, and the urging of hundreds who heard him, that drove him forward and brought about—after 30 years of labor, research and study—his translation of the Holy Bible from a branch of the ancient Aramaic language that the earliest Christians used. (It is a know fact that Jesus and his followers spoke Aramaic.)

There were times that he was temporarily stopped in his translations when the idioms in the manuscripts could not be given correct English equivalents. It was Lamsa's firm belief that his translation from Aramaic would bring people closer to the Word of God and would facilitate understanding between the East and the West. For forty years, he produced commentaries and many other works based on the Aramaic language. The last ten years of his life, Dr. Lamsa tutored and prepared Dr. Rocco A. Errico to continue with the Aramaic approach to Scripture. He left this earthly life on September 22, 1975, in Turlock, California.

246

ABOUT THE AUTHOR
Rocco A. Errico

Rocco A. Errico, Th.D., D.D., is the founder and president of the Noohra Foundation of Smyrna, Georgia. The Noohra Foundation is a nonprofit, nonsectarian, spiritual educational organization of Aramaic biblical studies, research and publications. Dr. Errico is an ordained minister, lecturer, author, Bible authority, translator, Aramaic instructor, educator and spiritual counselor. He is also Dean of Biblical Studies at the Rev. Dr. Barbara L. King's School of Ministry in Atlanta, Georgia.

For ten years Dr. Errico studied intensively with George M. Lamsa, Th.D., world-renowned Assyrian biblical scholar and translator of the *Holy Bible from the Ancient Eastern Text*. He is proficient in Aramaic and Hebrew exegesis—Old and New Testaments—and in the customs, idioms, psychology, symbolism and philosophy of Semitic peoples. Dr. Errico has translated the Gospel of Matthew from Aramaic into English. He is also fluent in the Spanish language and has translated his book *The Ancient Aramaic Prayer of Jesus* into Spanish.

Dr. Errico holds a doctorate in Letters from the College of Seminarians, The Apostolic Succession of Antioch and the Church of the East—American See, a doctorate in Philosophy from the School of Christianity, Los Angeles, a doctorate in Divinity from St. Ephrem's Institute, Sweden, and a doctorate in Sacred Theology from the School of Christianity, Los Angeles. He also hold a special title of Teacher, Prime Exegete, *Malpana d'miltha dalaha,* among the Federation of St. Thomas Christians of the order of Antioch.

Dr. Errico has served as a professor and dean of Biblical Studies in schools of ministry for many denominations and is a regular feature writer for Science of Mind magazine, Los Angeles. He formerly served as an editor and writer for *Light for All*, a religious magazine. He has held advisory positions with many boards of ecumenical religious organizations. Dr. Errico lectures extensively throughout the country and is widely known for his numerous radio

247

and television appearances.

Under the auspices of the Noohra Foundation, Dr. Errico continues to lecture for colleges, civic groups and churches of various denominations in the United States, Canada, Mexico and Europe.

For a complimentary catalog of Aramaic Bible translations, books, audio and video cassettes, and a brochure of classes, retreats and seminars, or for any other inquiries, write or call the Noohra Foundation. Those interested in scheduling Dr. Errico for a personal appearance may also contact:

Noohra Foundation
4480H South Cobb Drive PMB 343
Smyrna, GA 30080

E-mail: noohrafnd@aol.com

Phone: 770-319-9376
Fax: 770-319-9793

Noohra Foundation web-site: www.noohra.com

In addition to this commentary and the previous two in this series, *Aramaic Light on the Gospel of Matthew* ($29.95) and *Aramaic Light on the Gospels of Mark and Luke* ($26.95), the Noohra Foundation is pleased to offer the following books by Dr. Rocco A. Errico and Dr. George M. Lamsa.

<u>BOOKS BY DR. ERRICO:</u>

LET THERE BE LIGHT: THE SEVEN KEYS

In this illuminating work, Dr. Errico equips the reader with seven key insights to understand the allusions, parables, and teachings of the Bible, opening the door to the ancient Aramaic world from which the Bible emerged. $17.95

AND THERE WAS LIGHT

Like its predecessor, *Let There Be Light*, this book unlocks puzzling passages with the Seven Keys. The Bible now becomes clearer and more relevant for Western readers, and the teaching ministry and parables of Jesus come alive as never before. $19.95

SETTING A TRAP FOR GOD: The Aramaic Prayer of Jesus

Dr. Errico explains the meaning of the Lord's Prayer based on the Aramaic language and ancient culture of the Near East. Discover the way of peace, health, and prosperity as you learn to "set a trap" for the inexhaustible power of God. $10.95

THE MYSTERIES OF CREATION: The Genesis Story

A challenging new look at the processes and mysteries of the primal creation account. Dr. Errico uses his own direct translation from the Aramaic-Peshitta text of Genesis 1:1-31 and 2:1-3. $16.95

THE MESSAGE OF MATTHEW: An Annotated Parallel Aramaic-English Gospel of Matthew

Dr. Errico's translation of the ancient Aramaic Peshitta text of Matthew with illuminating annotations. The English translation is on the left side of the page with footnotes. The Aramaic text is on the right. $24.95

CLASSICAL ARAMAIC: Book I

Learn to read and write the language of Jesus in a self-teachable format. Classical Aramaic is a practical grammar that prepares you to read the New Testament in Jesus' own native tongue. $24.95

LA ANTIGUA ORACIÓN ARAMEA DE JESÚS: El Padrenuestro

Dr. Errico's own translation into Spanish of his book *The Ancient Aramaic Prayer of Jesus.* $8.95

ACHT EINSTIMMUNGEN AUF GOTT: VATERUNSER

German translation and publication of *Setting a Trap for God.*

ES WERDE LICHT

German translation and publication of *Let There Be Light.*

BOOKS BY DR. LAMSA

THE HOLY BIBLE FROM THE ANCIENT EASTERN TEXT

The entire Bible translated directly into English from Aramaic, the language of Jesus. There are approximately 12,000 major differences between this English translation and the many traditional versions of the Bible. $35.00

IDIOMS IN THE BIBLE EXPLAINED and A KEY TO THE ORIGINAL GOSPELS

Two books in one. In Book 1 (*Idioms in the Bible Explained*) Dr. Lamsa explains nearly 1000 crucial idioms and colloquialisms of Eastern speech that will enrich reading of the Bible for student and general reader alike.

Book 2 (*A Key to the Original Gospels*) explains how the gospels were written, the reason for two different genealogies, the conflicting stories of the birth of Jesus, and more. $14.00

THE KINGDOM ON EARTH

With a warmth and understanding seldom equaled among contemporary scholars, Dr. Lamsa teaches the Beatitudes and the Lord's Prayer in the light of Jesus' own language, people and times. $14.95

THE SHEPHERD OF ALL: The Twenty-Third Psalm

Based on his own personal experience as a shepherd, Dr. Lamsa interprets what many consider the most beautiful, moving and meaningful psalm in the light of Eastern biblical customs. $5.95

NEW TESTAMENT ORIGIN

Dr. Lamsa presents his theory for Aramaic as the original written language of the New Testament. $5.95